A GIFT FROM
JOHN "L." WEBB

SHOUT TREASON
The Trial of Aaron Burr

AARON BURR

From an original drawing from nature, by Saint-Mémin

SHOUT TREASON

The Trial of Aaron Burr

by Francis F. Beirne

HASTINGS HOUSE · PUBLISHERS
NEW YORK

Acknowledgments

The story of Aaron Burr has been treated exhaustively by many writers in many ways. Oddly enough, aside from the stenographic report of the proceedings and a small volume which appeared nearly a century ago, there seems to have been no work dealing alone with the subject of Burr's trial in Richmond, Virginia, in the spring and summer of 1807, on charges of treason against the United States and high misdemeanor. Yet this marked the climax of Burr's public career and the presence of a former Vice-President of the United States as the accused, charged with such serious crimes, of the Chief Justice of the United States on the bench, and of distinguished leaders of the bar represented both in the prosecution and defense made this the most dramatic case in the history of American jurisprudence.

It is true there is likely to be no better account of the trial than that of Albert J. Beveridge, on whom this author has leaned heavily in feeling his way through legal technicalities and to whom he makes grateful acknowledgment. This scholarly treatment, however, is buried in the middle of Senator Beveridge's life of John Marshall where it cannot attract the attention it deserves from a larger audience both because of the trial's historical importance and its human and spectacular qualities. It was with the idea of reaching the general reader that this work, striving for historical accuracy but relieved of confusing technicalities, was undertaken.

For valuable assistance in its preparation thanks are due the staffs of the Virginia Historical Society and the Valentine Museum, of Richmond; of the Enoch Pratt Free Library, the Peabody Library and the Maryland Historical Society, of Baltimore; and of the manuscript room of the Library of Congress. I am indebted to my wife, Rosamond Randall Beirne, for her patience and encouragement over the years the work was in progress and for the many hours of research she devoted to it; and to my sister, Lisa Beirne Leake, who made available her library rich in material on old Richmond. Mention should be made of the courtesy of Mr. John S. Stanley, former president of the Maryland State Bar Association, and of Mr. Douglas H. Gordon, also of that Association, in providing copies of their papers respectively on Luther Martin and John Marshall; and of Mr. Henry G. Alsberg, chief editor of Hastings House, for revealing notes on General Wilkinson.

For answering specific questions thanks are due Judge Brockenbrough Lamb, of the Chancery Court of Richmond, Mr. Arthur W. Machen Jr., of the Maryland Bar, and Mr. Walkley E. Johnson, Clerk of the United States Court for the Eastern District of Virginia. The last named gentlemen, however, did not see the manuscript and are not responsible for any technical errors that may appear in it.

FRANCIS F. BEIRNE

SHOUT TREASON
The Trial of Aaron Burr

Prologue

I N HIS *Critical and Historical Essays* Lord Macaulay has left
to posterity a vivid account of the opening of the impeachment proceedings against Warren Hastings, late Governor-
General of India, before the House of Lords, for high crimes
and misdemeanors allegedly committed during his incumbency.

The event took place on February 13, 1788. The scene was
Westminster Hall, London, where thirty kings had been
crowned and where Charles I faced his accusers. Macaulay tells
us that the avenues were lined with grenadiers and kept clear
by cavalry, for a great throng had assembled to view the spectacle.

Some 170 Lords, robed in gold and ermine, and marshaled
by heralds under Garter King-at-Arms, marched in solemn order from their House to the tribunal. In the procession also were
the judges in their vestments of state. Bringing up the rear were
the Duke of Norfolk, the Earl Marshal, the brothers and sons
of King George III, and, last of all, the Prince of Wales, "conspicuous for his fine person and noble bearing."

The gray walls of the ancient building, says Macaulay, were
hung with scarlet. Benches draped in red were provided for
the Peers, and benches draped in green for the Commons.
Seated in the galleries were the Queen, surrounded by the "fair-
haired daughters of Brunswick," the ambassadors and ministers
of great countries, and such distinguished personages as Mrs.
Siddons, the actress and beauty, Sir Joshua Reynolds, the artist,

3

Georgiana Duchess of Devonshire, and other women of brilliance and fashion.

There, too, were the Managers, the great orators of the day —Edmund Burke, Charles James Fox, Richard Brinsley Sheridan, William Windham, and Charles Earl Grey. They were to conduct the prosecution.

There, too, in all his injured dignity was the man who was responsible for this glamorous exhibition of justice. Nearly eight years were to pass before the tedious performance came to a close and Warren Hastings went forth a free and vindicated man.

Meanwhile the world looked on at the drama. Not the least interested spectators were members of the bench and bar of the new nation across the sea. It had lately won its independence, but none the less, especially where the law was concerned, it clung to the tradition of its mother country.

Our ancestors brought English law with them when they founded the American colonies. During the colonial period those young men who could afford it journeyed to London to study the law at the Inns of Court. No revolution of a few years' duration could sever this stout line of descent. No greater compliment could be paid an American lawyer than to remark that he was capable of holding his own with the best in the spirited forensic encounters in Westminster.

It was only natural that our American bar, reveling in the Hastings episode, should yearn to put on a similar show. It was inevitable that an opportunity would arrive.

It first presented itself in the case of Samuel Chase, a justice of the Supreme Court of the United States and an ardent and outspoken Federalist who did not hesitate to express his low opinion of Thomas Jefferson's Republican administration even from the bench. The Republican leaders in Congress took up the challenge. In eight articles members of the House compressed all the complaints of his conduct that had been made since his appointment eight years before and laid the charges before the Senate of the United States.

On February 4, 1805, the Senate, sitting as a Court of Impeachments, convened to hear the case. Mark the influence of the trial of Warren Hastings. The Senate Chamber was re-modeled for the occasion. In the center of the scene was the chair of the President of the Court—in this case the Vice-President of the United States. To his right and left were two rows of benches with desks, the whole covered with crimson cloth, like those of the Lords in the trial of Warren Hastings. These were for the thirty-four senators who were to sit in judgment. Facing them were three rows of benches arranged in tiers and covered with green cloth, as had been those of the Commons. These were for members of the House of Representatives. On either side of the chair of the presiding officer were inclosures covered with blue cloth; respectively for the Managers, who were to prosecute the case, and for the lawyers of the defense. Present, too, were the Chief Justice and the associate justices of the Supreme Court.

The young Republic, alas, could produce no peers in gold and ermine. There were no brothers and sons of a ruling monarch, nor an heir apparent conspicuous for his fine person and noble bearing. Nor could the raw and straggling community that then went under the name of Washington present the same array of genius and fashion as London. But it did the best it could with the raw material it had. In the Senate Chamber a temporary gallery had been erected. Here were boxes provided with comfortable seats from which ladies dressed in the height of fashion followed the proceedings.

Who was responsible for this elaborate and colorful setting, so obviously imitating the spectacle of a few years earlier at Westminster? Senator Plumer, of New Hampshire, records that all the arrangements were in the hands of the Vice-President who also presided over the trial. And that Vice-President was Aaron Burr. One might have guessed that no other American statesman boasted the same dramatic instinct. Nor was the stage set without his awareness that he was to play a leading part on it. And he played it well. From at least one none-too-friendly critic he provoked the comment that: "He conducted with the dignity and impartiality of an angel, but with the rigor of a devil." Burr was greatly pleased with that remark and quoted it in a letter to his daughter, Theodosia.

Through February the arguments were heard. Then on March 1 the Senate voted on the charges. The Republicans could not muster enough votes to convict and Vice-President Burr closed the proceedings with the pronouncement that Samuel Chase, Esquire, stood acquitted of all the articles exhibited by the House of Representatives against him.

The impeachment of Chase was the prelude to another legal spectacle soon to follow. Once more the leaders of the American bar were to have an opportunity to emulate their English brethren. As Burr, half-angel and half-devil, presided while Samuel Chase awaited his fate at the hands of the United States Senate, did he have an inkling that in the next cause célèbre he would appear not as presiding officer, but in the role of the accused?

This time the leaders at the bar were to have as the subject of their contention not a mere associate justice of the Supreme Court but a former Vice-President of the United States. The charge against him was to be not just incompetence in office, but the high crime of treason. An effort was to be made to show that Burr, who had been honored by his countrymen with the second highest elective office in the land, had responded to that generosity by doing his best to split the nation in half while it was still struggling for survival.

The trial was to provide another battleground for the two new political parties—the Federalists, representing wealth and aristocracy and conservatism, and the Jeffersonian Republicans, recruited from the masses and led by a man of no small fortune who was regarded by the Federalists as a dangerous radical and a traitor to his class. It was to be the scene, too, of a fight for power between the executive and the judiciary reflected in the personalities of Thomas Jefferson and John Marshall—a fight not only of immediate moment but one whose outcome was to determine the relative positions of the two branches of government for years to come.

Finally, if the accused was found guilty he faced not simply dismissal from office, but death on the gallows. Even the colorful impeachment of Warren Hastings fell short of that.

Chapter I

AT DUSK ON THE evening of the twenty-sixth of March, in the year 1807, there arrived in Richmond, Virginia, over the road from Fredericksburg, a stagecoach bearing a party of seven men. It pulled up on Main Street before the Eagle Tavern, one of the leading hostelries of the town, where in the growing darkness the passengers descended without attracting great attention.

One of them was a tall, thickset man with a weather-beaten face whose air of authority marked him as leader of the group. His companion, of less than average height, lightly built and erect, wore a rough suit of homespun with pantaloons and a hat with a wide brim which drooped disconsolately over his refined features. Those unmistakable evidences of gentility were in striking contrast to the uncouth dress of a backwoodsman.

The large man bore the name of Nicholas Perkins. He was registrar of the land office of Washington County in faraway Alabama. The second man was Aaron Burr, lately Vice-President of the United States, and now a prisoner of the United States Army. The other five men were his guards, especially picked to assure the safe delivery of the prisoner wherever the authorities might direct. Theirs had not been an arduous task. With one minor exception the prisoner could not have been more co-operative and amenable.

7

The trip from Alabama had taken 21 days, but the journey which brought Aaron Burr to his present situation might be said to have begun when he first saw the light of day more than 51 years before. For nature had endowed him at birth with a fatal combination of brilliance and deviousness that in the end was to be his undoing.

No man could have been blessed with worthier forebears than was Aaron Burr. The first of the line to arrive in this country was one John Burr, a Puritan, who came to the Massachusetts colony with Governor John Winthrop in 1630. Aaron, born on February 6, 1756, in Newark, New Jersey, represented the fourth generation in descent from the immigrant. His father, whose name he bore, was president of the College of New Jersey, shortly to become Princeton. Aaron's mother was Esther Edwards Burr, daughter of the Rev. Jonathan Edwards, theologian, metaphysician and scholar. Because of his many descendants who achieved distinction, Jonathan Edwards was destined to go down in history as one of the greatest of New England progenitors. Following the death of his son-in-law, Edwards also held the office of President of Princeton.

When Aaron was still a child his father and mother died, and he and his older sister Sally were sent to live with an uncle, Timothy Edwards, of Elizabethtown. Uncle Timothy met his responsibility with Puritan zeal. Aaron's childhood was marked by strict discipline. Distasteful though it may have been it bore practical results. A precocious youngster to begin with, he progressed so rapidly in his studies that he was ready to enter the sophomore class at Princeton at the age of 13 years. In 1772, aged 16, he was graduated at the head of his class.

Already he was beginning to exercise an irresistible charm. The hazel eyes, which seemed to cast a hypnotic spell on whomsoever they fell, the regular handsome features, and an ingratiating manner made him a favorite among his fellows and aroused lively interest in those of the other sex.

Sister Sally by now had married Tapping Reeve, another person of outstanding intellect, who conducted a law school at Litchfield, Connecticut. To Litchfield Aaron repaired, to begin professional studies under his brother-in-law. Tradition has it that at Litchfield commenced the series of love affairs that were to earn Aaron the reputation of a philanderer. There he was when the Revolution broke out.

Fired with patriotism, Burr volunteered his services in time to join the expedition against Quebec which was led by Benedict Arnold. In that arduous and ill-fated campaign he conducted himself with courage and fortitude and was rewarded by being made a captain on the headquarters staff. He displayed signal gallantry in the heat of the battle and General Montgomery, Arnold's lieutenant, died in his arms.

Arriving in Albany flushed by his exploits in the Quebec campaign, Burr received word that General Washington would find it agreeable to see him in New York City where the Commander-in-Chief then had his headquarters. On Burr's appearance there the General invited him to join his official family and Burr accepted. The prospect was indeed a pleasing one.

On this occasion, however, the usually irresistible charm failed to work. Burr, young and impetuous and fired with enthusiasm, apparently expected to be taken into General Washington's confidence and to share in planning the grand strategy. On the contrary he was treated with no particular deference and saw himself nothing more than a clerk. Disappointed and discouraged he appealed to John Hancock, President of the Continental Congress, who arranged to have him transferred to General Putnam's staff. His stay at general headquarters lasted only about six weeks.

Other later contacts between General Washington and Burr proved to be equally unsatisfactory. In the retreat of the army after the Battle of Long Island Burr saved a brigade from capture and was annoyed when the incident passed unnoticed by the General. When, a year later, a letter came from the General notifying Burr of his promotion to lieutenant colonel, instead of expressing gratitude Burr wrote a petulant reply complaining of others who had been promoted ahead of him and asking whether the late date of the commission was due to any misconduct on his part.

In the winter of Valley Forge Burr proposed a raid on Staten Island which Washington turned down. When in the same winter Generals Conway, Lee, and Gates plotted to relieve Washington of command, Burr was counted in the camp of the conspirators. At the Battle of Monmouth just as Burr was about to attack, General Washington appeared on the scene and countermanded the order. Yet when soon thereafter Burr suffered a sunstroke which ended his military career, Washington accepted his resignation "with regret."

The most authoritative account of the relationship between Washington and Burr is found in the memoir of Matthew L. Davis, Burr's friend of many years and his literary legatee. Davis states that Burr's prejudices against Washington became so fixed and unchangeable that up to his dying day he referred to the retreat from Long Island with acrimonious feelings for the commander. It is equally certain, adds Davis, that for some reason Washington placed no confidence in Burr and was exceedingly hostile to him.

Following his retirement from military service Burr was admitted to the bar and opened a law office in Albany. He soon thereafter married Theodosia Prevost, a widow ten years his senior and already the mother of five children. She bore him two daughters. Little is known about one of them who appears to have died in early childhood. The other, bearing her mother's name, lived on, as we shall see, to play a major role in the life of her father.

Letters of the elder Theodosia to her husband reveal an almost pathetic adulation. On at least one occasion Burr reacted with an impatience such as he seldom showed to anybody. Still, the marriage appears to have been on the whole a happy one, and it lasted twelve years until the death of Mrs. Burr in 1794.

Burr's intellect, his political instinct, and his charm combined to speed him on his career. Casting his lot with the Jeffersonians, he was elected to the New York Assembly. He moved to New York City and soon was recognized as a leader at the bar. There he found Alexander Hamilton already firmly established both in law and politics, and soon to apply his power and genius to blocking Burr's further progress. Hamilton, like Burr, was a veteran of the Revolution and had served on Washington's staff; but, unlike Burr, Hamilton was highly esteemed by the Commander-in-Chief. The friendship and mutual confidence there cemented were carried on into civilian life and Hamilton, who shared Washington's conservative views, entered the first President's cabinet as Secretary of the Treasury. When Burr arrived in New York Hamilton was leader of the local Federalists and the Federalists controlled the town.

After the Revolution there was established in New York and other cities in the East an organization bearing the name of the Tammany Society. Its membership was composed of mechanics and like humble citizens and it was dedicated to social, patriotic, and charitable activities. Burr was the first man in public life to realize its potentialities as a political force and to use the New York organization for the advancement of his own political fortunes. Meanwhile he had been appointed Attorney General of the state and from that vantage point was elected to the United States Senate over General Schuyler, Hamilton's father-in-law. The victory, naturally enough, served to aggravate Hamilton's jealousy and increase his concern over this rising political rival.

So far had Burr progressed in popular esteem that, in the Presidential election of 1796, he received 30 electoral votes as against 71 for John Adams, the victor, and 68 for Thomas Jefferson. His term in the Senate having expired, he returned to the practice of law and also to the New York Assembly.

In the Presidential election of 1800 Burr's meteoric political career reached its peak. He and Jefferson, running as Republicans, received an equal number of electoral votes and the election was thrown into the House of Representatives. For the first and last time Burr was within one vote of winning the nation's highest honor. But, on the thirty-sixth ballot, Jefferson was elected. As was the rule in that day Burr, who had received the next highest number of votes, became Vice-President.

In the election Burr had put his political machine to such
effective use that the Federalist monopoly in New York was
broken and enough Republicans from the city won seats in the
Assembly to give their party control. Since the Assembly chose
New York's electors, and since in the election of 1800 New
York was the pivotal state, Burr could reasonably claim credit
for swinging the election which threw the Federalists out of
the government in Washington and put the Republicans in.

Hamilton was far from being a silent witness to these events.
By now he was thoroughly alarmed not only for himself but
for the safety of the nation whose future he saw in jeopardy if
the Presidency were to go to a man of the caliber he judged
Burr to be. With all the vigor at his command he threw himself into the contest to prevent Burr from winning the necessary votes. "As unprincipled and dangerous a man as any country can boast," "as true a Cataline as ever met in conclave," a
man whose "private character is not defended by his most partial friends," "bankrupt beyond redemption except by the
plunder of his country," his "public principles have no other
spring or aim than his own aggrandizement"—these were
among the extravagant epithets Hamilton applied to Burr in
letters to friends. As much as he disliked Jefferson there was no
question in Hamilton's mind that the rangy Virginian doc-
trinaire was the lesser of the two evils. Burr could lay his failure
to attain the Presidency to the violent animosity of Hamilton.

Burr's political success in New York was disturbing not only
to the Federalists but equally so to certain members of his own
party. The New York Republicans were then divided into
three factions made up of the followers of the Livingston and
Clinton families and of Burr. All three groups were steeped in
intrigue and so bankrupt of moral principle that there was little choice between them. Albert Gallatin, Jefferson's Secretary
of the Treasury and political mentor, was inclined to give a
preference to Burr. Not so Jefferson.

The presidental election over, Burr showed his pique by
kicking over the traces. In January 1802 a bill to repeal the
hated judiciary act, passed in the previous year by the Feder-

alists, reached the Senate. A motion to recommit led to a tie vote and left the decision to the Vice-President. Burr voted with the Federalists. Then a few weeks later, to add insult to injury, he appeared as guest at a dinner given by the Federalists and there proposed a toast to "the union of all honest men." It was abundantly clear to those present that in the select company of honest men Burr emphatically did not mean to include Mr. Jefferson and the rest of the "Virginia dynasty."

Such disloyalty to his party could not be overlooked. Within a few days the Republican press, led by DeWitt Clinton's New York *American Citizen* and William Duane's Philadelphia *Aurora*, was in full cry. There was no longer any doubt that Jefferson, the Clintons, and the Livingstons were determined to strip Burr of his power and drive him from the party.

Considering the conflicting temperaments of Burr and Jefferson the split between the two men was inevitable. Though Jefferson professed to believe that Burr had declined the blandishments of the Federalists to have himself elected President in 1801, a truer opinion of Burr is revealed in a letter written some years later to Senator William B. Giles. Jefferson denied having ever had any hostile sentiment toward Burr yet confessed that he had not thought him an honest, frank-dealing man but rather "a crooked gun, or other perverted machine, whose aim or shot you could never be sure of."

An election for Governor of New York was scheduled for the spring of 1804 and though Burr's term as Vice-President would not be up until March of the following year he announced himself as a candidate. But the Clintons and the Livingstons controlled the party machine. While the rank and file were for Burr the leaders saw to it that the nomination went to one Morgan Lewis. Since the Federalists had no candidate of their own and Burr was well liked by many of them, he decided to run as an independent candidate, counting on both Federalist and Republican votes. Here he met with violent opposition from Alexander Hamilton, who had no intention of being humiliated by Burr, whom he disliked and distrusted, winning the election with the aid of Federalist votes. In the bitter campaign which followed Lewis, with the support of the regular Republicans and a minority of Federalists, was swept into office. Burr's defeat, attributed largely to Hamilton's intervention, spelled the end of his political career.

In the course of the campaign Hamilton attended a dinner at the home of a friend in Albany. It was an assembly of intimates and Hamilton freely expressed his opinion of Burr. The matter might have ended there had not the remarks he was supposed to have made found their way into an Albany newspaper, from which they were picked up by other newspapers throughout the state and used extensively in the campaign. One remark was to the effect that Hamilton had said Burr was a "dangerous man and ought not to be trusted." The other credited Hamilton with having applied to Burr the term "despicable."

Burr waited until the campaign was over. Then he wrote Hamilton a letter stating that the remarks had been brought to his attention and demanding an explanation. Hamilton's reply was evasive. After further exchanges failed to give satisfaction, Burr's friend William P. Van Ness presented himself before Hamilton with a challenge to a duel. Hamilton accepted. The date set was July 11 and the place the heights of Weehawken in New Jersey across the Hudson River from New York City.

On July 4, according to its custom, the Society of the Cincinnati, composed of former officers of the American army in the Revolution, held a convivial celebration in honor of the Declaration of Independence. Both Hamilton and Burr were members and both attended. Those present recalled later that Hamilton was unusually gay, leading the others in song, while Burr was more serious than was his usual custom at these parties. Their conduct toward each other was so correct that nobody suspected that the two men shortly were to meet in a duel.

Early on the morning of the 11th Hamilton, accompanied by Nathaniel Pendleton, his second, and Dr. Davis Hosack, his surgeon, crossed the river and arrived at the rendezvous. They found Burr and Van Ness already on the ground, busy clearing away the underbrush and overhanging boughs. The formal greetings required by the "Code" were exchanged. The seconds loaded, inspected and approved the pistols, and agreed on the procedure.

The principals took their positions. In appearance they were evenly matched. Both men were short of stature, trim in figure, alert but calm. Whatever their shortcomings neither lacked physical courage. With pistols gripped they awaited instructions which were not long in coming.

The order "Fire!" was given by Pendleton in a loud voice, and two shots followed. Burr stood unmoved; Hamilton fell forward on his face. Pendleton and Hosack rushed to the wounded man's side. Burr made a motion as if to do likewise but was restrained by Van Ness, and after removing their hats in respect for their opponent they left the scene.

Hamilton managed to tell Dr. Hosack he believed the wound was fatal before he lost consciousness. The ball had passed through his liver and lodged in his spine. He was rowed back across the river to New York and, suffering great pain, lingered through the day and night and died the following afternoon.

An incident which occurred on Burr's return to Richmond Hill, his handsome country home outside the city, affords a momentary glimpse into the strange character of the man. A young relative, unaware of what had happened, dropped by and found Burr engrossed in ordinary household matters. He accepted an invitation to breakfast where the conversation was confined to general topics. After breakfast the young man said goodby and went down to Wall Street where a friend inquired if he had heard that Burr had killed Hamilton in a duel. "Impossible," exclaimed the relative, "I have just had breakfast with the Colonel and he said nothing about it."

Those who knew him well say that Burr would have expected no mourning had he, and not Hamilton, been killed.

But if Burr's conscience was clear, not so that of the local community. Before this meeting public opinion had turned strongly against dueling as a means of settling personal differences. Anger reached fever heat when the victim was so distinguished and popular a man as Hamilton. The public cried out for punishment. Burr was indicted for murder in New Jersey and for a misdemeanor in New York. To escape the action of the courts he had to leave home and, as he expressed it, "give a little time for passions to subside."

When men faced the possibility of death in a duel it was customary for them, on the eve of the meeting, to set down parting messages. Burr's on this occasion was a touching farewell to his daughter Theodosia. Hamilton's contained an apology for his attacks on Burr. Confessing that in some particulars he might have been influenced "by misconstruction of misinformation," he concluded: "It is also my ardent wish that I may have been more mistaken than I think I have been, and that he, by his future conduct, may show himself worthy of all confidence and esteem, and prove an ornament and a blessing to the country." Later events were to give a prophetic quality to the doubt expressed.

The situation in which he found himself did little to disturb Burr's natural buoyancy. He allowed himself to be involved in a romantic episode with a lady named Celeste and wrote gaily to Theodosia: "If any male friend of yours should be dying of ennui, recommend to him to engage in a duel and a courtship at the same time. *Prob. est.*"

Burr's objective at this time was a reunion with Theodosia, who had married Joseph Alston, a wealthy South Carolina planter. The Alstons, and their little son Aaron Burr Alston, had a home in Charleston. Before going there Burr spent a brief vacation at St. Simon's Island, Georgia. His traveling companion, who acted also as secretary and aide-de-camp, was Samuel Swartwout, whom Burr described as " a very amiable young man of twenty or twenty-one." Samuel was the younger brother of John Swartwout, onetime Collector of the Port of New York and a political ally of Burr who had been ignominiously discharged by Jefferson. More will be heard of Samuel.

In the journey from Georgia to Charleston Burr included a 200-mile canoe trip by inland waterways which revealed his exceptional powers of endurance at the age of 48 years.

Around the beginning of the New Year of 1805 Burr was back in Washington as presiding officer of the Senate. His admirable conduct of the impeachment trial of Justice Samuel Chase has been mentioned. But his official days were numbered. In the election of 1804 the Republicans chose DeWitt Clinton, his New York rival, for second place on the ticket. The Republicans were again the victors and Jefferson and Clinton took office on March 1, while Burr went out.

The Vice-President made a dramatic exit. On the eve of his departure he addressed the Senate. No scribe was at hand to record for posterity his exact words. He himself stated that he had made no previous preparation, but spoke merely from the heart. What posterity does know is that he spoke so earnestly, so eloquently, and so convincingly that some of his colleagues in that austere body broke down and wept unashamedly. When he had finished, in spite of the duel, in spite of political animosities and suspicions, they "Resolved, unanimously, that the thanks of the Senate, be presented to Aaron Burr, in testimony of the impartiality, dignity and ability with which he has presided over their deliberations, and of the arduous and important duties assigned him as President of the Senate."

Was he not to be excused if, with such impressive evidence of magic power over his fellow men, he was led to imagine that destiny still had great things in store for him?

Yet, for the moment, there were serious defects in his fortunes which called for immediate repair. He was out of political office. The indictments against him in New York and New Jersey made it impossible for him to return home to the practice of law which hitherto he had found lucrative. Always extravagant in his tastes, and chronically living beyond his means, he was now heavily in debt. Soon after the duel he had been obliged to sell Richmond Hill for $25,000 to meet his more pressing obligations. As one of his biographers says of him, he was at this point what is popularly described as "a ruined man." Under these discouraging circumstances Burr turned his eyes to the West.

Chapter II

THE UNITED STATES census of 1800 showed a population of 5,308,483 persons, of whom one fifth were slaves. The bulk of it was in the states along the eastern seaboard; west of the Allegheny Mountains were fewer than 500,000 settlers, chiefly in Ohio, Kentucky, and Tennessee. The mountains served as a rugged barrier cutting off the westerners almost completely from the East and giving them a sense of political as well as physical detachment.

The only means of communication overland were three crude highways largely limited to travel by horseback or by the great Conestoga wagons drawn by six horses which carried such commerce as there was between the two areas. One road led from Philadelphia to Pittsburgh, another followed the line of the Potomac River through Maryland to the Monongahela, and a third ran through Virginia and crossed the mountains into Kentucky and Tennessee.

Once the tributaries of the Mississippi River were reached river craft provided a more luxurious mode of travel and also transported freight. The staple products of the western country were floated downstream on flatboats to New Orleans to be sold there and shipped by sea. Sometimes their owners went along to market their goods in the thriving young cities of the East and returned home across country on horseback.

That was why Spanish control of the mouth of the Mississippi at New Orleans, involving refusal of the right to deposit goods there, had been so irritating to the people of the West. The westerners with considerable justification considered the easterners indifferent to their problem and felt they were getting precious little in return for the taxes they paid to the central government. During the period of the Confederation when the prospect of a solid, united nation was anything but sure, a separatist movement sprang up in Kentucky and Tennessee. Its object was an independent nation west of the Alleghenies under the protection of Spain, whose colonial officers encouraged the idea. Though the so-called "Spanish Plot" had the support of influential men, it was not accepted by the rank and file. The purchase of the Louisiana Territory in 1803, with the control of New Orleans, and the granting of statehood to Kentucky and Tennessee, served further to weaken the separatist urge.

Magnificent as the Purchase eventually proved to be, it had serious flaws. The original mission of Livingston and Monroe to France called for the acquisition of the Floridas. Yet the final settlement did not include East Florida and left the claim to West Florida in doubt. Equally vague, and therefore a cause for controversy, was the Texas boundary. These questions, of great moment to the South and West, were little understood or bothered about by the rest of the country. They did, however, give grave concern to President Jefferson. Acquisition of the Floridas became an obsession with him and, until the issue was settled, war with Spain was always an imminent possibility. The Spanish did not help ease the tension when they massed troops on the frontier. Meanwhile in Europe the Napoleonic wars were resumed and Spain, as an ally of France, returned to her irritating practice of seizing American merchant ships that were alleged to be carrying cargoes to Britain.

Thus it came about that in his message to the Ninth Congress in December, 1805, President Jefferson's charges against Spain were so violent and his warning of retaliation so strong that many interpreted it as being virtually the introduction to a declaration of war. It was so played up by the Republican press throughout the country. This widespread belief in the immi-

nence of armed conflict was to have an important bearing on
the activities of Aaron Burr in the West. The general public
did not know that the threats in the message were primarily for
Spanish consumption and that in a secret communication Jefferson was proposing simultaneously an amicable settlement of the
Floridas dispute through purchase.

In the spring of 1805, immediately after terminating his
duties in Washington, Burr set out on horseback along the high-
way for Pittsburgh, even then a flourishing center of trade.
There he purchased a commodious houseboat and began a journey down the Ohio River. The boat contained a dining room,
kitchen with fireplace, and two bedrooms; the roof, running
the length of the craft, served as a porch and a place for exercise. Burr's ultimate destination was New Orleans but he made
a leisurely progress, stopping frequently at settlements along
the river. In that remote country any visitor from the East was
welcome and none more so than the distinguished and charming ex-Vice-President. In the West no stigma was attached to
dueling, but rather admiration was bestowed on a man who had
practiced it. And, since most westerners were Jeffersonian Republicans, the fact that Burr's victim had been a Federalist
leader was more reason for applause than for condemnation.

One of Burr's stops was at an island a few miles below
Marietta, Ohio. It was owned by an Irish gentleman named
Harman Blennerhassett who had erected a handsome mansion
on it. The master was away but Burr was graciously entertained by Mrs. Blennerhassett. The island and its owners were
to figure prominently later in the alleged conspiracy.

At Cincinnati Burr was entertained by Senator John Smith
of Ohio, a versatile fellow who, in addition to representing his
state in the Senate, acted in such diverse capacities as Baptist
preacher, storekeeper, speculator, and army commissary. There
too Burr ran into his old friend Jonathan Dayton, former U.S.
Senator from New Jersey, a kindred spirit whom he had
known since college days at Princeton. Dayton, like Burr, was
now out of a job; and, like Burr, on the lookout for an im-
provement in his fortunes.

Burr left the river and proceeded by land to Frankfort, Kentucky, and from Frankfort to Nashville, Tennessee, where he was received with public honor and invited by General Andrew Jackson to be his guest at the Hermitage. Of his relations with Jackson more will appear later.

From Nashville Burr journeyed to Fort Massac, an army post on the Ohio River not many miles above its confluence with the Mississippi, where he had another significant meeting with an old friend of Revolutionary War days, Maj. Gen. James Wilkinson. They had served together on the expedition to Quebec. Wilkinson now held the important offices of Commander-in-Chief of the United States Army and of Governor of Louisiana Territory. In the previous winter Burr and Wilkinson had met in Washington and it was reported they spent much time studying maps of the Spanish territories that adjoined those of the United States in the South and Southwest. They had become sufficiently intimate to devise a cipher to be used in their personal correspondence and so protect it from prying eyes.

Wilkinson supplied Burr with a new houseboat equipped with sails and assigned to it a detachment of soldiers which enabled Burr to make an impressive entry into New Orleans in keeping with his station as a statesman temporarily out of a job. Wilkinson provided him as well with several letters of introduction. Wilkinson was to play a major role in the alleged conspiracy.

On his arrival in New Orleans Colonel Burr was cordially welcomed by Governor W. C. C. Claiborne as well as by the governor's numerous and vociferous enemies. He saw much of the leaders of the Mexican Association, an organization sympathetic with Mexico's aspirations for liberation from Spain. He was well received also by the Roman Catholic Bishop of New Orleans who favored this cause since at the time the Spanish rulers were threatening to confiscate church property in Mexico.

After three weeks in New Orleans Burr retraced his steps northward as far as St. Louis. Again he gave an impressive

demonstration of his physical fitness by traveling on horseback
from New Orleans to Nashville through the roughest sort of
country. By the end of the year he was back in Washington
dining with President Jefferson at the White House.

Late in the summer of 1806 he again set out for the western
country. Summer gave way to autumn and as the days grew
shorter alarming rumors about his doings spread through the
East. Some of them reached the White House. What was Burr
up to?

Foremost among the informants was Joseph Hamilton Daveiss, U. S. District Attorney for Kentucky, who owed his
appointment to President John Adams. As early as January he
was writing letters to the President warning him of a plot and
implicating Burr. But the President was not happy about this
source of information. Daveiss was aided and abetted by former U. S. Senator Humphrey Marshall of Kentucky. Both
were Federalists; both were brothers-in-law of the Chief Justice for whom Mr. Jefferson had no fondness. Humphrey
Marshall, a first cousin of John Marshall, and Daveiss had married John's sisters. Furthermore all the people they mentioned as being involved in the conspiracy were Republicans.
Naturally the President wondered why his political enemies
should be taking so much trouble to keep him informed, and
suspected their motives.

Receiving no encouragement from the President, Daveiss
and Marshall pursued their campaign alone. In July there appeared in Frankfort a publication under the name of the *Western World* with which Daveiss and Marshall were closely
identified. In its September issue it openly charged that there
was a conspiracy afoot to combine Kentucky, Tennessee,
Ohio, Indiana, Louisiana, and the Floridas into an independent
government. The newspaper added that while the majority of
the conspirators wanted to call a convention and obtain the
consent of Congress, a considerable number favored effecting
their purpose by force of arms. The statement turned out to
be pure speculation; nevertheless it was picked up and widely
republished in the East.

Burr by this time was in Lexington, Kentucky. Daveiss now took another step. In his capacity as district attorney he appeared in the Federal Court at Frankfort and accused Burr of having violated the laws of the Union by setting on foot an unauthorized expedition against Mexico, a country with which the United States was at peace. A similar charge was preferred against Senator John Adair of Kentucky. Adair, a veteran of the Revolution, had accompanied Wayne and Wilkinson on a campaign against the Indians in the Northwest in 1791. He enjoyed Wilkinson's confidence, met Burr through him, and seems to have taken the attitude that Burr was an advance agent of the Federal Government to arouse the West for a war with Spain and conquest of the Southwest.

Learning of the charge, Burr presented himself at Frankfort and demanded an examination. A grand jury was empaneled but Daveiss could not round up his witnesses and asked for its discharge. Thanks to his failure Daveiss was held up to public ridicule. Two weeks later the same performance was repeated. Another grand jury was empaneled, Daveiss again failed to assemble his witnesses, and again Burr was discharged. So too was Adair. To add to his accuser's mortification Burr's second victory was celebrated by a public ball.

The silence in Washington in the face of what was going on led to two possible conclusions. One was that the administration was too weak to put up a fight even against its own destruction. The other was that if Burr actually was leading an expedition against Mexico he was doing so with the co-operation and blessing of the Jefferson administration.

Burr's dinner at the White House of the winter before lent credence to that conjecture. The public could not know that Burr had requested the meeting and had gone to the White House to beg some important office in the administration, and to warn Jefferson that if he did not get it he was in a position to do him much harm. Mr. Jefferson had enough informants on Burr's trail to comprehend what the threat implied. But he was not to be bullied or frightened. He replied calmly that he had always realized Burr had talent and hoped he would put

it to the public good. However, Burr must be aware that the
public had lost confidence in him. Mr. Jefferson did not know
why Burr should wish to do him harm but he feared no injury.

This was not the first time Burr had enjoyed the hospitality
of the White House at his own solicitation. Two years before,
when he was about to retire from the Vice-Presidency, he had
dined with Mr. Jefferson, had proposed an alliance between
them, and on that occasion too had asked for an office. The
President had declined the request. He thought the meeting
sufficiently important to note it in his diary, remarking that
Burr's conduct had always inspired him with distrust. Evidently Jefferson was not to allow this distrust to forbid Burr
the White House. No doubt he hoped to derive information
from such contacts and was so confident Burr could do him no
harm that he was indifferent to the use which Burr might put
the show of intimacy. Unfortunately, at this critical moment
the policy left the country uncertain as to how far the administration was implicated in Burr's operations.

At last the Government at Washington acted. Following
discussions by the Cabinet on October 22 and 25, John
Graham, secretary of the Orleans territory, who was in the
East and about to return to his post, was ordered to stop in
Ohio and Kentucky on his way westward and inquire into
Burr's movements. He arrived in Marietta during the middle
of November where he was warmly welcomed by Harman
Blennerhassett who talked freely with him. It seems that in his
effort to impress Blennerhassett, Burr had told him that
Graham was concerned in the plot.

Graham proceeded to Chillicothe where the Ohio Legislature was sitting and persuaded that body to authorize the governor to use the militia to seize Burr's boats that were building
at Marietta. He then went to Kentucky and induced its legislature to take action to halt the conspiracy. He was too late,
however, to prevent a flotilla under the command of Blennerhassett from passing down the Ohio River to join Burr's contingent at the mouth of the Cumberland.

On November 27 the President issued a proclamation that was broadcast throughout the western country warning all good citizens to withdraw from unlawful enterprises. Thus he made it emphatic that whatever might be taking place was without the Government's sanction.

Simultaneously orders were dispatched to the civil authorities, from Pittsburgh to New Orleans, putting them on the alert and directing them to use regular troops and militia to thwart any illegal enterprise that might be brewing. The proclamation was disappointing to the public since it left the nature of the enterprise a mystery and did not so much as mention Burr's name.

On December 1 the President sent his regular message to Congress. He made casual reference to the conspiracy, but again supplied no names. Meanwhile the House of Representatives was growing restive. John Randolph of Roanoke, the brilliant but eccentric Virginia member, who had broken with the Jeffersonians and was now constantly looking for ways to embarrass the administration, introduced a resolution requesting from the President detailed information on the conspiracy.

Thus spurred to action, President Jefferson, on January 22, addressed a special message to the Senate and House of Representatives. He stated that in answer to their request he was transmitting to them information received by him touching on "an illegal combination of private individuals against the peace and safety of the Union, and a military expedition planned by them against the territories of a power in amity with the United States, with the measures pursued for suppressing the same."

At last the President was specific. The prime mover, he said, was Aaron Burr, "heretofore distinguished by the favor of his country."

As early as September, the message continued, the Government had received reports of agitation in the western country. Then in the latter part of October the objects of the conspiracy began to be perceived. But they were still so involved in mystery that nothing distinct could be singled out for pursuit. However, the Government had sent a trusted agent to investigate the plot.

Then, said the President, on November 25 the Government had received from General Wilkinson, Commander-in-Chief, a letter in which the General reported having been visited by a confidential agent of Burr, with communications partly written in cipher, and partly oral, setting forth his designs and offering Wilkinson such emolument and command as to engage him and his army in the unlawful enterprise.

But, declared the President, "The General, with the honor of a soldier and the fidelity of a good citizen, immediately dispatched a trusty officer to me with the information of what had passed. Thanks to the General's letter and other information received a few days earlier, it was possible to develop Burr's general design."

It appeared, said Jefferson, that Burr contemplated two distinct objects, which might be carried on either jointly or separately, and either the one or the other first, as circumstances should direct.

One of these was the severance from the Union of the states west of the Allegheny Mountains.

The other was an attack on Mexico.

The President mentioned also as a third object a settlement on what he called "a pretended purchase" of a tract of country on the Washita River in northern Louisiana. As the President interpreted it, this third object, however, was merely to serve as a pretext for Burr's preparations in collecting men, boats, and supplies, and as an allurement for such followers as really wished to acquire settlements in that country. It also was to serve as a cover under which to retreat in the event of the final discomfiture of both branches of his main design.

But, said the President, Burr had found that the attachment of the western country to the Union was not to be shaken. Its dissociation, therefore, could not be obtained through the consent of the inhabitants, and Burr's resources were inadequate to effect his purpose by force. So, instead, Burr had determined to seize New Orleans, plunder the bank there, take possession of the military and the naval stores, and proceed on his expedition to Mexico.

Burr, the message further charged, had seduced good and well-meaning citizens—some of them by pretending he enjoyed the confidence of the Government and was acting under its secret patronage, others by offers of lands on the Washita.

In response to his proclamation of November 27, reported the President, Governor Tiffin of Ohio and the Ohio Legislature had, "with a promptitude, energy and patriotic zeal, which entitled them to a distinguished place in the affection of their sister states, effected the seizure of all the boats, provisions and other preparations within their reach, and thus gave a first blow, materially disabling the enterprise at its outset."

The President went on to say that when the authorities of Kentucky and Tennessee received the proclamation and learned the true circumstances, they followed the admirable example set them by their sister state of Ohio. The governors of New Orleans and Mississippi also had been alerted. Great alarm had been caused in New Orleans by the exaggerated accounts of Mr. Burr disseminated there.

But, according to the message, the faithful General Wilkinson had arrived on the scene on November 24 and "immediately put into activity the resources of the place for the purpose of its defense." Great zeal had been shown by the inhabitants generally.

In the present state of the evidence, said the President, some of it delivered under the restriction of private confidence, neither safety nor justice would permit the exposing of names, except that of the principal actor.

Of Burr, he declared, his *"guilt is placed beyond question."*

Such was the Government's version of the conspiracy as conveyed by President Jefferson to the Congress. The report was supplemented with various letters and other confirmatory documents. It left no doubt that the conspiracy had been crushed, even though at the time of its writing the "principal actor" was still at large.

Meanwhile the "principal actor," commanding a small body
of men on flatboats, was on his way down the Mississippi
River. He had arrived at a place called Cole's Creek in Mississippi territory when he first learned of the hue and cry raised
against him by the President and General Wilkinson. A few
days prior to this he had voluntarily surrendered himself to the
territorial authorities and, after an inquest like the two earlier
ones in Kentucky, he had been dismissed by a grand jury. Instead of indicting Burr the jury rebuked the authorities for
their overzealousness in interfering with him and his men.

Burr had nothing to fear from the civil authorities of Mississippi, but the military under Wilkinson's command were
quite a different matter. According to his later testimony Burr
imagined his life was in danger. For the first and last time in his
life he acted in a manner that suggested cowardice. He deserted
his followers. Disguising himself as a backwoodsman he mounted
a horse and started his flight. By this time the alarm had been
broadcast and everywhere people were on the lookout for him.

It was Nicholas Perkins who, informed of the presence of a
mysterious stranger near Wakefield, in Washington County,
Alabama, set out to investigate. His keen eye noted that the
boots showing below the stranger's pantaloons were much too
fine for any ordinary countryman. Burr, on being challenged,
acknowledged his identity and agreed to go with Perkins who
turned him over to the military authorities at Fort Stoddart,
an army post north of Mobile.

The commander was a young Virginian, Lieutenant Edmund Pendleton Gaines. Gaines engaged Perkins to deliver his
prisoner to the Government in Washington. On March 5 the
party set out. The first part of the journey, made on horseback,
lay through the Cherokee Indian country in Alabama and
Georgia. Heavy rain increased the discomfort of the travelers.
Burr bore his hardships without a whimper and with but one
incident of insubordination. As a lawyer he knew his arrest was
highly questionable. South Carolina was the home of his son-
in-law where he might perhaps find sympathy. So, while passing through the little settlement of Chester in that state, Burr

leaped from his horse and shouted, "I am Aaron Burr, under military arrest, and claim the protection of the civil authorities." Perkins, with his superior size and strength, calmly took him around the waist, sat him back on his horse, and the party proceeded. Thereafter, Burr traveled in a gig. That is, until the party shifted to a stagecoach shortly before reaching Richmond.

The original destination had been Washington. But at Fredericksburg, Virginia, Perkins received counterinstructions from President Jefferson to deliver his prisoner to the authorities in Richmond. So on their arrival at the Eagle Tavern, Perkins' task was nearly ended.

That explains why and how a former Vice-President of the United States found himself in the toils of the law. The rumors of conspiracy that had spread throughout the country during the last two years had now been confirmed by the President of the United States. Burr's guilt, declared that highest authority, was "beyond question." And, but for the honor of Wilkinson the soldier and the fidelity of Wilkinson the good citizen, who acted in the nick of time, no telling where the country would be. Such was the official version.

No wonder the general public, in the face of the damning evidence, expected the ensuing trial to be a mere formality. No wonder a toast that became universally popular was drunk to "Aaron Burr—may his treachery to his country exalt him to the scaffold, and hemp be his escort to the republic of dust and ashes."

The gallows might loom before him. Burr surveyed the prospect with his accustomed calm.

Chapter III

WHEN FORTUNE thus rudely delivered Burr at its gates Richmond was a thriving community of over 5,000 souls. Of these from a third to a half were colored slaves. The town, situated on the falls of the James River, enjoyed the distinction of being the seat of government of a commonwealth which, despite the loss of Kentucky, still extended from the Atlantic coast to the Ohio River and included the present West Virginia. It ranked as one of the important cities of the young nation along with Boston, New York, Philadelphia, Baltimore, and Charleston, South Carolina.

Richmonders boasted that their city, like Rome, was built on seven hills. These overlooked the river on the north. The most conspicuous of them was the lofty promontory known as Capitol Hill on which stood the state capitol, an impressive structure with a columned portico facing the river and some hundred or more feet above it. Credit for the design was given to Jefferson who took as his model the Roman temple known as the Maison Carrée at Nismes, France.

Richmond owed its commercial prosperity to being the city in the state farthest inland on navigable water. It was dominated by Scotch merchants who imported manufactured goods from Europe and sold them to their fellow townsmen and the planters nearby. Then they bought from the planters grain and tobacco which they marketed abroad or in the cities to the north, taking a nice profit on each transaction.

The town had been laid out many years before by Col. William Mayo, a friend of the second William Byrd, its founder. The Colonel adopted a checkerboard plan, the streets running east and west paralleling the river, each on a higher level than the other, and intersected at right angles by streets running north and south. The capitol sat in the middle of an open space of several acres known as Capitol Square, whose steep slopes were scarred with unsightly gullies. Behind the capitol the ground leveled off into a plateau whose north side, bearing the name of Shockoe Hill, served as the fashionable residential section of the town.

The Eagle Tavern to which Burr had been conducted stood on Main Street, an east-west thoroughfare at the foot of Capitol Hill occupied chiefly by shops and other business establishments. A trifle less refined than the Swan Tavern at the top of the hill, it catered to a wide variety of guests, including sportsmen, legislators, and planters who came up to Richmond periodically for a brief respite from the monotony of their plantations. The hostelry was identified by a sign, eight feet by five, displaying a golden eagle. This was no ordinary bird. It had been painted by the artist Thomas Sully, who in his later years was to become one of the leading portraitists of his day and to number among his subjects the young Queen Victoria of England. Sully got $50 for the eagle, not an insignificant sum according to 1800 standards of value.

At the tavern Colonel Burr remained under informal arrest over the weekend waiting to be handed over by the military to the civil authorities. The warrant, issued by the Chief Justice of the United States and written in his own hand, was based on the charges of treason against the United States and of a high misdemeanor in preparing a military expedition against the dominions of the King of Spain, with whom the United States was at peace.

In the early days of the Federal judiciary there were no judges of appeal, the appellant functions being performed by the justices of the Supreme Court to each of whom was assigned a circuit. Virginia, in which state Burr's crimes were

alleged to have been committed, lay in the circuit assigned to
the Chief Justice. The Judiciary Bill of 1801, rushed through
the Congress by the Federalists, provided for appeals judges.
But it had been repealed by the Jeffersonians. Thus the presence of Chief Justice Marshall in Richmond on this occasion
was attributable to Jefferson's counterattack on the Federalists,
unmindful though he may have been of the particular effect it
was going to have on the trial of Aaron Burr.

The formal procedure took place on Monday, March 30. It
was a matter of note among the Jeffersonians that the Chief
Justice did not order the prisoner to be brought to court but
instead went himself to the Eagle Tavern. They saw in this
evidence of bias rather than a demonstration of John Marshall's
consideration for a fellow man once exalted and now humbled
and reduced.

Over the weekend Colonel Burr had supplied himself with
a suit and fresh linen more in keeping with his station as a
former Vice-President of the United States than the homely
disguise he had worn on making his entry into Richmond.
Shortly after mid-day Maj. Joseph Scott, the United States
Marshal for the Virginia district, appeared at Burr's quarters
and politely informed him that the time had come for the serving of the warrant. News of Burr's arrival had spread through
the town and attracted a crowd of the curious to the tavern.
It was "an awfully silent and attentive assemblage of citizens"
that looked on as the Colonel was conducted by Marshal Scott
to a retiring room where the Chief Justice was waiting to examine him.

Present in the room with Judge Marshall were Caesar Rodney, newly appointed Attorney General of the United States,
and George Hay, the District Attorney, representing the Government; and Edmund Randolph and John Wickham, attorneys for the defense. Present also, in addition to a few subordinates and friends of the accused, was Nicholas Perkins, who
had conducted the prisoner from Alabama to Richmond.

Of the principals the youngest man there was Caesar Rodney. He had just turned 35 and was an enthusiastic Jeffersonian

who had seen service in the United States House of Representatives. His situation was embarrassing since he had recently been on friendly terms with Burr. Next in order of youth was Hay. Not a brilliant lawyer but a plodder, and a determined one, he had rapidly forged to the front at the local bar. In his rise he had no doubt been assisted by his loyal adherence to Republican ideals. In an atmosphere that laid emphasis on birth it was not overlooked that he was the son of Anthony Hay, keeper of the Raleigh Tavern in Williamsburg. Richmond, however, was producing so many self-made men that while the fact of humble origin may have been noted, and perhaps mentioned privately, it placed no obstacle in the path of those who were on their way up.

In contrast to these rising luminaries was Edmund Randolph, the eldest in the group. Men developed early in those days and though Randolph was only 54 years old he was nearing the close of a distinguished career. He traced his descent from William Randolph of Turkey Island and his wife Mary Isham. In producing worthy descendants these two were to Virginia what Jonathan Edwards was to New England. They produced in quantity as well as quality, and were referred to as the Adam and Eve of Virginia. In the drama that was unfolding in Richmond both prosecution and defense were represented by a rash of their descendants. Proud though he may have been of his heritage, Aaron Burr could not complain that in Richmond he was not largely in the company of his social peers.

At the outbreak of the Revolution, leaving William and Mary College, where he had been an apt student of the law, Randolph through his breeding and ability gravitated to the staff of General Washington. His military service was brief. It soon was apparent that, like Jefferson, his talents were better suited to matters of state than to the battlefield. From the age of 20 he was not out of office during the succeeding 32 years. He served as mayor of Williamsburg, Attorney General of Virginia, member of the Continental Congress, Governor of his state, member of the Constitutional Convention, and Attorney General of the United States in Washington's Cabinet.

Now in the twilight of his career, he was present to add dignity to the defense. As a staunch Federalist he considered it no more than his duty to lend his talents to thwarting the Jeffersonians in their determination to convict Burr.

Ten years junior to Edmund Randolph was his colleague John Wickham. Wickham was something of an outsider to Virginia. Born on Long Island in the colony of New York, the son of Tories, he was educated in France for a military career. He returned home at the outbreak of the Revolution just in time to be arrested by the American patriots, but he was released in the care of a Virginia uncle. At the close of that conflict he gave up the idea of a military career and read law. Now, at the age of 44 years, he was the recognized leader of the Virginia bar.

Hay had measured swords with Wickham in the Richmond courts enough times to recognize that he lacked Wickham's skill and dexterity. Wickham's years abroad had endowed him with a sophistication unknown to the average Virginia squire or merchant who traveled little beyond the local frontiers. Tom Moore, the supercilious young Irish poet who paid this country a critical visit at the turn of the century and abused almost everybody from the President down, made an exception of Wickham. He said he was the only gentleman he had discovered during his American travels and that he would grace any court.

Yet in this galaxy of talent the Chief Justice was as usual the dominating figure. His commanding height marked him out. His ruddy, weather-beaten complexion setting off his fine dark eyes, his genial expression suggesting a quiet sense of humor, his obvious indifference to dress, and his loose-jointed awkwardness, all these combined to make a pleasing impression of naturalness and sincerity. He and Colonel Burr were not strangers. They had known each other in Washington when Burr was in the Senate and Marshall in the House. Marshall, too, when Chief Justice, had appeared both as spectator and witness at the Chase trial.

The proceedings at the tavern were brief. Hay had objected

to the locale in the first place—it was the strategy of the prosecution to keep popular emotion high by putting on a public spectacle. He consented to the meeting in the tavern only on condition that, if arguments were needed, they would be heard at the Courthouse behind the Capitol.

It was the not unwelcome task of Nicholas Perkins to give a dramatic account of the detection of Colonel Burr under his disguise, his arrest, and the long and tedious journey from Alabama to Richmond. He spoke his piece with evident relish. When he had finished Hay submitted a motion in writing that the prisoner be committed on the charges both of treason and high misdemeanor. Counsel agreed that argument would be necessary. Hay then moved adjournment to the Courthouse and the motion was granted. The Chief Justice released Colonel Burr on bail at $2,500 for his appearance there at 10 A.M. on the morrow. Until then he was free to go about the town as he pleased.

When, next day, at the appointed hour the Chief Justice took his seat on the bench, the courtroom was filled to overflowing while a large crowd outside clamored for admission. It was a half hour after the time set for the hearing when Colonel Burr at last arrived. He apologized for keeping the Court waiting, explaining that he had misapprehended the hour.

Rather than disappoint those who could not find a place in the courtroom, the Chief Justice consented to move the hearing to the great hall of the House of Delegates in the Capitol nearby. This was a shabby chamber, unimpressive except for its size; it could accommodate a large crowd and, before the trial was over, all its space was going to be needed.

It may be imagined that Colonel Burr observed with a critical eye the drabness of the setting. Had he been in charge of the arrangements, as in the trial of Justice Chase, surely he would have ordered things differently. Colored hangings would have cheered up the premises no end and perhaps even some artistic embellishment could have been thought up for the plain sand boxes distributed around the hall at intervals for the convenience of the tobacco chewers. In this austere atmosphere all the proceedings of the trial thereafter were to take place. It was notorious that counsel on both sides, like actors in a play, addressed their remarks to the audience as much as they did to the bench.

Virginia was a big state with a variety of people. Since the crimes with which Colonel Burr was charged were alleged to have taken place on the western frontier, that territory was well represented both with respect to witnesses and spectators. So it was that in the trial room dignified gentlemen with hair powdered in the old style, and dressed in fine ruffled linen, black silk and knee breeches, rubbed shoulders with long-haired frontiersmen in leather hunting shirts and pantaloons.

The argument was opened by Mr. Hay who quoted the act of Congress which made it a high misdemeanor for any person in the United States territory to prepare an expedition against a nation with whom this country was at peace. As evidence of Colonel Burr's violation of the act he cited a letter written by the prisoner to General Wilkinson.

Hay's motion also asked that Burr be committed on a charge of treason. He based this request on the Burr letter to Wilkinson, to an affidavit given by the General, and also on an affidavit of one William Eaton. Eaton too bore the title of General, but its authenticity was questioned.

Burr's letter to Wilkinson had been written in Philadelphia in a cipher previously agreed upon between them. It was dated July 29, 1806, and read:

"Your letter, postmarked 13th May, is received. At length I have obtained funds, and have actually commenced. The eastern detachments from different points, and under different pretences, will rendezvous on the Ohio, 1st of November. Everything internal and external favors our views. Naval protection of England is secured. Truxton [Commodore] is going to Jamaica to arrange with the admiral on that station. It will meet us at the Mississippi. England, a navy of the United States, are ready to join, and final orders are given to my friends and followers.

"It will be a host of choice spirits. Wilkinson shall be second to Burr only, and Wilkinson shall dictate the rank and promotion of his officers. Burr will proceed westward 1st of August, never to return. With him go his daughter and his grandson. The husband will follow in October, with a corps of worthies. Send forthwith an intelligent friend with whom Burr may confer. He shall return immediately with further interesting details: this is essential to harmony and concert of movement. Send a list of persons known to Wilkinson west of the mountains, who could be useful, with a note delineating their character. By your messenger, send me four or five commissions of your officers, which you can borrow under any pretence you please.

"Already are orders given to the contractor to forward six months' provision to points Wilkinson may name; this shall not be used until the last moment, and then under proper injunctions. Our project, my dear friend, is brought to a point so long desired. Burr guarantees the result with his life and honor, with the lives, and honor, and the fortunes of hundreds of the best blood of our country.

"Burr's plan of operation is to move down rapidly from the falls on the 15th of November, with the first five hundred or one thousand men, in light boats now constructing for that purpose, to be at Natchez between the 5th and 15th of December, there to meet you, there to determine whether it will be expedient, in the first instance, to seize on, or pass by, Baton Rouge [then held by the Spaniards]. On receipt of this send Burr an answer. Draw on Burr for all expenses, etc. The people of the country to which we are going are prepared to receive us; their agents, now with Burr, say that if we will protect their religion, and will not subject them to foreign Power, that in three weeks, all will be settled. The gods invite us to glory and fortune: it remains to be seen whether we deserve the boon.

"The bearer of this goes express to you; he will hand a formal letter of introduction to you, from Burr; he is a man of inviolable honor and perfect discretion, formed to execute rather than project, capable of relating facts with fidelity, and incapable of relating them otherwise. He is thoroughly in-

formed of the plans and intentions of ——, and will disclose
to you, as far as you inquire, and no further. He has imbibed
a reverence for your character, and may be embarrassed in
your presence; put him at ease, and he will satisfy you."

To make doubly sure the letter would reach Wilkinson Burr
made two copies of it, one to go overland and the other by
sea. Bearer of the overland message was Samuel Swartwout,
who will be recalled as Burr's companion on the trip south
following the duel. Bearer of the copy of the letter going by
sea was one Dr. Justus Eric Bollman, a German and a soldier
of fortune. Bollmann was distinguished chiefly for a desperate
attempt at rescuing General Lafayette from imprisonment in
Austria during the French Revolution.

Swartwout accomplished his mission first, coming up with
Wilkinson in camp at Natchitoches in northern Louisiana,
where Wilkinson was standing guard against a threatened
crossing by the Spaniards of the Sabine River, boundary between Louisiana and the present State of Texas. Bollman presented himself to Wilkinson shortly thereafter in New Orleans.

But, so President Jefferson's message to Congress declared,
the indignant and patriotic Wilkinson, instead of listening to
Burr's blandishments and preparing to take second rank on the
treasonable expedition of which the letter treated, sent a warning to Washington, arrested both Swartwout and Bollman,
and packed them both off to the capital charged with high
misdemeanor and treason. On their arrival in Washington, in
order to hold them, William B. Giles, Jefferson's leader in the
Senate, got a bill through that body suspending the writ of
habeas corpus. But the House refused to go along. The Chief
Justice then issued the writ, heard the charges, and released
the two men, declaring that charges had not been proved. The
uncooperative behavior of the Chief Justice on this occasion
did not improve Mr. Jefferson's opinion of him.

Equal in importance with Burr's letter was the affidavit of
William Eaton. A Connecticut Yankee, Eaton first appeared
on the public scene as a captain in the United States Army. In
1804 he was serving as United States Consul at Tunis. It was

a time when the infant United States Navy was waging sporadic warfare with the Barbary States. Commodore Samuel Barron, commanding our Mediterranean fleet, dispatched Eaton on a mission to Alexandria where one Hamet, former Pasha of Tripoli, had taken refuge after being driven from his throne by his elder brother. Eaton's mission was to restore Hamet to the throne.

Assembling a tatterdemalion force of Greeks, Italians, and Arabs to the number of 500, Eaton led them on a gruelling march across the Libyan desert to Derne. The expedition made the 600 miles in fifty days and on top of it assaulted and captured the city.

But here the United States policy changed. New negotiations led to recognition of the usurping brother. This altered state of affairs caused a break between Barron and Eaton and the latter returned home, indignant over the manner in which he had been treated and demanding from an indifferent Congress remuneration for his services. Through his military exploits he had acquired the title of General, but he held no such commission from the United States Government.

Where a man had a grudge against the Government there repeatedly was found the trail of Burr. So it was in the case of Eaton. In the winter of 1805–06, following Burr's return from his first trip to the West, he and Eaton lived in the same boarding house in Washington and were much in each other's company. According to Eaton's affidavit, Burr told him he was organizing a military expedition against the Spanish provinces on the southwestern frontier, giving him to understand he was acting under the authority of the Federal Government. Eaton recalled that at this time the controversies with Spain and the tenor of the President's message to Congress led to the conclusion that war with that country was imminent. Having lately returned from Africa, he was unaware, he said, of any suspicions against Burr and did not question his patriotism. This, Eaton explained, was why at first he consented to embark on the enterprise and pledged himself to Colonel Burr's confidence.

But, Eaton continued, as time passed certain indistinct expressions and innuendoes aroused his suspicions that Burr had other projects in mind. He noted in particular that Burr was critical of the administration, accusing it of want of character, energy, and gratitude. Eaton suspected Burr of arousing his resentment by dilating on the harsh treatment Eaton had received on the floor of Congress in connection with his African expedition, and the delay in adjusting his financial claims against the United States.

By this time, declared Eaton, he had begun to suspect that Burr's expedition was unlawful, but he had pretended to be impressed in order to draw Burr out. It was then, he said, that Burr laid open his proposal of revolutionizing the territory west of the Alleghenies and establishing an independent empire there. New Orleans, said Eaton, was to be the capital and Burr was to be the chief, organizing a military force on the Mississippi and carrying the conquest to Mexico.

Eaton said he protested that the western people were attached to the present administration and that Burr would be opposed in his designs by the regular army of the United States stationed on the frontier. To this, he said, Burr replied that he had the preceding season made a tour through the country and attached to his person the most distinguished citizens of Tennessee, Kentucky and the Orleans territory; that he had inexhaustible resources and funds; that the United States Army would act with him; that he would be reinforced by from 10,000 to 12,000 men from the aforementioned states and territories; and that he had powerful agents in the Spanish territory.

Eaton said he told Burr he had known Wilkinson during the Revolution and ventured the opinion that he would act as lieutenant to no man in existence. Burr assured him he was wrong and led him to believe that the plan of the revolution had been made in concert with Wilkinson.

The affidavit then mentioned a plan for overthrowing the Government in Washington, assassinating the President, and revolutionizing the eastern states.

Eaton said Burr had given him nothing on paper, nor did he know of anybody to whom Burr had made similar advances.

It was, therefore, his word against Burr's. He did not dare place his testimony in the balance against the weight of Burr's character, fearing that Burr would turn the tables on him. He was therefore uncertain which way to proceed. He at last decided that the best way to save the country was to get Burr out of it. That was why he approached President Jefferson with a suggestion that Burr be sent abroad as an ambassador. He mentioned Paris, London, or Madrid. The President, according to Eaton, signified that the trust was too important and expressed something like doubt about the integrity of Burr.

Perceiving that the subject was distasteful to the President, said Eaton, and to impress him with the danger, he told him there would be insurrection in the Mississippi area within eighteen months. He quoted the President as replying that he had too much confidence in the integrity and attachment to the Union of the citizens of that country to admit any apprehension of that kind. Such, in substance, was Eaton's affidavit.

Mr. Wickham was the first lawyer of the defense to open the attack on it. There was, he declared, no evidence of treason in it. As for an attack on the Spanish settlement, if Burr had such an intention it was not only innocent but meritorious. He reminded the court that at that time there were strong circumstances pointing to a war with Spain and he cited the President's message at the opening of the Ninth Congress in December, 1805, in which the provocations were mentioned.

Wickham was followed by his colleague Randolph who, in a reminiscent mood, stated that though he had long been conversant with criminal jurisprudence, never before had he heard of anybody attempting to prove an overt act of treason from a supposed intention.

Colonel Burr now made clear his intention to act as his own counsel in the trial. Addressing the court he ventured the opinion that there was no cause for all this concern. He charged that Wilkinson had alarmed the President and that the President had alarmed the people. When he, Burr, heard that charges were being preferred against him while he was in the West, had he not voluntarily hastened to meet investigation both in Ken-

tucky and Tennessee? Yes, he had fled later, but only after he
had learned that military orders had been issued to seize his person and his property. He protested that there was no proof of
his guilt other than the affidavits of Wilkinson and Eaton. As
for these they were "abounding in crudities and absurdities."

Attorney General Rodney next addressed the court. He had,
he said, looked upon Colonel Burr as his friend and, in fact, had
received him in his house. But now the chain of circumstances
showed without doubt that he was guilty. He thought that the
evidence presented was sufficient for commitment. It was his
contention that for a mere commitment no such complete testimony was needed as in an actual trial. This brief comment from
the Attorney General proved to be the last words he was to
utter in the case. In a day's time illness in his family—or such
was the excuse given—took him from Richmond and the trial
and he did not return. Whatever part he played in it was performed in Washington.

Thereafter the burden of the prosecution fell on the con-
scientious and hard-working Hay. The District Attorney, too,
had had family sorrow. A week before Burr's arrival in Richmond he lost his wife, Rebecca, a young woman of 25 years.
But the bereaved husband had little time for mourning. Nor
did he allow his grief to interfere with the performance of his
official task with all the effectiveness his limited talents could
command.

When the arguments were over Judge Marshall introduced
a procedure he was to follow steadfastly throughout the trial.
He adjourned court and promised that he would deliver his
opinion the following day. He was as good as his word. The
opinion was in writing. He had had the evening before in which
to review the arguments and from them arrive at his own conclusions. Like all his opinions, this one was closely reasoned and
carefully drawn. Nobody was going to be given grounds for
charging him with such arbitrary and high-handed behavior on
the bench as had brought about the impeachment of Justice
Chase. Again a numerous audience was on hand to hear what
the Chief Justice had to say.

Judge Marshall quoted Blackstone to the effect that only if it was manifest that no crime had been committed or that the suspicion was wholly groundless would it be lawful to discharge a prisoner. Otherwise he must be committed to prison or released on bail. By that, he continued, he did not mean to say that the "hand of malignity may grasp any individual against whom its hate may be directed." His audience picked up their ears, especially those who were anxious to catch the Chief Justice in a false step. Was not the hand of malignity to which he referred that of President Jefferson? It sounded suspiciously like it. One man who put that interpretation on it informed the Chief Justice who, immediately after adjournment, called to the bench those who were reporting the trial and stated explicitly that the observation had no allusion to the Government's conduct in the case before him.

The Chief Justice's conclusion was that enough evidence had been presented to warrant a commitment for a high misdemeanor. But a commitment for treason was a different matter. He pointed out that the assembling of forces to levy war was a visible transaction. Numbers must witness it. If, therefore, in November or December last a body of troops had been assembled in Ohio, it was impossible to suppose that affidavits establishing the fact could not have been obtained by the last of March. The evidence that had been given proved the loyalty of the western people to their eastern brethren. How strange then that no man could be found who would voluntarily depose that a body of troops had actually assembled for an object which had been detested by these people. He concluded: "I cannot doubt that means to obtain information have been taken on the part of the prosecution; if it existed, I cannot doubt the practicability of obtaining it; and its non-production, at this late hour, does not, in my opinion, leave me at liberty to give to those suspicions which grow out of other circumstances, the weight to which at an earlier day they might have been entitled. I shall not, therefore, insert in the commitment the charge of high treason."

On the commitment on the charge of high misdemeanor the

Chief Justice set bail at $10,000. Hay thought it too low and said so. Wickham commented that Burr had few friends in Richmond. What is more he had heard several gentlemen of great respectability say they were unwilling to appear as bail for him for fear of being regarded as enemies of their country. The defense was careful to lose no opportunity to emphasize the popular prejudice against their client.

Nevertheless, in spite of Mr. Wickham's concern, sureties were found and Colonel Burr was released for his appearance at the next meeting of the Court of Appeals for the Virginia District on May 22. In the initial skirmish the prosecution had met with a setback. The prisoner was not to be treated as a man who had tried to destroy the nation and who might still be dangerous if permitted to roam at large.

From the White House the proceedings in Richmond were being closely watched. Details were reported as fast as messengers on horseback could carry dispatches from Attorney Hay to President Jefferson. The President was hardly surprised at the direction events were taking. The Chief Justice had been a thorn in the flesh from the moment Mr. Jefferson took office. His latest ruling was strictly according to form. Well, some day he would overstep the mark. The President must be on the alert to seize the opportunity when that day came.

Chapter **IV**

To Thomas Jefferson and John Marshall history has assigned positions in the first rank of the nation's great men. Their backgrounds show a remarkable similarity. Both were Virginians, Jefferson being twelve years senior to Marshall. Both were the sons of frontiersmen, Peter Jefferson having established himself in Albemarle County and Thomas Marshall in Fauquier County, a short distance to the north, when those counties were still outposts of the Virginia colony. Both were tall and loose-jointed, but where Marshall was dark, Jefferson was sandy-haired and freckled. Jefferson's indifference to dress matched that of Marshall.

They were, according to Virginia's intricate way of determining relationship, "third cousins once removed," being descended through their mothers from the famous William Randolph and Mary Isham. Both were educated to the law and both were students of Virginia's most distinguished law teacher, Chancellor George Wythe, though Marshall's instruction under him was only for a few weeks. In short there was every reason why these two highly gifted Virginia cousins should share the same attitudes and prejudices and hold the same opinions on the great issues of the day.

But fate had decreed otherwise. Early in their relationship distrust and antagonism developed. Marshall's biographer Beveridge traces it to the harsh days of the American Revolution.

45

The Marshalls, father and son, were warriors who volunteered their services on the outbreak of hostilities. They fought at Great Bridge, the first engagement of the Revolution on Virginia soil. They later were present at the battles of Brandywine and Germantown. John was at Valley Forge and by then promoted to captain. According to all accounts he was a shining light in that winter of gloom, spreading good cheer through the camp and idolized by his men. In the next campaign he fought at Monmouth and Stony Point.

During the ordeal of Valley Forge General Washington is said once to have inquired, "Where is Jefferson?" Jefferson had, of course, been serving his country in a different way as a member of the Continental Congress. In retrospect it is obvious that he served it better as author of the Declaration of Independence than he might have as a mediocre soldier. Allowances for Jefferson's military ineptitude are easy to make now in the light of his other great accomplishments; they were not so easily made by those of his contemporaries who had to do the fighting.

Whatever prejudices the Revolution may have sparked between the two cousins were fanned into flame by the subsequent events which shaped their careers. Jefferson went to France as American Minister where his theory of the liberty and equality of men pronounced in the Declaration found startling application in the revolution taking place there. Very naturally Jefferson's sympathy was with the revolutionists.

Meanwhile at home the masses of the people were reveling in their new-found freedom, ignoring their responsibilities as citizens, disregarding property rights, refusing to meet their debts, and showing so little willingness to join in united action that many thoughtful men feared for the survival of the new nation.

Among the latter was John Marshall. By now he was married to Mary Ambler, daughter of Jacquelin Ambler, state treasurer, who had moved with the capital when in 1779 Governor Jefferson transferred it from Williamsburg to Richmond. The elder Ambler died some years before 1807 but the fashionable quarter of Shockoe Hill was dominated by his children and relatives. The Marshalls occupied a charming brick house which John Marshall built for his wife in 1788. He enjoyed a lucrative law practice, his clients being for the most part the well-to-do merchants and members of the creditor class. Marshall's interests and his sympathies turned in their direction. He himself came to the conclusion that the country's only salvation rested in a strong central government. He shared this opinion with Washington and Alexander Hamilton and the other conservatives who sought to replace the loose and ineffective confederation with a compact and articulate union. These men and others with kindred ideas evolved as Federalists.

Jefferson returned home from France to join Washington's Cabinet as Secretary of State. It soon became apparent that an ideological gulf separated him from his colleagues. There had been political factions before but now for the first time the two divergent attitudes toward government became so clear-cut that two political parties were the inevitable outcome. Jefferson assumed the leadership of the party of revolt against the Federalist domination that had developed during Washington's administration and continued under that of John Adams. The issue reached a climax with the victory of the Jeffersonian Republicans in the presidential election of 1800 and Jefferson's elevation to the presidency.

Defeat threw the Federalists into a panic. Already the civilized world was shaken to its depths by the events in France where the original respectable movement to suppress tyranny and substitute for it democratic institutions had degenerated into a reign of terror, culminating in the execution of the king and queen. And now the government of the United States, insecure at best, was about to be placed in the hands of a man who approved the French Revolution and in other ways had revealed his indifference to established institutions. As the Federalists saw it, in a few weeks the House of Representatives would be "Jacobin" while in a few years the Senate too would be in the hands of the radicals.

From the Federalist point of view one hope remained. Thus far not a single Republican tainted the national judiciary. In his message to the expiring Congress on December 3, 1800, President Adams urged its expansion. The message, incidentally, though bearing the signature of the President had been written by Secretary of State Marshall. The Federalist Congress, following the advice of the President, passed the bill which increased the number of district judges and created an entirely new system of circuit courts with three judges to each circuit. The Republicans, perhaps because they thought the Federalists would not have time to make use of the measure before leaving office, put up only a mild opposition. They reckoned without the fierce determination of the rival party to seize this last opportunity to curb the Republican President and Congress.

Meanwhile Marshall had been named Chief Justice, and until the Federalists went out of power he was to have the distinction of holding at one and the same time the offices of Chief Justice and Secretary of State. So it came about that far into the night on the eve of Jefferson's inauguration President Adams nominated from his own party judges and other court officers created under the new law, the judges to hold their seats for life. As fast as he nominated them the Senate confirmed them. Then John Marshall, in his capacity as Secretary of State, signed and sealed the commissions of the Federalists who were to form the officers and rank and file of the judiciary army which he in his capacity as Chief Justice was to lead!

Marshall's law practice and his political prejudices might throw him with the wealthy elements of Richmond society, but neither these nor his growing importance in the world relieved him of the common touch. His simplicity of manner, his carelessness about dress that bordered on slovenliness, his humor and good fellowship appealed to all classes. It was the custom in those days for the man of the household to do the marketing. Mr. Marshall was a familiar figure in the early morning at the market at 17th and Main streets where he bartered with the country folk who brought in their fresh vegetables, meats, and other supplies. His market basket filled, he would, like other gentlemen, stop in at the booth of Joseph Darmstadt, the

Hessian, who kept boiling hot coffee on the stove to which customers were free to help themselves, and there gossip over the affairs of the day. Darmstadt had valuable connections with the Pennsylvania Dutch farmers who had drifted into the Valley of Virginia and brought choice provisions to market, making the long trip in Conestoga wagons. Or Mr. Marshall might be seen on horseback, a bag of clover resting on the pommel of his saddle, setting out for a farm he owned on the outskirts of the town.

Many of his political opponents—among them Patrick Henry and George Mason—held him in deep affection. The sad exception was Jefferson. With all his democratic principles, Jefferson was not a good mixer. He had an innate reserve that made ordinary men self-conscious in his company. When reports reached him that John Marshall was the most popular man in Richmond, he could not contain himself. Was not Marshall, by thus cultivating the good will of the masses, poaching on territory Jefferson regarded as peculiarly his own? In the autumn of 1795 he wrote to his friend Madison: "His lax lounging manners have made him popular with the bulk of the people in Richmond; and a profound hypocrisy with many thinking men of our own country. But having come forth in the plenitude of his English principles the latter will see to it that it is high time to make him known." Anger did not help Jefferson's clarity of expression but his meaning is obvious. Marshall, as Jefferson saw him, was a hypocrite.

Yet in spite of his dislike for Marshall, Jefferson was careful to observe the amenities. When Marshall returned from a mission to France in 1797, unsuccessful as the mission had been, he was given an ovation on his arrival in Philadelphia, then the seat of government, and a public dinner was arranged in his honor. Jefferson was in Philadelphia at the time and promptly called on Marshall. Not finding him at home he left a note expressing disappointment at not seeing him and regret that a previous engagement would prevent his attending the dinner. Marshall, not to be outdone in courtesy, sat down next day and penned a reply stating that "J. Marshall begs leave to accompany his respectful compliments to Mr. Jefferson with assurance of the regret he feels at being absent when Mr. Jefferson did him the honor to call on him. J. Marshall is extremely sensible of the obliging expression contained in the polite billet of yesterday."

These sentiments were hardly in keeping with "J. Marshall's" true feelings. For once he was not exercising that candor which his friends considered his strongest attribute. For if Jefferson distrusted Marshall, that distrust was in no measure greater than Marshall's distrust of Jefferson. When in the presidential election of 1800 Jefferson and Burr received an equal number of electoral votes and the election was thrown into the House of Representatives, Hamilton, displaying his usual animosity toward Burr, appealed to Marshall, then a member of the House from Virginia, to support Jefferson. To Hamilton's appeal Marshall replied on New Year's Day, 1801: "To Mr. Jefferson whose political character is better known to me than that of Mr. Burr, I have felt insuperable objections. His foreign prejudices seem to me totally to unfit him for the chief magistracy of the nation which cannot indulge those prejudices without sustaining deep and permanent injury. Your representation of Mr. Burr, with whom I am totally unacquainted, shows that from him still greater danger than even from Mr. Jefferson may be apprehended. But I can take no part in the business. I cannot bring myself to aid Mr. Jefferson."

Here then was Jefferson, afraid that Marshall and his followers would turn the nation's government into an hereditary monarchy; and Marshall equally afraid that Jefferson and his party, unless restrained, would soon reduce the nation to anarchy. To such absurd extremes can political partisanship drive otherwise highly intelligent men.

In spite of his anxieties and misgivings, Marshall, in his capacity as Chief Justice, performed his official duty in administering the oath of office to President Jefferson. How painful that duty must have been is revealed by a letter he wrote on the same day to his friend Charles Cotesworth Pinckney, of South Carolina: "The Democrats are divided into speculative theorists and absolute terrorists. With the latter I am disposed to class Mr. Jefferson. If he ranges himself with them it is not difficult to foresee that much difficulty is in store for the country—if he does not, they will soon be his enemies and calumniators." Strong words for the Chief Justice to use against the President of the United States so soon after the Chief Justice had administered the oath to the President.

During the first nine months of his administration Jefferson had sufficient evidence of the animosity of the Federal bench, largely directed by Marshall, to write to a friend: "The Federalists have retired into the judiciary as a stronghold . . . and from that battery all the works of republicanism are to be broken down and erased."

The Republicans were not slow in taking up the Federalist challenge. Their first major offensive was the impeachment of Justice Chase. The blustering, choleric Chase, with his violent partisan comments from the bench, had provided just cause for complaint, Heaven knows. Yet his trial by the Senate and his exoneration from the charges leveled at him by the House indicated that impeachment was a dull and unreliable weapon. The verdict left Jefferson more than ever convinced that a grave error had been committed in the Constitution by granting to the judiciary authority equal to that of the executive and legislative branches. Marshall's epochal decision in the case of Marbury versus Madison, confirming the Supreme Court's right to pass on the constitutionality of laws enacted by Congress, strengthened that belief. Nowhere was the presumption of the judiciary better exemplified than in the person and actions of John Marshall. Jefferson's unerring political instinct told him that the quickest and surest way to cut the judiciary down to size was to get rid of Marshall, either by impeachment or by amending the Constitution to make Federal judges removable from office at the will of the President and Congress.

But a case must first be made against Marshall. The Burr trial presented a perfect opportunity. Of this the President and the Chief Justice were both well aware, and the party leaders no less than the President and the Chief Justice. So it was that, at Rich-

mond in the spring of 1807, Aaron Burr did not stand at the
bar alone. The Chief Justice also was on trial.

President Jefferson had taken his time in acting against the
alleged conspirators. He had been waiting for tangible evidence
that would stand up in a court of law. Once he was convinced
that he had it he moved with dispatch and determination to
find Burr guilty. Otherwise, after the unequivocal charge of
"guilt beyond question" proclaimed to the nation in his special
message to Congress, he and his administration would be made
to look ridiculous. If the Chief Justice cooperated to this end,
all well and good. If on the contrary, as Jefferson foresaw, the
Chief Justice raised obstructions in favor of the prisoner, he
would do well to look to his own head. It was already being
rumored that the President was so set on getting rid of Marshall, and so confident that doing so was a mere matter of time,
that he had already chosen a successor in Spencer Roane, another Virginian, but one consecrated to the cause of Republicanism.

And here at the very outset of the trial the Chief Justice was
prejudging the charge of treason by stating that if there had
been treason there must by now be evidence of it. But no evidence had been produced before the court. In a letter to his
friend Senator Giles, the President unbosomed himself on the
unreasonableness of the decision.

"In what terms of decency can we speak of this?" he asked.
"As if an express could go to Natchez, or the mouth of the
Cumberland and return in five weeks, to do which has never
taken less than twelve! . . . But all the principles of law are to
be perverted which would bear on the favorite offenders who
endeavor to overturn this odious republic! . . . The nation
will judge both the offender and the judges for themselves. If
a member of the Executive or Legislative does wrong, the day
is never far distant when the people will remove him. They
will see then and amend the error in our Constitution which
makes any branch independent of the nation. . . . If their protection of Burr produces this amendment, it will do more good
than condemnation would have done . . . and if his punish-

ment can be commuted now for a useful amendment of the Constitution, I shall rejoice in it."

If letting Burr go scot free resulted in checkmating Marshall and putting the judiciary in its place, Mr. Jefferson was willing to pay even that price. As for the lack of witnesses the Government, if the Chief Justice would only give it reasonable time, would take care of that. From Washington, Attorney General Rodney sent out printed circulars for wide distribution throughout the western country urging every good citizen to step up and communicate to the Government any information which might "contribute to the general welfare." The allusion was obvious. A deputy marshal and special messenger were dispatched to Wood County, Virginia, to round up witnesses from the vicinity of Blennerhassett Island where the overt act of treason was alleged to have occurred.

Secretary of State Madison and the Attorney General solicited the help of General Andrew Jackson to the same end in Tennessee. Wilkinson, in New Orleans, sent agents in search of information through Louisiana and Mississippi. This governmental dragnet brought results. Witnesses and depositions combined reached an impressive total of close to 150.

Whether they would all be heard was a different matter. They still had to pass an exacting test contrived by counsel for the defense, sufficient to convince the Chief Justice that the admission of their evidence was strictly within the letter of the law. Let the public make whatever deductions it pleased about the trial at Richmond, John Marshall did not intend to deviate one inch from what he considered to be the sacred duties of a judge in the execution of justice.

Chapter V

COLONEL BURR in a letter to Theodosia complained: "The Democratic papers teem with abuse against me and my counsel, and even against the Chief Justice. Nothing is left undone or unsaid which can tend to prejudice the public mind, and produce a conviction without evidence."

His complaint must have included the Richmond *Enquirer* whose editor, Thomas Ritchie, was coming to be recognized as one of the leading Republican editors of the nation. Ritchie had been born in Tappahannock, Virginia, when that town was a thriving port on the Rappahannock River. His father, Archibald Ritchie, was a Scottish merchant who was charged with being a Tory during the Revolutionary War. His mother was Mary Roane and through her he was related to the best families in that section. Archibald Ritchie died when Thomas was still young and the widowed mother put the lad to the study of law with her kinsman Spencer Roane, the rising lawyer and ardent Republican who, as has been mentioned, was believed to be Jefferson's choice for Chief Justice if disaster should overtake John Marshall.

But Thomas did not like the law. He switched to medicine only to discover that he liked that even less. A spell of school teaching, followed by one of bad health, brought him to Richmond where he opened a small bookstore. Then, at the urging of Thomas Jefferson and his cousin Spencer Roane, he established there a newspaper supporting the Republican cause. The first issue of the bi-weekly *Enquirer* appeared on May 9, 1804. It was kept alive by party patronage in the rarefied atmosphere of Richmond where most of the prosperous people who could afford the luxury of a $5 per annum subscription were Federalists and subscribed to *The Gazette*.

Ritchie was by no means a party hack. If he thought the administration in Washington was at fault he said so. In fact, his occasional outbursts of independence provoked from that indefatigable party regular, William Duane of the Philadelphia *Aurora*, the charge of being "a wolf in sheep's cloth."

By 1807 Ritchie was firmly established in the editor's chair and also in Richmond society to which his birth entitled him. In that year he married Isabella, daughter of Dr. William Foushee, first mayor of Richmond and one of the leading doctors. Isabella, before her career as mother ended, was to bear him twelve children, threatening the supremacy of Eliza Wickham who had a brood of seventeen.

Emaciated, sallow, long-nosed, thin-lipped, and unsmiling, Thomas Ritchie looked the part of a crusader. In his treatment of Burr in the columns of *The Enquirer* he was regular enough to have met the most exacting specifications of Duane. It is true that a few days after Colonel Burr's arrival in Richmond *The Enquirer* piously declared: "It is difficult for us to distinguish all those cases in which we ought to speak from all those where we should be silent. Perhaps the editor of the *National Intelligencer* has nearly struck the proper line of discrimination: like him we shall abstain from all 'impassioned representations'—and like him—we shall 'unhesitatingly give all new facts as they offer themselves' without any regard to the party whom they favor."

Contrary to this impressive declaration of impartiality *The Enquirer* had not hitherto shown itself altogether free from bias. On March 13, for example, it had reprinted from the *Intelligencer*, that other vehement mouthpiece of the administration which was published in Washington, the statement: "That Aaron Burr has formed a treasonable plan leveled at the destruction of every ingredient of our felicity cannot be disputed."

On March 24, two days before the arrival of the Colonel in Richmond, *The Enquirer* again quoted the *Intelligencer:* "Let us not hereafter hear it said that a Republican government is deficient in vigilance. . . . That it [the conspiracy] was deliberately formed we have reason to believe from the character of its author, and from the deposition of General Eaton, which shows that his mind had long dwelt upon it and had contemplated it in its various aspects."

Nor did *The Enquirer* let its impartiality go to the point of withholding from its columns a dispatch from Baltimore quoting an extract from a letter from a "gentleman of unquestionable character," dated "New Orleans, February 17" and declaring: "I must acknowledge that Burr is the most consummate scoundrel and artful liar that I ever had an acquaintance with." *The Enquirer* followed this with a squib from the Philadelphia *Aurora,* which, under the heading "An Outlaw Emperor," said in part: "The Federalists have now an opportunity of exhibiting new evidence of their sympathy and attachment to traitors."

On the other hand the Federalist press could not boast that its hands were altogether clean. As the trial got under way, *The Gazette,* speaking for the conservative element, presented in its columns an extract from a letter allegedly received from Caroline County, between Richmond and Washington—no doubt penned by a gentleman of as "unquestionable character" as *The Enquirer's* gentleman from New Orleans—whose subtle aim was to discredit the Government's witnesses. It stated that a man on his way to Richmond as a witness for Mr. Jefferson against Colonel Burr had been detected in an attempt to start an insurrection among the Negro slaves in that county. Since the Virginia countryside was still in a state of alarm over an abortive uprising led by a slave named General Israel several years before, no more serious charge against a witness could have been made.

That, warned *The Gazette,* "ought to make the court and

jury extremely cautious in giving credence to witnesses on both sides until characters are examined. Such a man would not scruple to swear away a man's life for a few dollars."

In announcing his policy of impartiality Editor Ritchie had reserved to himself the right "unhesitatingly to give all the new facts as they offer themselves." While Colonel Burr was free on bail an opportunity presented itself such as would delight the heart of any editor.

Richmonders in those days lived well. The farms outside the city provided a varied supply of meats, poultry, vegetables and fruits in season. The town was sufficiently close to salt water to be supplied with oysters and other seafood in spite of primitive methods of refrigeration. Mrs. David Randolph, who conducted a fashionable boardinghouse and was famous as cook and provider, was credited with having devised a cold box that served as a model for the first refrigerator in this country. Ships from abroad that dropped anchor at City Point, below the town, brought in consignments of the finest wines that, along with the rest of their cargo, were poled on flatboats upstream to the city market. In the spring of the year the James was alive with shad which came up to fresh water to spawn. For a naturally hospitable people the temptation to entertain was overwhelming.

A popular custom among the members of the legal profession was "lawyer dinners" at which the lights of bench and bar sat down together to partake of good food and drink and to engage in sparkling conversation. In this form of entertainment John Wickham excelled. He was among the élite who dwelt on Shockoe Hill and no household there enjoyed a higher reputation for serving the best of food. None boasted more capable servants than Bob, the butler, and Bob's wife, the cook, who, under the guidance of Eliza Wickham, could prepare the most complicated dishes. No one, except for the most impelling reason, would decline an invitation to attend one of the Wickham dinners.

During the more than seven weeks between Colonel Burr's commitment and the convening of the court on May 22, time was hanging heavy on the hands of the principals. It was not surprising that Mr. Wickham should have seized the opportunity to give a lawyer dinner and to introduce his distinguished client to this delightful local custom.

No one enjoyed a lawyer dinner more than the Chief Justice, whose wit and good humor made him a welcome guest. His house was within a stone's throw of Mr. Wickham's. He and the Chief Justice were good friends as well as neighbors and the Chief Justice had often been a guest of Mr. Wickham. What then was more natural than that Mr. Wickham should extend an invitation to Judge Marshall? Judge Marshall accepted the invitation and attended the dinner.

What none of them seems to have grasped was the obvious impropriety of the judge who was to preside at the trial appearing as a guest at a dinner given by the leading lawyer for the defense at which the defendant also was a guest!

The significance of the incident, however, was not lost on Editor Ritchie. The story of the dinner was soon public property. There appears to have been no attempt to conceal it. So for the issue of *The Enquirer* of Friday morning, April 10, Mr. Ritchie did not have to rack his brains to find an idea suitable for his acid pen. This issue contained an article signed "A Stranger from the Country." It did not require a gift of clairvoyance to perceive that the "Stranger" was none other than Mr. Ritchie himself.

Said the Stranger: "In the *Argus* of the 7th it is stated, and the fact is now too notorious to be doubted, that the Chief Justice has dined with Aaron Burr at Mr. Wickham's, since he himself solemnly decided that there was probable cause to believe Burr guilty of a high misdemeanor against his country."

The editor first directed his attack at Mr. Wickham. He alluded to the old charge of Mr. Wickham having been a Tory in the Revolutionary War, indifferent to the fact that the same charge had been made against his own father. The people of Virginia, observed Mr. Ritchie, had generously forgiven that error of his youth. But Mr. Wickham "should modestly have refrained from recalling it to our recollection by entertaining a suspected traitor to the Union as his guest, a report so defamatory to his own fame."

Having thus disposed of Mr. Wickham, the editor dipped his quill in acid and set to work on Judge Marshall. "I have never," he confessed, "had any the least confidence in the political principles of the Chief Justice. I have never discovered in his public (for I am ignorant of his private) character, any of that noble candor which his friends have made the theme of such extravagant eulogium. I cannot discern in him, for my soul, those splendid and even Godlike talents, which many of all parties ascribe to him, his book certainly displays none such." The allusion was to Judge Marshall's recently published *Life of Washington*.

The Stranger continued: "But I have always been informed, and until now have believed, that he was a man of excellent judgment, most consummate prudence, and of a deportment highly decorous and dignified. I took his merits upon trust and bountifully gave him credit for good qualities I find he does not possess." Mr. Ritchie now shook an accusing finger at Judge Marshall. "Let me inform the conscience of the Chief Justice that the public do not view his dining with Burr as a circumstance as trivial as he himself may incline to consider it. . . . We regard such conduct as a willful prostration of the dignity of his own character, and a wanton insult he might have spared his country."

The writer then asked several questions that were on the tongues of many Richmonders and which for years after the event were to provide a subject for popular speculation. "I have searched in vain in my own mind for some apology for conduct so grossly indecent. . . . Was the Chief Justice ignorant that Burr was to be of the party to which Wickham invited him? If so, what are we to think of Mr. Wickham's delicacy toward his friend? If so, why did not the judge leave the house as soon as he discovered the indignity imposed upon him?"

Then came the peroration: "Has the Chief Justice forgotten

or neglected the maxim which is on the mouth of every tyro of the law—that *the administrator of justice should not only be pure but unsuspected*?"

The editor was not yet through with the Chief Justice. The incident continued to be "news" around the city, for in the issue of *The Enquirer* of Tuesday, April 28, Ritchie returned to the subject. This time his comments were contained in a column headed "Extract from a letter written by a resident of Richmond Hill to his friend in the country." The Resident said he had been informed that Judge Marshall had been apprised of the invitation to Colonel Burr. But, commented the Resident, that could not have deprived him of his faculty of locomotion "unless he had been touched by the transforming wand of Circe." Richmond was full of witty classicists. The reference to Circe's wand, which turned men into swine, and its application to the magical effect of Mr. Wickham's dinner on the Chief Justice could not have been lost on them.

"But," continued the Resident of Richmond Hill, "perhaps the imagination of the judge was stronger than his appetite, and he had not fortitude enough to tear himself away from the prospect before him. In this the judge must pardon me if I am reminded of one of Goldsmith's dishes of tongue with a small garnish of brains. Many judges have been condemned for the errors of the heart and the head, but I hope, dear F., that the list is not enlarged by errors of the appetite."

At that point Editor Ritchie brought his torment to a close. As for the Chief Justice, he no doubt thought much, but he said not a word.

Professor George Tucker, Jefferson's biographer, was present at the dinner and an eyewitness to what went on there. He made a report on what he saw, and what he did not see he said he got "from an authentic source." According to Professor Tucker's version, a few days after Colonel Burr had been released on bail Mr. Wickham invited him to dine with a large party, among whom was the Chief Justice, a neighbor and personal friend. But, on the morning of the dinner, realizing that there might be some impropriety in the situation, Mr. Wickham informed Judge Marshall that Colonel Burr would be among the guests.

Judge Marshall, however, being a man of delicate feeling, was afraid that if he were to withdraw at that late hour, after having accepted the invitation, he might be regarded as being unduly fastidious, and that such action might be interpreted as a censure on his friend. So he went to the dinner. "But," testified Professor Tucker, "he had no communication whatever with Burr, sat at the opposite end of the table, and withdrew at an early hour after dinner."

One version of the incident had it that the Chief Justice asked the opinion of his beloved wife Molly and that she advised against his going. But it was not like the judge to act contrary to her judgment. At any rate, concludes Professor Tucker, no one was more sensible of the indecorum than the Chief Justice, "but it was not an act of deliberation, but merely inconsiderate."

As to the effect of the incident on the subject of his biography Professor Tucker remarks: ". . . it no doubt contributed to increase the alarm and apprehension of Mr. Jefferson, always sufficiently disposed to judge the Federal party with the same harshness that they judged him." And well he might. Contemporary comments make it clear that then, as today, a judge dining in company with the man he is about to try and at the home of the chief lawyer for the defense is, to say the least, an inexcusable act of impropriety. As Editor Ritchie declared at the time, it is not the sort of thing that would be expected of a man of "excellent judgment, most consummate prudence, and of a deportment highly decorous and dignified."

Chapter VI

ON MAY 22 the Circuit Court of Appeals for the District
of Virginia, before which Aaron Burr was to face the
charges of treason and high misdemeanor, convened at 12:30
o'clock. But first a grand jury would have to be picked and
pass on the charges. Far ahead of the hour a throng moved on
the hall of the House of Delegates where the session was to be
held. It was a throng composed solely of men, for a court of
law in Virginia in those days was no place for a lady. Save in
Virginia's great debate on the ratification of the Constitution
in the convention of 1788 Richmond had never before seen
such a colorful and distinguished assemblage.

For days strangers had been descending on the city from all
sides until the taverns and inns were filled to capacity. The
hardier stock from the western outposts of the Commonwealth
did not even try to find accommodations: they brought tents
with them and camped on the low ground beside the river.
Some came out of curiosity, others were there on court business. The administration's offensive to counter the Chief Justice's demand for witnesses to Colonel Burr's alleged criminali-
ties, directed by the Federal officials in the western country and
spurred on by the tireless efforts of the patriotic Wilkinson,
had borne results. It was estimated that persons concerned in
the trial as counsel, witnesses, and in other official capacities
reached a grand total of 200.

So large was the crowd in the hall that lawyers of long service at the local bar were forced out of their rightful places by officious interlopers. This was no commonplace gathering. Here and there could be distinguished men who had already made their names in history and others who later were to become famous.

Anybody who was familiar with the Navy would have recognized two veteran sailors, their faces bronzed by wind and sun and salt spray, who had served their country well. They were Stephen Decatur the elder and Thomas Truxtun, commodores both. Decatur boasted commendable service as a privateersman in the Revolutionary War, but he was to be overshadowed by his son of the same name. Truxtun, too, began his naval career as a privateer in the struggle for independence. Later he supervised the building of the frigate *Constellation* and, on her completion, took command and mustered her first crew. His latest exploits were the capture of the frigate *L'Insurgente* and the defeat in battle of the frigate *La Vengeance* in the quasi-war with France.

Present, too, was William B. Giles, loyal party man and President Jefferson's leader in the Senate. He was there, oddly enough, under a summons of the United States Marshal for the Virginia District to be a member of the panel from which the Grand Jury was to be chosen. Burr thought it unreasonable, considering Giles's politics. Soon he was going to say so.

There, too, was "General" Eaton, author of the affidavit, now present in person. The "Hero of Derne" wore a broad scarlet sash around his middle which provided an exotic touch to his costume and a silent rebuke to those who questioned his title and his fame. Eaton was a great talker and, so it was said, when not attending court spent the better part of his time at the tavern bars.

One might have marked a handsome young man with blue-gray eyes and a head of abundant chestnut hair. He was a stranger to Richmond and his accent betrayed a northern background. His name then meant nothing to anybody save the little group of Burr's friends who had come down from New

York to lend the prisoner moral support during the trial. This was Washington Irving, lately returned from a European tour. He had read law and been admitted to the New York bar; there was a report to the effect that he had actually had a client. But even at this early stage in his career he was more active with his pen. He and his older brother William, and William's brother-in-law James K. Paulding, had just launched a sprightly magazine satirizing New York society under the title of *Salmagundi*. Brother William and Paulding were having to carry the burden while Washington was away.

William was a Republican, Washington's sympathies were Federalist. Fastidious by nature, Washington rose superior to the unpretentious merchant family into which he had been born. The Irvings, on the other hand, were immensely proud of their precocious son and all too glad to give him a helping hand in his rise in the world. They liberally financed the trip to Europe and it had been a great success. There young Irving made the grand tour and lived in style in the Paris of Napoleon's empire. He had himself fitted out by the best tailor. He sat for the rising young American painter, John Vanderlyn, then resident in Paris. The work seems to have been undertaken out of the sheer delight of the artist in having such a pleasing model.

On his travels Irving had made the acquaintance of two Virginia gentlemen of the bluest blood, a Mercer of Fredericksburg and Joseph Cabell, the Governor's brother. He looked forward to renewing the acquaintance on his trip south, particularly that with Cabell who had just married Mary Walker Carter. Irving was told she was one of the wealthiest young women in the state. The young New Yorker was there on a literary retainer. It was said that some of Burr's friends thought he might help the cause through his writings. But if any of his accounts of the trial ever got into the newspapers the record of them has been lost.

A familiar figure to most of the Virginians in the hall was a tall, gaunt man with absurdly long legs for so short a body who spoke in a high falsetto voice. His leather breeches and his riding boots identified him as a country squire. In actual fact he had ridden up to Richmond from his estate, Bizarre, some sixty miles to the south. This was the brilliant and eccentric John Randolph, master as well of Roanoke. A horse, he once said, was to him what a ship was to a sailor. A member of Congress, Randolph had acted none too astutely as one of the Managers, or prosecutors, in the impeachment trial of Judge Chase. He, too, had received a summons from the Marshal to appear for jury duty. Like the Chief Justice and Edmund Randolph, he was a part of the lengthened shadow of the prolific Turkey Island pair, William and Mary Isham Randolph.

Standing out conspicuously in that dense throng was still another youth. His height alone would have distinguished him, for he was 6 feet 4½ inches tall. Not content with looking over the heads of the crowd he climbed up on the great lock of the entrance door of the hall in order to get an unobscured view of the proceedings. From his perch he had a good look at the accused. Colonel Burr saw him, too. The young man was Winfield Scott. Years later, when he had become one of the nation's great soldiers, the two met again and Burr reminded the general of the encounter. Contemporaries described Scott as the most magnificent youth in all Virginia.

At the time of the trial young Scott was reading law in the office of David Robertson, of Petersburg. Not only was Robertson well grounded in Blackstone and Coke and the intricacies of the Virginia statutes, he also was an accomplished linguist with a knowledge of five languages. What is more, he had trained himself to take notes in shorthand, and he was present at the trial to record the proceedings. Thanks to David Robertson, posterity has in two fat volumes a reliable verbatim account of much that was said at the trial. It was at Robertson's suggestion that young Scott came to Richmond to get a first-hand impression of the leaders in what he then intended to be his chosen profession.

Better known to the Richmonders of the day than he was to be known to posterity was a queer Scotsman named James Ogilvie who was to be a regular attendant at the sessions. According to local gossip he was heir to an earldom and had passed up the title to become an impoverished schoolteacher in Virginia. Elocution was his forte and he not only came to the trial himself but brought his pupils along so that they could have a practical demonstration of the art of oratory from the greatest practitioners of the day. Ogilvie was in bad repute with the local clergy. Either an atheist or an agnostic, he traveled about delivering "infidel lectures." He was blamed for shaking the religious faith of a number of Virginia's young men. But the Devil got him in the end. As an elocutionist he failed to live up to his own exacting standards, grew melancholy, and committed suicide. Or so it was said. A less romantic account of his death attributed it to an overdose of laudanum, a drug to which he had become addicted.

On this day there were new faces both among the counsel for the defense and for the prosecution. Now associated with Edmund Randolph and John Wickham was Benjamin Botts, the youngest lawyer on either side, bubbling over with the wit and sprightliness of youth. Already he had made his mark at the Virginia bar.

When Caesar Rodney peremptorily retired from the case President Jefferson at once recognized that the plodding District Attorney Hay needed reinforcement. William Wirt seemed the ideal choice; the summons went out from the White House and Wirt accepted. Wirt's Swiss and German background, which he inherited respectively from his father and his mother, showed itself in his curly blond hair, his blue eyes, and his fair complexion. He was built in heroic proportions, over six feet tall, broad-shouldered, with thick eyebrows, a wide forehead, a prominent nose, and ample chin. With his agreeable countenance he combined rare good humor and graciousness. A young woman who came under his spell remarked that Wickham was handsome but that he seemed insignificant in contrast to the manly beauty of Wirt. The same young woman observed that while Wickham went out of his way to please he could not suppress an air of condescension. Wirt, on the other hand, contrived to give the flattering impression, not that he was trying to please, but that he himself was being entertained.

Like Hay, Wirt was self-made. His father, too, was an innkeeper in the 1770's, at Bladensburg, Maryland, a few miles north of the future site of the national capitol. At an early age William was left an orphan, but from the start he had the gift of making friends. Among other accomplishments he sang and played the violin. His schooling completed he read law, moved to Virginia, and was admitted to practice in Culpeper County. There he met and married a daughter of Dr. George Wilmer, a man of prominence in the community and a friend of Thomas Jefferson. Through his father-in-law Wirt was introduced to Jefferson and also to Madison and Monroe and was an ardent follower of what was known in the political world as "the Virginia dynasty."

These early associations, combined with his own superior talents, played an important part in the fashioning of Wirt's career. Five years after their marriage Wirt's young wife died and the rising young lawyer moved to Richmond. For a time he held the office of clerk of the House of Delegates, then served briefly as Chancellor of Virginia. He was a frequent visitor at Gray House, the home of Colonel Robert Gamble, a prosperous merchant. This imposing dwelling, on a hill overlooking the James River and commanding an extensive view of the river valley and the rolling country of Chesterfield County on the other side, had been built for Colonel Gamble by Benjamin Latrobe, an architect recently arrived in this country from England. In 1802 Wirt took as his second wife Colonel Gamble's daughter Elizabeth, and through that connection became the brother-in-law of Governor William H. Cabell who married Elizabeth's older sister Agnes.

Wirt was well known to the Richmond bar where he had appeared in a number of important cases. A notable one was in defense of the nephew of Chancellor Wythe, law teacher of Jefferson and Marshall. The nephew was charged with the murder of his uncle by putting arsenic in his coffee. Wirt was reluctant to take the case and did so only under a sense of

duty. He handled it so successfully that the nephew was exonerated. If that constituted a gross miscarriage of justice, as many
then believed, the blame could not be put on Wirt. He was
now to have an equally spectacular chance to show whether
he would be as good a prosecutor as he had been a defender. At
the time of the trial the Wirts were sharing the Gray House
with the Gambles senior and the Cabells. It was a gay and
accomplished household.

Present also with the prosecution was Alexander MacRae,
who held the honorable office of Lieutenant-Governor of Virginia. One of the seven sons of a Scotch parson who was an
ardent Tory in the Revolution, MacRae showed his independence by embracing the American cause and ending as an equally
ardent Republican. He had a reputation at the local bar for a
sharp tongue and a sour disposition. One observer remarked
that where Wirt used a rapier MacRae's favorite weapon was a
meat axe. In contrast to Wirt's bonhomie MacRae gave the impression of being completely indifferent to popularity. MacRae
was among the elect in residence on Shockoe Hill. His house
was within a stone's throw of those of the Chief Justice and
Mr. Wickham. Neighborly though they may have been, neigh-
borliness did not extend to Mr. MacRae being included in Mr.
Wickham's notorious dinner.

So dense was the crowd in the courtroom that it was with
difficulty that Chief Justice Marshall, clad in his robes of office,
made his way to the bench. He was accompanied by Judge
Cyrus Griffin, of the Federal district court, who sat with the
Chief Justice throughout the trial.

Cyrus Griffin was no ordinary man. He was fortunate in
being born the son of Col. Leroy Griffin, of Lancaster County,
Virginia, and his wife, Mary Anne Bertrand. His parents sent
him to be educated in England, a privilege that was reserved
for the sons of the well-to-do. He studied law in the Temple,
then met and married Lady Christina, daughter of John Stuart,
sixth Earl of Traquair, in the Scottish peerage. On his return
to this country, in spite of his years in England and his Scottish
wife, he adhered to the American cause, was elected to the

Continental Congress, and for a time served as its president. In politics he was a Federalist.

Now he sat beside Chief Justice Marshall. Once in the course of the long trial the Chief Justice inquired of Judge Griffin about past procedure, in a minor incident leading up to the trial, on which his recollection was vague. From Judge Griffin he received an answer. If the Chief Justice ever deferred to him again, if the Chief Justice so much as asked his colleague how he was bearing up under the heat, the record is silent on the matter.

At the time of the trial Judge Griffin had been on the Federal bench for 18 years. In the course of that long service there were many times when he had had to render decisions. In rendering them he must perforce have had to think. Cyrus Griffin was not a wax effigy. There must have been a heart beating under his judicial robes. He must have taken pride in his office. But if the Chief Justice, other than on the occasion mentioned, reflected that it would be considerate at least to make a pretense of consulting his fellow jurist, the record does not show it.

All we are told is that Judge Griffin sat on the bench with the Chief Justice. So he goes down in history as a footnote. But he should be a footnote in heavy black type. For in his humble position in that famous trial he was the perfect symbol of all the poor mortals whose fate it is to be just important enough to occupy a place on the stage, but to be given no speaking lines and to serve merely as background for the star performers.

But the chief object of attention was the prisoner at the bar. To many there Burr was already a well-known figure; others were seeing him for the first time. They craned their necks out of curiosity to learn what manner of man this was who had set to work to carve an empire in the Southwest and in so doing disrupt the nation. If Burr had been denied the opportunity to arrange the setting dramatically, as he had done for the impeachment proceedings against Justice Chase, he still was at liberty to give attention to his personal appearance. He had selected a suit of fine black silk and he wore his hair powdered, a picture of scrupulous neatness. His manner was calm, col-

lected, and dignified, his mind apparently concentrated on the
proceedings and indifferent to the stares of the curious. To
Winfield Scott, who was watching him from the far end of the
hall, he looked "as composed, as immovable as one of Canova's
living marbles."

Impressive too was the Chief Justice. His admirers had accustomed themselves to the carelessness of his dress. They centered their attention on his majestic head, without a single gray
hair, set on broad shoulders, his ruddy weather-beaten face, his
dark luminous eyes approached in beauty only by the hazel
eyes of Burr. It was frequently remarked during the trial that
never before had two such pairs of eyes beheld each other.

Marshall's friends spoke of him as the soul of dignity and
honor, prudent, courageous, immovably resolute to do the
right, "the Washington of the Bench." Not so the champions
of Jefferson. They saw him on the contrary as "suave, almost
unctuous, wearing the mask of impartial benevolence" which
was "to slip conspicuously more than once in the course of the
trial . . . revealing a partisan as malevolent as any that Jefferson ever faced."

When the courtroom had quieted down proceedings were
opened by the clerk calling the names of those who had been
summoned for the Grand Jury. Burr was on his feet at once.
He lost no time in making it clear that he was going to act as
his own counsel. Learned in the law and thoroughly at home
with court procedure he was not going to hesitate to interpose
when he saw a chance to make a point in his favor. When he
spoke his remarks were crisp and to the point.

Selection of the jury was now the object of his attention.
Only a week before Burr had written to Theodosia: "The
grand jury is composed of 20 Democrats and 4 Federalists.
Among the former is W. C. Nicholas, my vindictive and
avowed personal enemy—the most so that could be found in
this state!" He referred to Colonel Wilson Cary Nicholas, a
former member of Congress. By "the grand jury" Burr meant
the panel of 24 men from whom the jury of 16 would be
chosen. His immediate aim was to use every legal means to

overcome the disadvantage of having the charges against him heard by a group composed chiefly of Jeffersonians and among them men he knew harbored a personal animosity toward him. He therefore begged to point out to the court that under the law the Marshal was required to summon twenty-four free-holders. But if any of them had been stricken off the list and others substituted in their places the act was illegal. He asked if such had been the case.

This afforded the first opportunity of the day for opposing counsel to warm to their task, and they debated the issue for more than an hour. At the conclusion of the arguments the Chief Justice ruled in favor of Colonel Burr and the names of the men substituted for the original twenty-four were removed.

Burr now was to exercise his right of challenge. The first juror to be dealt with was Senator Giles. It was he who, a few weeks before, in direct violation of Republican principles of the days of the Federalist alien and sedition laws, introduced the bill to suspend the writ of habeas corpus in the cases of Swartwout and Bollman and nursed it through the Senate. It was no fault of his that it met with ignominious defeat in the House.

However, in this instance he was no part of a plot to rob Burr of justice. He was there because the Marshal had called him. No sooner had Burr questioned his fitness to serve than Giles admitted prejudice and volunteered to withdraw.

Nicholas, who was questioned next, proved equally tractable. He made no attempt to conceal his dislike and suspicion of Burr. He recalled how he had opposed him when the presidential vote was thrown into the House of Representatives of which Nicholas was then a member. He declared that he had no desire to serve on the Grand Jury. But word had come to him that if he tried to withdraw an effort would be made to embarrass him by publishing certain things against his reputation. He hesitated therefore to retreat in the face of his enemies. Burr here interrupted to deny that any of his followers had made any such threat. Following this exchange Nicholas withdrew.

Joseph Eggleston, another member of the panel, did not wait

to be challenged. Veteran cavalry officer who had followed Light Horse Harry Lee in the Revolution, former member of Congress and of the Virginia Assembly, he confessed that, after reading Eaton's deposition in the newspapers, he had expressed himself with great warmth and indignation. He therefore asked to be excused.

The situation was perfectly made for Burr's claim that it was impossible to get a fair trial in the light of the public prejudice against him. He was quick to take advantage of it.

"Under different circumstances," he said, "I might think and act differently, but the industry which has been used through this country to prejudice my cause, leaves me very little chance indeed of an impartial jury."

Pausing a dramatic moment for reflection he continued: "There is very little chance that I can expect a better man to try my cause. His desire to be excused, and his opinion that his mind is not entirely free upon the case, are good reasons why he should be excused; but the candor of this gentleman, in excepting himself, leaves me ground to hope that he will endeavor to be impartial." Could the Colonel, by any chance, have been calculating that Eggleston would show him the consideration that one gallant officer of the Revolution might expect from another?

And now the name of John Randolph was called. Randolph appealed to the Court, protesting and begging to be excused, pleading that he had the impression the prisoner was guilty of the charges preferred against him. It was ridiculous to suppose that in the face of this frank admission of bias Randolph's participation in the case would be given consideration.

But there were extenuating circumstances. Randolph's enthusiasms and loyalties seldom lasted long. At an earlier time he had been one of the President's most ardent hero-worshippers. Once the leader of the Jeffersonians in the House he had now broken with his party and was neither fish, flesh, fowl, nor good red herring. A master of caustic epithet he had tagged Mr. Jefferson with the name "St. Thomas of Cantingbury." On the other hand of late he had on occasion expressed admiration for the Chief Justice. Now not only was this man with admitted prejudice against the accused to be put on the jury but the Chief Justice was to make him its foreman. And this without protest from Colonel Burr.

No wonder the Jeffersonians interpreted this as a clever move on the part of Judge Marshall to place in a key position a man who could be expected to counterbalance the strongly Jeffersonian flavor of the jury.

Politics aside, if the United States Marshal for the District of Virginia had spent a lifetime at the task of assembling a panel he could not have brought together one more representative of the best brains, blood, and ability in the Commonwealth. The descendant of Jonathan Edwards, who stood at the bar, had no reason to complain that the Grand Jury which was to pass on the charges preferred against him was not composed of his peers in the most literal sense of the term.

John Randolph and Joseph Eggleston have been mentioned. Another juryman was Joseph Carrington Cabell, brother of the Governor and a finely educated man who shortly was to collaborate with Thomas Jefferson in founding the University of Virginia. This was the Cabell whose acquaintance young Washington Irving had made in Europe.

Equally worthy in that select company were Littleton Waller Tazewell, James Barbour, and James Pleasants. All three were to be governors of Virginia, Tazewell and Barbour were to represent Virginia in the U.S. Senate, and Barbour was to enter the Cabinet of John Quincy Adams as Secretary of War.

In less spectacular company James Mercer Garnett would have been outstanding. His claims to distinction were membership in the Virginia Legislature, in the U.S. House of Representatives, and as first president of the United States Agricultural Society. For variety the jury included one banker, John Brockenbrough, who had abandoned the medical profession to become the treasurer of the Bank of Virginia. Later he was to be its president. Perhaps his rarest achievement was that he made and kept the friendship of the fickle John Randolph of Roanoke. Interestingly enough it was a boast that in this company he shared with Tazewell who also managed to hold Randolph's affection.

Another member of the jury bore an unusual relationship to the foreman. This was Robert Barraud Taylor, of Norfolk. Years before as hot-headed youths at William and Mary College the two had a falling out which led to a challenge followed by a duel in which Taylor was wounded. He still carried in his side a slug fired from Randolph's pistol. The record does not show that their meeting on the jury revived the animosity.

Numbered among the sixteen were Edward Pegram, member of a family prominent in Petersburg and shortly to become mayor of that busy commercial city, and John Mercer, whose family was honorably associated with Fredericksburg. There was Mumford Beverley in whose veins ran the blood of the Byrds of Westover. There was John Ambler, first cousin of the Chief Justice's wife and a Shockoe Hill neighbor. Finally there were three jurymen who left no conspicuous public record behind them—Thomas Harrison, Alexander Shephard, and William Daniel. But they all bore good names. Looking at the sixteen chosen men as they arose from their seats and proceeded to the Grand Jury room Burr might have flattered himself that few prisoners had ever been honored with a jury of such quality.

However, it was not characteristic of Burr to acknowledge favors. Quite the contrary. He was up and addressing the Court again, this time to ask the Chief Justice to advise the jury on the admissibility of certain evidence he assumed Hay would place before them. Hay retorted that he trusted the Court would grant no indulgence, but treat Burr like any other man who had committed a crime.

Here was another chance for Burr to assume a posture of injured innocence. Rising to his feet he exclaimed: "Would to God that I did stand on the same footing with every other man. This is the first time I have been permitted to enjoy the rights of a citizen. How have I been brought hither . . . ?"

Here the Chief Justice interrupted Burr's soliloquy to remark that such digressions were improper. After a little more of such skirmishing between counsel Court was adjourned while all Richmond was held in suspense as to whether the Grand Jury would indict and, if so, what crimes the indictment would include. Burr may not have liked the complexion of the jury, yet he might have gone farther and fared worse.

Simultaneously with the adjournment a tall, cadaverous frontiersman was reported to be haranguing a crowd from the steps of a grocery store just off the Capitol Square, in the same breath damning Jefferson's administration and declaring that Colonel Burr was a victim of its persecution. The name of the speaker meant little to most Richmonders, though it was already well known in Washington and in the speaker's home state of Tennessee. The man was Andrew Jackson. What was he doing in Richmond? And why had he taken it on himself to deliver this public excoriation of Jefferson and defense of Burr?

Chapter VII

ON MAY 29, 1805, on his first visit to the West, Aaron Burr arrived in Nashville, Tennessee. There he was heartily welcomed as was becoming a former Vice-President of the United States, a member of the ascendant political party in that section of the country, and one who in the best frontier tradition had met his man on the field of honor.

Still another potent reason for the warmth of the reception was Tennessee's gratitude to Burr who, as a member of the Senate, had actively supported her successful appeal for statehood.

Foremost among those greeting the statesman was Andrew Jackson, Nashville's first citizen, businessman, planter, sportsman, former judge, and major general of militia. The two had met before in Philadelphia when that city was the seat of the Federal Government and Jackson appeared there briefly as Senator from Tennessee. The General retained vivid recollections of a magnificent dinner he had attended as a guest of Colonel Burr—a dinner featuring foods and wines which reflected the Colonel's reputation as an epicure. Jackson was only one of many guests and Burr did much entertaining. It is not improbable that in the intervening years Burr had forgotten the tall, lanky frontiersman who had not at that time made his mark on the national scene. But even if that were the case Burr was far too astute to let Jackson know it. He saluted him as an old friend.

The bustling young town did itself proud in entertaining its distinguished visitor. There were military reviews to the sound of martial music, the firing of salutes, and the cheers of the crowds along the way. Crowning the celebration was a banquet at which General Jackson undertook to repay Burr's hospitality in kind, and where toasts were drunk until late in the evening.

After the public festivities were concluded Burr stayed on for five days as a guest of Andrew and Rachel Jackson at the Hermitage. The Jacksons had only recently moved in and the dwelling that was to become so intimately associated with them was a mere blockhouse consisting of a single room downstairs, two rooms upstairs, a kitchen, and a detached guest house in the yard.

From Nashville Burr proceeded to New Orleans where his welcome was as cordial as that extended him in Kentucky and Tennessee. In August he was back in Nashville after a strenuous journey on horseback through wild country that would have tested the physical vigor of any man and satisfied the Tennesseans that here was no effete easterner but a red-blooded individual who could keep pace with the best of them. This was not the Burr of the drawing room but the veteran warrior of the Quebec campaign and numerous pitched battles of the Revolution.

On this occasion Burr was a guest at the Hermitage for eight days. Of the second visit the Colonel wrote in glowing terms to Theodosia: "For a week I have been lounging at the house of General Jackson, once a lawyer, after a judge, now a planter; a man of intelligence, and one of those prompt, frank ardent souls whom I love to meet."

What bond held the two men together? No formal record was kept of their conversations but more than a year later, when much had happened, the General wrote a letter to a friend in Washington, George W. Campbell, that throws light on the two meetings.

Prevalent throughout the western country was the belief that war with Spain was inevitable and imminent. Spain had been forced against her will to consent to the sale of Louisiana by Napoleon to the United States. New Orleans, though now an American possession, was flanked by the Floridas on one side and by Mexico on the other, both still Spanish territory. A Spanish army stood threateningly on the Sabine River which separated Texas from Louisiana. Acquisition of Louisiana Territory, too, brought on a renewed fever for expansion in the western country. Underlying the spirit of unrest was the fact of an aged dying empire faced by a young and virile country. The West was so confident of itself and so contemptuous of the Spaniards that it longed for action. No person there was more impatient than Andrew Jackson who looked scornfully at the dilatory policy in Washington. In Aaron Burr he thought he saw the dynamic leader needed to put an end to dilly-dallying.

According to what Jackson said in his letter to Campbell, Burr told him the expedition he was planning was primarily to settle the Wachita lands to which he claimed a title. However, if on the way down the Mississippi River war with Spain were to break out, as seemed probable, his force could be diverted to march into Mexico, support the patriots there, and effect the country's independence from Spain. For this plan of action Burr assured the General he had the support of the Washington administration. It was a plan which fired the General's imagination, and, as Burr outlined it, bore no taint of illegality. By November Burr was again in the East, spending part of his time in Washington and there dining with the President at the White House.

On March 24 Burr wrote a letter to Jackson which contained several mischievous passages. First he reported what he knew would be unpleasant news to the General—that the Administration was against a war with Spain, "if it can be avoided with honor, or even without." Equally irritating to the fiery Tennessean must have been Burr's report that Jefferson was trying to wring from Congress an appropriation of $2,000,000 for the purchase of the Floridas. Why, the General might have asked, was the nation proposing to hand out all that money for what it could get by the use of its strong right arm?

Yet, continued Burr, in spite of the pacific attitude of the Administration there still was reason to expect hostility. He argued that Spain, aroused by Miranda's activity in behalf of the independence of her American colonies, which the United States Government was suspected of supporting, would attack this country.

Whether Burr actually believed that or not it gave him a chance to get in a little flattery. He observed that he had often said that a brigade could be raised in West Tennessee capable of driving double the number of Frenchmen off the earth. Would General Jackson care to select officers for two regiments from colonel down? If so, and in case troops should be called, Burr would recommend the list to the Department of War ". . . and I have reason to believe that on such occasion my advice would be listened to. . . ." Burr had no such reason. He was vague, as usual, but the implication was strong that he was acting with the knowledge and consent of the Administration.

Burr closed his letter on a critical note that played up to Jackson's prejudice against the occupant of the White House. He had been told, he said, that Mr. Randolph had charged the President with duplicity and imbecility. "All these things, my dear Sir, begin to make reflecting men to think, many good patriots to doubt, and some to despond." Just what did he mean? Burr was again resorting to innuendo which he handled so skillfully.

While Burr was in the East General Jackson had been fully occupied. In April his thoroughbred stallion Truxton won a classic race against Joseph Erwin's Ploughboy, earning a stake of $3,000, which the General greatly needed, and establishing his owner as the leading turfman of the West. This sporting event was followed by the General's meeting with Charles Dickinson in a duel in which Dickinson was killed. On the way to the duelling ground the General was not too preoccupied with the business in hand to discuss the Spanish matter with his second, General John Overton. He doubted that the conquest of Mexico would be as easy as Burr imagined. "Burr," he commented, "is as far from a fool as ever I saw, and yet he is as easily fooled as any man I ever knew."

Jefferson's help the General did not value highly. He was then under the impression, which had been encouraged by Burr, that the Government was a silent partner in the plotting against Spain. He prophesied that the Federalists, when they learned about it, would assail the policy tooth and nail. And, he observed, when they did so Mr. Jefferson would "run like a cottontail rabbit." Here was the rugged frontiersman's scorn for the timidity of the intellectual in the White House.

In the autumn of 1806, more than a year after his first visit, Burr returned to Nashville. His welcome was as cordial as ever. Another banquet and a ball were given in his honor. Burr entered the hall on the arm of Jackson, resplendent in the uniform of a major general of militia. The General had seen to it that all his friends were on hand to pay their respects to the distinguished visitor. The tall, raw-boned Jackson and the trim, diminutive Burr made a striking contrast. When time came for the drinking of toasts, Jackson arose and offered the always popular one: "Millions for defense; and not one cent for tribute." Did he have in mind the two millions Jefferson was just then trying to get from Congress for the purchase of the Floridas?

On this visit Burr gave Jackson an order for five large boats and provisions sufficient for the complement of men they would carry. In payment he tendered $3,500 in Kentucky bank notes. Jackson turned over the execution of the contract to his faithful friend and partner, John Coffee. Meanwhile another friend of Jackson's, one Patton Anderson, set to work in earnest raising a company of young men to go with the Burr expedition down the river, whatever the destination might be.

On Colonel Burr's appearance in Nashville in late September he imparted confidential information to Jackson which led the latter to believe that war with Spain was about to break out. On the strength of it the General on October 4 took it upon himself to issue a proclamation to the Tennessee militia stating that the menacing attitude of the Spanish forces already inside the American boundary required that the militia be called out and made ready for instant duty. He then notified President Jefferson of his readiness to tender his services:

"Sir: In the event of insult or aggression made on our government and country from any quarter, I am well convinced that the public sentiment and feelings of the citizens within this State, and particularly within my division, are of such a nature and such a kind that I take the liberty of tendering their services, that is, under my command; and at one moment's warning, after your signification that this tender is acceptable, my orders shall be given conformably." There could not have been a more generous and loyal gesture.

To a man of Jackson's impetuous temperament Jefferson's reply was like a dash of cold water in the face. "Always a friend of peace," wrote the President, "and believing it to promote eminently the happiness and prosperity of mankind, I am ever unwilling that it should be disturbed as long as the rights and interests of the nation can be preserved. But whenever hostile aggressions on these require a resort to war, we must meet our duty, and convince the world that we are just friends and brave enemies."

This noncommittal philosophizing was hardly agreeable to the ears of a man whose command was already drawn up under arms and waiting impatiently for the proper authorities to give the word "go." It could not have failed to increase Jackson's distaste for Jefferson.

The friendly relations between Burr and Jackson continued as late as November 3. Then, within a week, Jackson's attitude underwent a sudden reversal. The change came with the visit to the Hermitage of a Captain Fort, a stranger to the General. Fort stayed for the night and part of a day. By this time the country was seething with rumors of a conspiracy, and the conversation between the master of the Hermitage and his guest turned on that subject. Captain Fort ventured the opinion that part of the plot was the division of the Union.

The General asked him how it would be done. Captain Fort replied that it would be done by seizing New Orleans and the bank there, closing the port, conquering Mexico, and uniting part of the Union to that country. It was to be accomplished, he said, with the aid of Federal troops under the command of General James Wilkinson. Jackson inquired if Burr was involved. Fort replied that he did not know. Asked where he got his information, he said it came from Col. John Swartwout of New York. At this the General pricked up his ears, for Swartwout was well known as a political lieutenant of Burr.

Impressed and shocked, Jackson acted with characteristic directness. He ordered Coffee to accept no more contracts from Burr. He penned a letter to Burr in strong terms, telling him of his suspicions and warning him that until they were cleared from his mind he wished no further intimacy to exist between them.

While Jackson had only suspicions of Burr he appears to have been convinced of the guilt of Wilkinson, whom he had known in years past, with whom he had had business dealings, and for whom he had no love. To Gov. William C. C. Claiborne, of the New Orleans territory, he dispatched a dramatic warning: "Indeed I fear treachery has become the order of the day. . . . Put your town in a state of defense. Organize your militia and defend your city as well against internal enemies as external. . . . Be upon the alert; and keep a watchful eye upon the General [Wilkinson] and beware of an attack as well from our own country as Spain." In his idle moments at the Hermitage between horse races and duels General Jackson must have been dipping into Shakespeare. The letter continued: "I fear there is something rotten in the State of Denmark. . . . Beware the month of December. I love my country and government, I hate the Dons; I would delight to see Mexico reduced; but I will die in the last ditch before I yield a foot to the Dons, or see the Union disunited. This I write for your own eyes, and for your safety; profit by it and the Ides of March remember."

To Jackson's demand for an explanation Burr gave prompt attention. According to the General he answered "with the most sacred pledges that he had not, nor never had, any views inimical or hostile to the United States, and whenever he was charged with the intention of separating the Union, the idea of insanity must be ascribed to him."

General Jackson was not the only one demanding reassurances from Burr. When Burr was about to appear before the Kentucky Grand Jury at Frankfort he asked Henry Clay to defend him. Clay, too, wanted to hear from Burr's own lips whether there was any substance to the charges that had been preferred by Daveiss and the *Western World* before accepting the commission. From Burr he got this categorical denial: "I have no design, nor have I taken any measure, to promote a dissolution of the Union or a separation of any one or more States from the residue . . . I do not own a musket nor a bayonet, nor any single article of military stores, nor does any person for me, by my authority or with my knowledge. . . . Considering the high station you now fill in our national councils, I have thought these explanations proper, as well as to counteract chimerical tales, which malevolent persons have so industriously circulated, as to satisfy you that you have not espoused the cause of a man in any way unfriendly to the laws, the government or the interests of his country."

Burr's friend Senator John Smith, of Kentucky, also had expressed misgivings. To him Burr wrote: "I was greatly surprised and really hurt by the unusual tenor of your letter of the 23rd [October], and I hasten to reply to it as well for your satisfaction as my own. If there exists any design to separate the Western from the Eastern states, I am totally ignorant of it. I never harbored or expressed any such intention to anyone, nor did any person ever intimate such design to me."

Following his exoneration by the Grand Jury in Kentucky, Burr went back to Nashville and called once more at the Hermitage. The General was not at home, but the visitor got a cool reception from Rachel. She evidently was not entirely satisfied by his written explanation to the General. Burr then put up at the tavern at nearby Clover Bottom where Jackson had a store. There he was confronted by Jackson and John Coffee and again protested he had no object in view except what was sanctioned by legal authority, and that, when the time came, he would produce the Secretary of War's orders. According to one account not mentioned by Jackson in his letter to Campbell, Burr drew from his pocket a blank commission signed by Jefferson saying, "Gentlemen, I suppose this will satisfy you."

Jackson concluded his letter to Campbell ". . . if he [Burr] is a traitor, he is the basest that ever did commit treason, and being tore to pieces and scattered to the four winds of heaven would be too good for him."

Campbell turned the letter over to Jefferson. It may well have been responsible for the President's declaration that Tennessee was faithful and "particularly General Jackson."

At Clover Bottom Burr's persuasiveness and apparent frankness dissipated the worst of Jackson's suspicions. So much so that when Burr, using the boats that Jackson's firm had built, dropped down the river, Rachel Jackson's 17-year-old nephew, Stokely D. Hays, was permitted to go along. In later years Hays testified that he carried a letter to Governor Claiborne and that he had instructions from the Jacksons to leave the expedition if he should discover any action on its part that was inimical to the Government.

Jefferson's expressed confidence in General Jackson, inspired by the letter to Representative Campbell, alas! came too late. All sorts of rumors were reaching the Government in Washington. One which was taken seriously came from a Captain Read, of Pittsburgh, who asserted that upon his honor he was firmly persuaded that "large bodies of troops from Tennessee, with General Andrew Jackson at their head, were in full march to join the traitors." Perhaps Washington had also received reports of Burr's visits to the Hermitage, which would have lent color to the charge. Indeed, Jackson's complicity in the plot was so fully accepted in the East that the Richmond *Enquirer*, while rejoicing that Wilkinson had been "tampered with unsuccessfully" added that "we must acknowledge that we have entertained involuntary suspicions of him as well as of a militia general in Tennessee." It regretted that it could not also withdraw its suspicions of the militia general.

So it came about that when Secretary of War Dearborn found it necessary to communicate with his subordinate in Tennessee on the subject of the nation's defense, he assumed he was writing to a man whose loyalty was seriously questioned.

Prefacing his letter on his belief that an unlawful enterprise against the Government had been commenced, Dearborn stated hesitantly that "it is presumed that the Proclamation of the President . . . will have produced every exertion . . . and that you will have been among the most jealous opposers of any such unlawful expedition." He then went on to say: "About Pittsburgh it is industriously reported among the adventurers, that they are to be joined, at the mouth of the Cumberland, by two regiments under the command of General Jackson." He concluded: ". . . such a story might afford you an opportunity of giving an effectual check to the enterprise if not too late."

Little did the Secretary of War understand the man to whom he was writing. The suspicion of guilt contained in the letter would have been calculated to arouse even the mildest of men. But Andrew Jackson was not a mild man. He was least mild when his honor was in question. The General took up his pen, but his emotions were too aroused to permit orderly thinking. He had to make several drafts of a reply before he settled on one that satisfied him. It would require an exhaustive search to find anywhere as bold and unrestrained an answer from a subordinate to his superior as the one Jackson directed to the Secretary of War.

Wrote Jackson: "You stand convicted of the most notorious and criminal acts of dishonor, dishonesty, want of candour and justice. You say, Sir, that it is industriously reported among the adventurers that they are to be joined at the mouth of the Cumberland by two regiments under the command of General Jackson. Such a story might afford him an opportunity of giving an effectual check to the enterprise, if not too late.

"After I have given the most deliberate consideration to your expressions . . . I cannot draw from them any other conclusion but this: that you believe me concerned in the conspiracy and that I was fit subject to act the traitor of traitors, as others have done [the reference was to Wilkinson], and that the Secretary of War could buy me up without honor." Dearborn did not answer the letter.

To his friend Patton Anderson, Jackson wrote: "I have received some communications from the President and the Secretary of War. It is the merest old-woman letter from the Secretary you ever saw." Then he turned on Wilkinson: "Wilkinson has denounced Burr as a traitor, after he found that he was implicated. This is deep policy. He has obtained thereby the command of New Orleans, the gunboats armed; and his plan can be executed without resistance. But we must be there in due time, before our fortifications can be erected, and restore to our government New Orleans and the western commerce." Then, as an afterthought: "The Secretary of War is not fit for a granny."

General Jackson had taken one other precautionary measure. He had sent a messenger to Captain Bissell, who commanded the Federal post of Fort Massac on the Ohio River a short distance above its confluence with the Mississippi, warning him of the approach of Burr's forces and urging him not to let any warlike party go past him down the river. He added that if Bissell should need help his troops were ready to march.

From Captain Bissell he shortly received a curt reply to the effect that Burr had already arrived at Massac, that his party showed no evidence of being on a warlike mission and had been permitted to proceed down the river.

Already Burr's protestations of innocence had begun to have their effect on the General and now this report from Bissell strengthened his conviction of Burr's sincerity. From then on in Jackson's judgment Wilkinson, and not Burr, was the real culprit, and he acted accordingly.

In the ambitious roundup of witnesses that followed the Chief Justice's demand on the prosecution for more evidence, General Jackson was caught and summoned by the lawyers of the Government to testify against Burr. But, contrary to the

Government's expectations, he turned out to be the noisiest of
Burr's champions, in the same breath attacking the Government
and defending Burr in the very shadow of the Capitol for the
benefit of anybody who chose to hear. Richmond's best people
already were aligned with Burr and needed no exhortations.
But Jackson's arguments were directed to the masses who up
to this time had been clamoring for Burr's blood. Jackson, too,
spoke as a Republican to Republicans. Such a man was highly
dangerous. To his friend Patton Anderson he wrote from Richmond on June 17: "I am sorry to say that this thing has in part
assumed the shape of a political persecution." No wonder then
that, after bringing him all the way from Tennessee to Richmond, once the Government's lawyers had heard about the
speech, the prosecution decided it was best not to let him testify.

But the mischief went beyond the Burr trial. The break between Jackson and the Jefferson Administration was never
mended. It was inherited by James Madison with the result
that when the War of 1812 broke out the Government was reluctant to use their most competent general when he was sorely
needed. Had Jackson commanded on the Canadian front the
story might have been different.

Chapter VIII

THE GRAND JURY had been selected. Counsel for the prosecution and the defense were present with the one important exception of Luther Martin. The audience was packed into the courtroom, impatient for the spectacle to go on. But there was an impelling cause for delay—the Government's star witness had not turned up. Government's counsel offered reassurances, yet they could not hide the fact that they did not know just where General Wilkinson was.

It is a considerable distance from New Orleans to Richmond, and, at the turn of the nineteenth century, transportation was primitive. One route Wilkinson might take was overland through wildernesses and by tortuous roads and trails. It had taken Burr and his captors three weeks to make the journey from Alabama to Virginia. It was more probable that the portly Major General, who liked his comfort, would choose a sea voyage. But that would put him at the mercy of wind and tide. To add to the uncertainty, the General was an inveterate procrastinator with an utter disregard for time.

Counsel for the defense made the most of the prosecution's embarrassment. They enlarged upon the great inconvenience members of the Grand Jury were being put to, and that of the many witnesses waiting to be called. They expressed doubt as to whether Wilkinson would ever show up. Many thought him as guilty as Burr. Might he not prefer to flee the country rather than face Aaron Burr in person and possible exposure in Richmond?

Hay pleaded that allowance be made for a man "of General Wilkinson's age and bulk to travel to this city." To which Mr. Randolph of the defense retorted: "Surely there is enough time to travel from New Orleans to this city in seventeen days, even with the gigantic 'bulk' of General Wilkinson himself."

General Wilkinson's protracted absence left a void that somehow had to be filled. Mr. Hay of the prosecution was the first to try to fill it. When court met on the morning of Monday, May 25, he offered a motion that Colonel Burr be committed for treason. His contention was that new evidence had appeared since the Chief Justice refused commitment for treason earlier in the proceedings.

The defense immediately protested, Mr. Botts acting as spokesman. The motion, he declared, took them completely by surprise. It was their understanding that no such action was to be taken by either side without previous consultation. And here was the prosecution breaking the agreement. What was more, if Mr. Hay's motion were granted it would mean taking away from the Grand Jury a task obviously its responsibility and giving it to the Chief Justice.

Here Mr. Randolph, the elder statesman, intervened to reinforce young Botts. Never, he asserted, in his thirty years of practice at the bar had he heard such an astounding proposal.

Mr. Hay explained that his purpose for making the motion was merely to get the prisoner's bail raised. Borrowing the explanation of Burr's friends for Wilkinson's absence, he said that with the bail as low as it was Burr, knowing he would soon have to face Wilkinson, might be tempted to run away. He intimated that he would not put it beyond Burr to make his exit in that craven manner.

Mr. Wickham scoffed at this. Afraid that Burr would run away, indeed! What the prosecution was actually trying to do was to introduce evidence in order to ruin the character of his client before the trial had even begun.

To Wickham's conjecture Wirt retorted: "Evidence, Sir, is

the greatest corrector of prejudice. Why, then, does Aaron
Burr shrink from it?"

Mr. Randolph charged that the Government had issued an
order "to treat Col. Burr as an outlaw, and to ruin and destroy
him and his property." Then the Colonel himself took up the
argument opposing the introduction of affidavits at this point.
He called attention to the great disadvantage he, as an individual, suffered in contrast to the Government of the United
States which could exercise a compulsory process to obtain
them.

The strategy of the defense was making itself clear. Burr was
to be portrayed as the victim of a ruthless government which
denied him his civil rights and employed the military to seize
his property and threaten his life. It was to charge the Jefferson
Administration with brutal disregard of the dignity of the hum-
blest citizen, whose equality before the law was Jefferson's
proudest boast.

Next day the Chief Justice presented his opinion, and it was
a victory for the prosecution. The Court, he declared, had the
right to commit even after the Grand Jury had been chosen.
Mr. Hay's motion was sustained and now he could proceed to
present the new evidence he claimed to have on Burr's alleged
treason.

On hearing the opinion, however, Hay stated that he did not
wish to present evidence at this time, provided the prisoner's
bail were raised. He proposed that counsel for both sides meet
to see if an agreement could be reached. The proposal was accepted and the meeting was held, but it ended in a deadlock.
Hay then proceeded to present his evidence while the defense
challenged each affidavit and witness. Its objection to the Wilkinson affidavit was sustained. Peter Taylor, Blennerhassett's
gardener, and Jacob Allbright, a laborer on the island, were
permitted to testify. But when the affidavit of one Sergeant
Dunbaugh was offered the defense again protested.

Judge Marshall here interposed to remark that it was becoming highly embarrassing to him to be issuing opinions on the
admission of evidence before the trial had actually begun. To

this Burr replied that if the Chief Justice was embarrassed he would consent to a higher bail. The sum of $10,000 was agreed upon, which put an end to this quite unnecessary sideshow. That is, unnecessary so far as the legal proceedings were concerned. But it had provided an opportunity for the counsel on both sides to posture before the audience and to do their best to influence public opinion for or against the accused according to the side they were on.

The digression did result in setting forth a statement of the fundamental issue that was to be iterated and reiterated during the trial: what was treason? In the course of his argument Mr. Botts outlined the definition of treason as it is set forth in the Constitution.

He stated that treason is either levying war against the United States or else giving aid and comfort to the enemy. But since in the present instance the United States was at peace with the world, giving aid and comfort to the enemy was ruled out.

That left the charge of levying war. But, says the Constitution, there must be an "overt act." Further that act must be proved by two witnesses, and it must have occurred in the district in which the case was being tried. All of these things, insisted Mr. Botts, had to be proved by the Government against Burr if he was to be found guilty of treason.

Mr. Botts contended further that the first obligation of the prosecution was to prove the overt act. Until that act was proved, no other evidence was admissible.

Nothing would be more damaging to the prosecution than a ruling of the Court sustaining the contention of the defense. The prosecution's plan was to present the evidence chronologically, introducing all the scheming and plotting that had been common gossip during the past few years, and gradually working up to a climax. Colonel Burr and his counsel touched a tender spot when they challenged this procedure.

At this juncture the defense received valuable reinforcement through the arrival of Luther Martin of Maryland. Mr. Martin was a lawyer of exceptional talent. A native of New Jersey, he had been educated at Princeton from which he graduated with high honors in the class of 1766, six classes ahead of Aaron Burr. At the age of thirty he was Attorney General of Maryland, from which high office he resigned to build up a lucrative practice in Baltimore. Elected a delegate from Maryland to the Constitutional Convention, he showed his courage and his scorn for conformity by defying the powerful Virginia delegation, headed by Washington, and championing the cause of the smaller states. His service in the Convention, valuable as it turned out to be, had more recently been overshadowed by his stalwart defense of Judge Chase in the impeachment proceedings.

Another asset for the business in hand was Mr. Martin's warm friendship for Burr and his inveterate hatred of Thomas Jefferson. In politics Martin was a Federalist; added to his political differences with the President was a personal grudge resulting from an injury quite unconsciously inflicted by Mr. Jefferson.

Luther Martin married Maria Cresap, a daughter of Col. Michael Cresap, a frontiersman of Allegheny County, Maryland. In his "Notes on Virginia" Jefferson included the eloquent speech of the Indian chieftain Logan, who had befriended the early settlers yet whose wife and children had been butchered by the whites. Jefferson's purpose in introducing this classic piece of rhetoric was to call attention to the nobility of the red man. He was not aware that responsibility for the murder had been pinned on Colonel Cresap, Martin's father-in-law. Martin voiced his resentment in a bitter letter to a Philadelphia newspaper, but this public outpouring was not sufficient in itself to erase the grudge he held against Jefferson.

Mr. Martin's brilliance was offset by an untidy dress, coarseness of speech and manner, and an addiction to spirits that earned him the nickname "Old Brandy Bottle." His capacity was phenomenal, and though he imbibed freely this did not seem to dull his wit or befuddle his mind. He made his entrance into the lists in Richmond as a foreigner, but, had he wished, he might have claimed kinship with his Virginia colleagues as a former student of Chancellor Wythe in Williamsburg and a member of the Virginia bar practicing briefly on the state's eastern shore.

The business of Hay's motion absorbed the attention of the Court for the better part of a week, but Wilkinson's failure to appear continued to hold up proceedings. To a friend in New York Washington Irving wrote impatiently: ". . . you can little conceive the talents for procrastination that have been exhibited in this affair. Day after day we have been disappointed by the non-arrival of the magnanimous Wilkinson; day after day have fresh murmurs and complaints been uttered; and day after day are we told that the next mail will probably bring this noble self, or at least some account of when he may be expected."

Finally the Court gave up hope of the immediate arrival of the General. The Chief Justice granted a recess of the Grand Jury for a week so that, as Irving put it, "they might go home, see their wives, and flog their Negroes."

On Tuesday, June 9, the Jury was recalled and Court reconvened, but it had nothing to do. It was now the turn of the defense to provide diversion to keep the case from dying of inanition. Colonel Burr set things in motion by stating that he thought he might need for his defense a letter of General Wilkinson of October 21, 1806, addressed to President Jefferson, which had been mentioned by the President in his special message to Congress, and the President's reply to the same. He also would like to have copies of the orders with reference to himself which had been issued to the Army and the Navy.

The Colonel said he had asked for the papers in Washington but without result. Therefore he requested the Chief Justice to issue a *subpoena duces tecum* to the President of the United States demanding either that he supply the papers or else come into court with them himself.

Burr's request called for quick thinking on the part of the District Attorney. How was Hay to protect his master from the indignity of a summons yet at the same time prevent his being exposed to a charge of concealing evidence? How was he to offer assurances without pledging the Government to go farther than the President might want it to go?

Mr. Hay settled on a delaying action. He expressed confidence that the Government would comply with the request if the Court should consider the papers pertinent. On the other hand he doubted whether the Court had the power to issue a *subpoena duces tecum* to the President of the United States. And, suggested Mr. Hay, since the Government was perfectly willing to produce the papers if the Court decided they were pertinent, what need was there for issuing a subpoena at all? Such procedure he thought would be a waste of precious time.

Mention of time wasting brought a shout of derision from the defense. The prosecution, they retorted, had wasted enough of it. And suppose the Government in Washington—by which they meant Mr. Jefferson—turned out to be less obliging than the District Attorney? The Chief Justice here remarked somewhat wryly that the *subpoena duces tecum* usually was requested in cases where it was anticipated that the papers asked for would not be produced. He inquired directly of the District Attorney whether the prosecution would consent to the issuance of the subpoena. On Hay's refusal to consent the Chief Justice called for argument.

There followed a prolonged debate, in which the Chief Justice allowed each lawyer to say his say with no apparent time limit. The situation was a delicate one for Mr. Jefferson. If he were to answer the subpoena by complying with a demand to appear in court in person the executive branch of the Government would be making abject surrender to the judiciary. If, on the other hand, he were to claim an exemption, he—the champion of equality of all men—would be claiming a special privilege which even the King of England hesitated to exercise.

The Government's counsel therefore did not go so far as to deny that the President could be called. But Mr. Hay insisted that the defense had to show that the papers were relevant and material. Further, he contended that the President had a right to reserve any portion of the letters requested whose production in court he considered detrimental to the interests of the United States. Nor was Mr. Hay sure the President was under any obligation to present a letter that had been addressed to him privately. To this, lawyers of the defense replied that in his message to Congress Mr. Jefferson had stated that the letter was addressed to him not as a private individual but as President of the United States. Mr. Hay suggested that a copy of the letter might do. Mr. Wickham of the defense said they would not have it that way. They demanded the original.

The debate gave Luther Martin the opportunity to chastise Mr. Jefferson for which he had impatiently been waiting since his entry into the proceedings. The President, he asserted, had undertaken to prejudge Mr. Martin's client by declaring that "of his guilt there can be no doubt." He had assumed the knowledge of the Supreme Being himself, and pretended to search the heart of Mr. Martin's highly respected friend.

The President, declared Mr. Martin, had proclaimed Colonel Burr a traitor in the face of the country which had rewarded him. He had "let slip the dogs of war, the hell-hounds of prosecution to hunt down my friend." And would the President of the United States, who had raised all this absurd clamor, pretend to keep back the papers which were wanted for this trial where life itself was at stake?

It was, continued Mr. Martin, a sacred principle that in all such cases the accused had a right to all the evidence needed for his defense. Then, releasing his venom on Mr. Jefferson, he exclaimed: "Whoever withholds willfully information that would save the life of a person charged with a capital offense, is substantially a murderer, and so recorded in the register of Heaven."

Mr. Wirt of the prosecution jumped to his feet to express his astonishment at the unrestrained language used by Mr. Martin. He even had the temerity to attack the Chief Justice for permitting it in his Court. Suppose, he said, there were foreigners present accustomed to regular government in their own country. What would they infer from hearing the Federal Administration thus reviled before the Federal judiciary and the Administration likened to "blood hounds hunting the man with a keen and savage thirst for blood"?

"Sir," protested Wirt, looking squarely at Judge Marshall, "no man, foreigner or citizen, who hears this language addressed to the Court, and received with all the complacency at least which silence can imply, can make any inference from it very honorable to the Court." He hoped the Court would compel a decent respect for that government of which they themselves formed a branch.

As for tracking the accused with bloodhounds thirsting for blood, Mr. Wirt wished to make it clear that, for their part, the prosecution wished only a fair trial of the case. "If the man be innocent, in the name of God let him go; but while we are on the question of his guilt or innocence, let us not suffer our attention and judgment to be diverted and distracted by the introduction of other subjects foreign to the inquiry."

For three days opposing counsel held forth until the Chief Justice, with a sigh of exhaustion, announced that he had heard enough arguments on which to base a sound opinion. He then proceeded to deliver it. If, said Judge Marshall, upon any principle the President could be construed to stand exempt from the general provisions of the Constitution, it would be because his duties as chief magistrate demanded his whole time for national objects. But, he observed, it was apparent that this demand "was not unremitting."

The last remark was a sly dig at Mr. Jefferson for spending several months every summer away from Washington at Monticello, his country estate in Albemarle County, Virginia.

Now, continued Judge Marshall, if the public's demand on the President's time should exist when his attendance at court was required, it could be sworn to on the return of the subpoena. It might serve as an excuse for not obeying the Court. But it did not serve as a reason for not issuing the subpoena.

The Chief Justice now assumed an apologetic attitude. It could not be denied, he said, that to issue a subpoena to a person filling the exacting position of chief magistrate was a duty which would be dispensed with much more cheerfully than it would be performed. But if it was a duty the Court could have no choice in the case. He recognized that the right to call the President into court could be abused. But, he assured, "the guard furnished to this high officer to protect him from being harassed by vexatious and unnecessary subpoenas, is to be looked for in the conduct of the Court after those subpoenas have been issued."

In short, what Judge Marshall said was that the decision as to whether it was appropriate for Mr. Jefferson to appear in Court rested with the Chief Justice, not with the President.

The Chief Justice went on to defend his position. "It is not," he said, "for the Court to anticipate the event of the present prosecution. Should it terminate as is expected on the part of the United States, all those who are concerned in it should certainly regret that a paper, which the accused believed to be essential to his defense; which may, for aught that now appears, be essential, had been withheld from him . . . it would justly tarnish the reputation of the Court which had given its sanction to its being withheld."

He therefore ordered that the *subpoena duces tecum* be issued to the President of the United States, or such of the secretaries of the departments as might have the paper mentioned.

The Chief Justice had hardly finished delivering his opinion when Mr. MacRae was up, clamoring for recognition. Unless his ears had deceived him, he said, he had heard the Chief Justice remark that should the case terminate "as is expected on the part of the United States." Against any such remark Mr. MacRae protested with all his might.

"The impression," he said, "which has been conveyed by the Court that we not only wished to have Aaron Burr accused, but that we wished to convict him, is completely abhorrent to our feelings." The prosecution, he insisted, was interested only that Burr be tried.

Judge Marshall did not immediately repudiate the comment. On the contrary, he defended it on the ground that he had inferred as much from remarks made by them assuming the guilt of the prisoner. But later, after reflection, he thought better of it. At the close of Court he called the reporters to him and observed that he had no desire that the words complained of by Mr. MacRae should remain in the written opinion and so he had expunged them.

However impelling the demand on the President may have been to give his time to other official matters, it did not keep him from paying close attention to what was going on in Richmond. Messengers were constantly passing back and forth between him and the District Attorney bearing suggestions from the President for trying the case and reports of the proceedings from Hay. No sooner, therefore, had the request for the papers been made by Colonel Burr than the President was so apprised.

Mr. Jefferson replied promptly that, reserving his right to decide independent of all other authority, what papers coming to him as President the public interest permitted to be communicated, he assured his readiness voluntarily to furnish on all occasions whatever the purposes of justice might require.

Mr. Jefferson said he was under the impression that General Wilkinson's letter of October 21 and all other papers relating to the charges against Burr had been turned over to the Attorney General when he first went to Richmond in March. He took for granted they had been left with Hay. Since he could not remember exactly what was in the papers he would leave it to Mr. Hay to exercise his discretion as to what part to communicate and what part to withhold.

As to the requests for the orders to the Army and the Navy, the President observed that supplying them would amount to laying open the whole executive books. But he would get the Secretary of War to look at the records. He added that if the defendant supposed there were any facts within the knowledge of the heads of departments, or of himself, which could be useful to the defense he would be glad to provide depositions.

"As to our personal attendance at Richmond," the President informed Hay, "I am persuaded it is sensible that paramount duties to the nation at large control the obligation of compliance with their summons in this case, as they would, should we receive a similar one to attend the trials of Blennerhassett and others in Mississippi territory, those instituted at St. Louis and other places on the western waters . . . to comply with such calls would leave the nation without an executive branch."

Feeling as he did the President was greatly annoyed when Judge Marshall's opinion was reported to him, still obstinately maintaining that he should appear in court. After reflection he sat down and framed a letter to Hay presenting his arguments against obeying the subpoena. The Chief Justice, he complained, as was usual with him when an opinion was to be supported, right or wrong, dwelt much on smaller objections and passed over those which were solid. He had laid down the general position that all persons owe obedience to subpoenas. But, argued Mr. Jefferson, if the Constitution enjoined a particular officer to be always engaged in a particular set of duties, did not that supersede the general law, subjecting him to minor duties inconsistent with these? "The Constitution enjoins his constant agency in the concerns of six millions of people. Is the law paramount to this which calls on him in behalf of a single one?"

Mr. Jefferson applied the Judge's doctrine to his own case. Suppose, he said, the sheriff of Henrico County (in which the Judge was domiciled) should summon him from court to quell a riot. Would the Judge abandon major duties to perform lesser ones? Then he got down to the root of the matter, which was the battle being waged between the executive and the judiciary.

"The leading principle of our Constitution," he reminded, "is the independence of the legislature, executive and judiciary of each other, and none are more jealous of this than the judiciary. But would the executive be independent of the judiciary if he were subject to the commands of the latter, and to imprisonment for disobedience; if the several courts could bandy him from pillar to post, keep him constantly trudging from north to south and east to west, and withdraw him entirely from his constitutional duties?"

The President now came to the most personal part of the opinion in which the Chief Justice intimated that his duties were not unremitting. "If," said Mr. Jefferson, "he alludes to our annual retirement from the seat of government, during the sickly season, he should be told that such arrangements are made for carrying on public business that it goes on as unremittingly there as if he were at the seat of government. I pass more hours in public business at Monticello than I do here every day and it is much more laborious, because all must be done in writing."

Thus Mr. Jefferson excused himself from casting aside his official duties in Washington and departing posthaste to Richmond at the request of Aaron Burr and on the order of Judge Marshall. He still had to deal with his other tormentor, Luther Martin. The President was not very successful in concealing the fact that the vindictive attack of the Baltimore lawyer had gotten under his skin.

While Mr. Martin was shouting invectives against the President in Richmond there came into Mr. Jefferson's hand a letter from a Mr. Graybill of Baltimore. Inquiry revealed that the writer was an old Revolutionary soldier who had set up as a flour merchant. According to the information reaching the President, Mr. Graybill was a man of respectable character whose word could be trusted implicitly. In his letter Mr. Graybill said that for more than a year it had been believed in Baltimore that Burr was engaged in some criminal enterprise and that Luther Martin knew all about it.

In his haste to even the score with Martin the President was carried away by the Graybill letter. He proposed to Hay that a subpoena be issued to Graybill to appear as a witness against Burr and, while Graybill was on the way, Hay might be considering how best to use his testimony. Then the President put forward a fantastic idea. How about summoning Luther Martin as a witness against Burr, meanwhile holding Graybill ready to confront Martin? How about the prosecution moving to commit Luther Martin as *particeps criminis* along with Burr? Graybill, Mr. Jefferson was assured, would fix upon him misprision of treason at least. Mr. Jefferson did return to realities sufficiently to admit that there might be some doubt whether the prosecution could legally examine a witness to discredit its own witness. He recognized, too, that lawyers considered themselves privileged from being forced to breaches of confidence.

"At any rate," concluded Mr. Jefferson, "his [Graybill's] evidence will put down this unprincipled and impudent Federal bulldog, and add another proof that the most glamorous defenders of Burr are all his accomplices. It will explain why L.M. flew so hastily to the aid of his 'honorable friend,' abandoning his clients and their property during a session of a principal court in Maryland, now filled, so I am told, with the clamors and ruin of his clients."

The District Attorney, wisely perhaps, ignored these chimerical suggestions from the White House.

Still another incident illustrated the zeal of the President of the United States to win a conviction against Colonel Burr. It will be recalled that Dr. Eric Bollman, the German adventurer, was one of the messengers dispatched to Wilkinson with the fateful letter which Wilkinson later disclosed; that when the conspiracy collapsed Wilkinson arrested him and Swartwout and shipped them east to Washington under arrest on charges of treason. Bollman shortly thereafter went to the President and denied some of the exaggerated charges against Burr that were being published in the newspapers. Bollman's purpose was to show that the plan did not involve a division of the Union, but only an expedition against Spain. He was received by the President in the presence of Secretary of State James Madison, who listened sympathetically to what he had to say. The President suggested that Bollman put his oral statements in writing, which Bollman did. The German admitted later that, because of his difficulties with the English language, some of his statements may have been misleading. It was his understanding that Mr. Jefferson promised not to use them against him or to let them out of his keeping. Mr. Jefferson appears to have understood differently.

As early as May 20 the President wrote Hay that he was sending him some blank pardons that were to be filled out at Hay's discretion "if you should find a defect of evidence and believe that this could supply it." However, he cautioned Hay that they were not to be given to gross offenders "unless it be visible that the principal will otherwise escape."

Bollman evidently was regarded by the President as a man whose testimony would be sufficiently important to justify his being given a pardon should he consent to turn State's evidence. A week after sending the blank pardons to Hay he wrote him that: "If a bill [against Burr] be found and a trial had, his [Bollman's] evidence is deemed entirely essential, and in that case his pardon is to be produced before he goes to book." In short, Bollman was to be offered a pardon if he would testify against Burr. But Bollman was not so keen to betray his friend. Hay filled out the pardon; Bollman spurned it. Hay then wrote the President for instructions.

"You ask," replied the President, "what is to be done if Bollman finally rejects his pardon, and the Judge decides it to have no effect. Move to commit him immediately for treason or misdemeanor." There were times when the mild-mannered "Sage of Monticello" could be tough.

At this point the side play was interrupted by the arrival of the Government's star witness, Major General James Wilkinson, Commander-in-Chief of the United States Army. In the excitement caused by his martial entry the *subpoena duces tecum* was brushed aside and almost forgotten.

On the original subpoena, now in the Federal Courthouse in Richmond, is an indorsement in Burr's handwriting indicating that he did not expect to bring the President into court. On the other hand, the language used by the Chief Justice in his opinion certainly indicated that he expected the President to appear in person. Certainly the President, in setting forth in his letter to Hay his reasons for not coming, indicated that he thought he had been summoned to appear. However, when the writ itself was drawn up it stated that neither the personal attendance of the President nor the other officers of government mentioned was required. When the critical moment came Marshall recoiled from a direct challenge.

Nevertheless a void of several days had been packed with

dramatics. The lawyers had been given a chance to exercise their eloquence and the audience had been well entertained. More to the point, Mr. Jefferson had been unmercifully badgered. That probably was as much as Colonel Burr and his counsel expected anyway.

Chapter IX

JAMES WILKINSON was born of good English stock on a farm near Benedict, in southern Maryland, in 1757. A medical career was planned for the boy and he was put under a relative to study for the profession. This was followed by formal training in Philadelphia. A brief adventure into medicine was interrupted by the outbreak of the Revolution when young Wilkinson was seized with patriotic zeal, volunteered in a rifle company, and marched off to join the American forces in Boston.

This transition from a medical to a military career proved permanent. Wilkinson's genius for self-advancement soon manifested itself. He was an extrovert who did not believe in hiding his light under a bushel. There may have been some doubt among his comrades as to his enthusiasm for engaging in hand-to-hand combat or making a desperate last stand, but none whatever as to his ability in ingratiating himself with his superiors.

He was aide successively to General Nathanael Greene and General Benedict Arnold and took part with the latter in the campaign against Quebec. On that strenuous expedition he first made the acquaintance of Aaron Burr. Unlike Burr he did not enjoy the distinction of having a general die in his arms, but his services were sufficiently noteworthy to lead to a promotion to lieutenant colonel.

The warrior's next assignment was on the staff of General Horatio Gates who made him deputy adjutant general of the Army of the Northern Departments. It was then he first exhibited a fatal quality for appearing wherever intrigue was in the air. This instance was the Conway Cabal whose object was to cashier Washington and put Gates in his place. The Commander first got wind of it when Wilkinson, arriving in a garrulous mood at Lord Stirling's headquarters, let out the contents of an incriminating letter from Conway to Gates. Wilkinson's later version of the incident was that he deliberately made the disclosure. He was to develop an exceptional gift for shifting from the role of conspirator to patriot when the going got hot.

However deeply he may have been involved in the plot it did not interfere with his continued rise in the military. He was promoted to brigadier and appointed clothier-general of the American Army, but he neglected his work, drew a rebuke from Washington, and shortly thereafter resigned from the service.

Meanwhile Wilkinson had married Ann, daughter of John Biddle of Philadelphia, a merchant and innkeeper. His devotion to his wife was the one sincere and admirable feature of his life. He bought an estate in Pennsylvania and made a brief entry into local politics, serving as member of the State Assembly.

Like Burr, Wilkinson was extravagant, loved display, and lived beyond his means. In an age when heavy drinking was not uncommon his indulgence was sufficiently conspicuous to provoke comment. He was soon overwhelmed with debt and, following the example of many other men in the same predicament, decided to go west to recoup his fortunes. It was in Kentucky and the Southwest that he was destined to spend the rest of his life.

The Spaniards were then in possession of New Orleans, parts of the present Louisiana, the Floridas, Texas, and Mexico. They dreaded the crude American frontiersmen as the decadent Romans dreaded the Vandals and the Visigoths, expecting them at any time to swoop down, loot, destroy, and conquer. One of their defense measures was to seek out friends and informers among the Americans. In Wilkinson they found a willing collaborator. The Spaniards about this time closed the Mississippi to American goods coming down from the territories and the frontiersmen were indignant with the Spaniards—and with the indifference of their own government to their plight. It was then that the Spanish Plot took shape. Esteban Miro, Spanish Governor of Louisiana, fostered it by calling attention to the advantages to be gained by an establishment of a nation beyond the Alleghenies under the protection of Spain.

Wilkinson, one of the American leaders in the plot, saw the chance to turn Spanish fears to his account. He made two trips to New Orleans, ingratiated himself with Miro, and wrung from him a concession to deposit his goods at New Orleans and to enjoy other special commercial privileges. In return he swore allegiance to the Spanish crown and engaged to act as a secret agent. In the Spanish reports he was thereafter to be designated as "Number Thirteen." It was a relationship Wilkinson was to maintain with Miro and his successors for more than a decade. The Spaniards agreed also to grant Wilkinson a pension of $2000 a year. But communications on the frontier were primitive; a pension payable in silver dollars did not always get through.

In spite of this new source of income Wilkinson's extravagance kept him on the verge of bankruptcy. To add to his difficulties, the Spaniards reversed their policy and withdrew his trading privileges. Wilkinson was driven to selling most of his personal possessions. In this extremity he accepted a commission in the United States Army, took part as second in command in General Anthony Wayne's invasion of the Wabash country, burned and pillaged with the best of them, and gained quite a reputation as an Indian fighter. At this time President Washington, making a summary of the general officers of the army, damned Wilkinson with faint praise, commenting that "little can be said of his abilities as an officer. He is lively, sensible, pompous and ambitious, but whether sober or not is unknown to me."

Wayne learned of Wilkinson's Spanish connections and

warned the Government. When President Washington, toward the close of his administration, sent Andrew Ellicott out as commissioner to put into effect a treaty with Spain, he directed him to investigate Wilkinson. Ellicott did not at that time find reason to take the rumors seriously, but Wilkinson himself did. In alarm he wrote to Gayoso, governor of Natchez, "For the love of God and friendship enjoin great secrecy and caution in all our concerns. Never suffer my name to be written or spoken. The suspicion of Washington is wide awake."

On the death of General Wayne in 1796 Wilkinson became senior officer in the army. Though John Adams, the incoming President, knew of Wayne's charges against Wilkinson, he kept him on and gratified his suspicion with true New England frugality by holding him to the rank of brigadier.

Seeing how the political wind was blowing against the Federalists, Wilkinson set to work ingratiating himself with Thomas Jefferson. This turned out to be a highly profitable speculation. Thereafter he enjoyed the support and at least the professed confidence of Jefferson, yet it is hard to believe that a man of Jefferson's sagacity did not at times entertain unpleasant doubts about his protégé.

When on December 20, 1803, pursuant to the terms of the Purchase, the United States took over Louisiana from the French, Wilkinson, as commanding general of the United States Army, shared with Governor William C. C. Claiborne, of the Mississippi Territory, the honor of representing the United States when the French Tricolor was lowered from the flagstaff in the Place d'Armes in New Orleans and the Stars and Stripes were hoisted in its place.

In 1804 Governor Don Vincente Folch of West Florida turned up in New Orleans. A nephew of old Miro, he had been a party to the intrigues with Wilkinson to which he referred as "the ancient history." The two took the occasion to renew secret relations. Wilkinson, for a price, volunteered to recommend a course Spain might pursue to prevent the United States from profiting by the cession of Louisiana. Asserting that he had not received his pension for ten years he asked for

$20,000 in arrears. Actually he is estimated to have received from the Spaniards $26,000 prior to 1796. Wilkinson also offered to supply Folch with a text of "reflections" and to ascertain and report on the plans and purposes of President Jefferson and his cabinet. Simultaneously, in his capacity as commander of the American forces, he was writing Secretary of War Dearborn that he was "collecting topographical information in all directions and at some expense which I am persuaded you will find highly interesting." The reference to expense bore the unmistakable odor of a request for compensation.

Folch, for his part, replied that he did not have the money Wilkinson asked and suggested that he apply to the Marquis de Casa Calvo, the boundary commissioner, who was known to be possessed of a generous supply of cash. Calvo accepted Wilkinson's offer but refused to bid higher than $12,000 for his "Reflections." These, written and translated, advised Spain to hold on to the Floridas or exchange them for the west bank of the Mississippi, and meanwhile to fortify strongly the Texas and Florida borders. This from the man who, as commander of the United States Army, might soon be called upon to lead his men against those same fortifications! No wonder he begged the Marquis, upon his loyalty, honor, and friendship, to avoid the use of his name and instead employ the designation "Number Thirteen."

In spite of his secret work for the Spaniards, and his duties as army commander, Wilkinson still found time for another job as Governor of the Louisiana Territory to which he was appointed by President Jefferson, and to curry favor with his benefactor by presenting him with a twenty page memorial describing the country between the Mississippi and the Rio Grande.

On a trip east in 1799 Wilkinson renewed his acquaintance with Aaron Burr whom he visited in New York. Burr was instrumental in placing Wilkinson's son James in Princeton. In the spring of 1804 Wilkinson again came east. On his arrival in Washington he lent welcome color to the dreary newborn capital by leading a cavalcade through the streets, mounted on a blooded mare and magnificent in the uniform of a major general of his own designing, his stirrups and spurs of gold, his saddlecloth a leopard's skin with dangling claws, his son and namesake James as military aide riding a respectful distance behind him.

Again Wilkinson sought Burr's company, addressing a letter to him at Richmond Hill and asking a bed for the night "if it may be done without observation and intrusion." Burr had broken with the Republicans by this time and Wilkinson evidently considered it unwise for President Jefferson's protégé to be discovered on intimate terms with so prominent an enemy of the Administration. Burr just then was smarting under his defeat in the campaign for Governor of New York and his next step was uncertain. The possibilities of fame and fortune deriving from an invasion of the Spanish possessions could well have served as an engaging topic for gentlemen of their adventurous temperament and vivid imagination.

Returning to Washington Wilkinson satisfied his gregarious impulses by rubbing shoulders with Congressmen, especially those from the Southwest, and discussing the prospects of war with Spain, lamenting that it was not already being waged. "Mexico," he commented, momentarily shifting his loyalty from Spain to the United States, "glitters in our eyes—the word is all we wait for."

In July the duel between Hamilton and Burr was fought. In his flight from the New Jersey authorities Burr sought refuge in the home of Charles Biddle, a cousin of Ann Wilkinson and a warm friend of the General.

During the following winter in Washington, while Burr was closing out his term as Vice-President, he and Wilkinson saw much of each other. It was then that Wilkinson got his appointment as Governor of Louisiana. He picked as his secretary a Dr. Joseph Brown who had married the late Mrs. Burr's sister. The Vice-President and the General spent much time together. It was said they were copying maps of the Floridas, New Orleans, and the Louisiana Territory.

Mention has been made that when, in the summer of 1805,

Burr first journeyed to the West he met with Wilkinson at Fort Massac and St. Louis. As further evidence of their intimacy at this time Wilkinson gave Burr letters of introduction to Daniel Clark, a former partner and one of the wealthiest men in New Orleans, and to other friends there. Speaking of Burr in his letter to Clark, Wilkinson wrote: "To him I refer you for many things improper to letter, and which he will not say to any other." In a letter to a Spanish friend he described Burr as a "brave, learned, eloquent, gallant, honorable, discreet gentleman, rich in the best affections of the human heart —in short a man who has filled the second place in the Government of the United States with dignity and admiration."

To Senator John Adair, Kentucky leader, he penned an intriguing note in which he said, "He [Burr] understands your merits, and reckons on you. Prepare to visit me, and I will tell you all. We must have a peep at the unknown world beyond."

Innocent though these letters may have been, the cryptic terms in which they were couched were enough to arouse suspicion. People were beginning to talk. In September Clark sent a warning to Wilkinson, cautiously expressed, for letters in those days were common property; no telling who might read one before it reached its destination. Said Clark: "Many absurd and evil reports are circulated here and have reached the ears of the officers of the late Spanish Government, respecting our Vice-President. . . . You are spoken of as his right hand man. . . . What in the name of heaven could give rise to such extravagancies? Were I sufficiently intimate with Mr. Burr and knew where to direct a line I should take the liberty of writing to him. . . .

"The tale is a horrid one if well told. Kentucky, Tennessee, the State of Ohio, with part of Georgia and part of Carolina, are to be bribed with plunder of the Spanish countries west of us to separate from the Union; this is but part of the business. Heavens, what wonderful doings there will be in those days. . . . Amuse Mr. Burr with an account of it." Clark's letter as much as said that General Wilkinson and Burr would do well to hold their tongues.

On Burr's visit to Wilkinson in St. Louis after his return from New Orleans the relations between the two men appeared to be as cordial as ever. But newspapers were asking whether there was a conspiracy on foot to disrupt the Union. Then came Clark's letter. Wilkinson grew disturbed. According to his later story, he then wrote to the Secretary of the Navy cautioning him to keep an eye on Burr. There is no evidence that such a letter was ever received by the Secretary. Nor, at that time, was there any indication that Burr was conscious of any change in Wilkinson's cordial attitude. Thus matters stood during the winter of 1806 and into the summer when Burr set out for the West with the intention, in his own words, "Never to return."

On his arrival in Pittsburgh Burr dispatched the two copies of his letter to Wilkinson, dated July 29. This was the incriminating document a copy of which President Jefferson sent to Congress along with his special message. It was the one on which the Government counted heavily in proving its charge of treason. Mention has been made that one copy went by sea to New Orleans in the hands of the German, Dr. Erich Bollman; the other by land in care of Samuel Swartwout, younger brother of John Swartwout, Burr's political ally in New York. Swartwout was accompanied by another young man, Peter Ogden, nephew of Burr's friend, former Senator Dayton of New Jersey. Dayton, now out of office, was deeply involved in the intrigue. Ogden carried a letter from Dayton to Wilkinson.

At this point the forces of Spain and the United States were drawn up opposite each other on the Sabine River which separated Texas from Louisiana. General Wilkinson headed the American force and was at his headquarters at Natchitoches in western Louisiana when, on October 8, Swartwout and Ogden arrived with the letters.

The contents of the cipher letter from Burr has been set forth. Though Burr may not yet have begun to doubt Wilkinson's steadfastness, he and Dayton evidently felt that he needed prodding. With that in mind, Dayton wrote that he had it on good authority that Wilkinson was to be replaced at the next session of Congress. "Jefferson," he declared, "will affect to yield reluctantly to the public sentiment, but yield he will; prepare yourself, therefore for it; you know the rest." Then, further to stiffen the General's morale, he added: "You are not the man to despair, or even disposed, especially when such prospects offer in another quarter. Are you ready? Wealth and glory. Louisiana and Mexico."

Wilkinson spent the better part of the night decoding Burr's letter and pondering his next step. By morning he had reached a decision, if he had not done so already. Timidity had prevailed over adventure and avarice. He would abandon Burr and cling to the Government. But he needed all the shrewdness and skill at his command to make the transition convincing and lend credence to the story he would tell. How would an innocent man behave? The General's first act was to summon his subordinate, Col. Thomas Cushing, and inform him that Swartwout was Burr's agent and that Burr was the head of a widespread conspiracy. He said he would make what terms he could with the Spaniards so that his hand might be free to deal with the conspirators.

But Wilkinson did not reveal his betrayal of Burr to Swartwout. For the next ten days he kept the young man at Natchitoches while he pumped him dry of information and considered his next move. By October 20 he had sufficiently mapped his course to write Jefferson that he had discovered that a powerful association, extending from New York through the western states, had been formed for the purpose of leading an expedition against Vera Cruz. Judging it inadvisable to name names at this stage he stated that it was "unknown under whose authority" the enterprise had been projected. This ten days after he had announced to Colonel Cushing that Burr was the man!

The following day, in another confidential dispatch, he reiterated that, "I am not only uninformed of the prime mover and ultimate objects of this daring enterprise, but am ignorant of the foundations on which it rests." This letter professing complete ignorance was the one Burr asked the court to get from Jefferson through the *subpoena duces tecum*. No wonder.

Then in his heart-searching dilemma the General seized upon a fantastic scheme which he thought might enable him at one and the same time to demonstrate his loyalty to the Government without at the same time abandoning his friends. In a postscript he asked, "Might not some plan be adopted to correct the delirium of the associates and by a suitable appeal to their patriotism to engage them in the service of their country?"

If he supposed the Government would countenance an invasion of Spanish territory he was wrong. Jefferson's policy just then was not one of war, but of negotiation by purchase.

Wilkinson's immediate concern was that Jefferson might lose faith in him. Added to other rumors of his guilt was the open charge of the Kentucky newspaper, *The Western World*, that he was an "intriguer and pensioner of Spain, now associated with Aaron Burr in reviving the old Spanish conspiracy." There was little chance that, with all its avenues of communication, the White House would not be informed of the articles running in *The Western World*. Wilkinson, with an initiative he seldom showed on the battlefield, decided to take the offensive and strike without waiting for Jefferson to inquire.

So in another letter to the President on the same day Wilkinson called attention to the attacks, stating that he had been "bespattered with obloquy and slandered with a degree of virulence and indecency surpassing all example."

"I have at times been fearful," he confessed, "your confidence might be shaken by the boldness of the calumnies leveled at me: but the reflection that I have not only enjoyed but merited the confidence of George Washington [which was far from the truth] and his administration . . . and that the same illustrious character died my friend; and that the honest but wrong-headed President Adams approved my conduct in opposition to his ministers, combined with the consciousness that the wealth and power of the wide world could not for the moment divert my course from the path of honor, dissipated my apprehensions and determined me not to descend to the task of refuting by . . . testimony and authentic documents every imputation alleged against me, from the most frivolous to the most sane; I therefore contented myself by directing my attorney to bring action for slander against the printers, to test their authorities in a court of law." Fine words but, like the warning to the Secretary of the Navy there is no record that such a suit was ever brought.

Whatever his other shortcomings the General was not lacking in eloquence, especially when he was proclaiming his own virtues. He continued: "My ultimate views are limited to the acquisition of an honorable fame—I have ever condemned the sordid interest of the world, and estimate property by its immediate utility only." This from a man in a position of high public trust who had not hesitated to sell out to a foreign government! He went on: ". . . and it is the highest ambition of my soul on a poor occasion, to spend my last breath in the cause of my country—a frail character, but a just one." Finally a modest tribute to Mr. Jefferson: "To you I owe more than I will express, lest I should be suspected of adulation, which I detest."

Wilkinson need not have worried about Jefferson. Almost a year before the President had had very definite warning from District Attorney Daveiss who wrote him that he was convinced Wilkinson "has been for years, and now is a pensioner of Spain." Jefferson showed the letter to Gallatin, Madison, and Dearborn, but took no further action for reasons that later were made clear by his cabinet officers.

By November the General had effected a treaty with the Spaniards. His lieutenant, Colonel Cushing, was marching to the defense of New Orleans and Wilkinson was in the throes of patriotic emotion. To Cushing he wrote, "My God! What a situation has the country reached. Let us save it if we can. . . . Hurry, hurry after me, and, if necessary, let us be buried together in the ruins of the place we shall defend!"

Now that the die had been cast Wilkinson exerted every effort to lend authenticity to his declarations. To Governor Claiborne of New Orleans he dashed off a startling message of warning: "You are surrounded by dangers of which you dream not, and the destruction of the American Government is seriously menaced. The storm will probably burst in New Orleans, where I shall meet it and triumph or perish."

The Governor must have been impressed by the similarity between this message and the one he had previously received from Andrew Jackson. The one striking difference was that in Jackson's message the warning had been to watch not Burr or unknown conspirators, but Wilkinson. Then the man who had designated himself to save the nation in its hour of peril took up his pen and indited another dispatch to President Jefferson in his most florid style. He wrote:

"This is a deep, dark and widespread conspiracy, embracing the young and the old, the Democrat and the Federalist, the native and the foreigner, the patriot of '76 and the exotic of yesterday, the opulent and the needy, the ins and the outs." But let not the President despair. Wilkinson was there and ". . . nothing shall be omitted which can be accomplished by indefatigable industry, incessant vigilance and hardy courage; and I gasconade not when I tell you that in such a cause, I shall glory to give my life to the service of my country; for I verily believe such an event is probable."

Wilkinson informed the President that 7000 men were descending the Ohio River, bringing the sympathies and good wishes of that country. This exaggerated estimate no doubt was intended to justify his declaring martial law when he should arrive in New Orleans.

As emotionally aroused as Wilkinson appeared to be, he still was sufficiently the hard-headed businessman to devise as clever a bit of scheming as can be found in his long and illustrious career of intrigue. While at Natchitoches he had taken on as military aide one Walter Burling, a local planter. Burling asked Wilkinson's permission to enter Spanish territory to buy mules. Wilkinson assented, then told Burling he had long wanted details of the route from the United States to Mexico City and directed him to use the trip as an excuse for reconnaissance, and to return by water.

Wilkinson then gave Burling a letter to José de Iturrigary, Spanish Viceroy at Mexico City, in which he related the intentions of Burr against Mexico. He laid great stress on the measures he had taken at the risk of his life, fame, and fortune to save the Spanish possession. His services he valued at $121,000. Simultaneously he wrote to President Jefferson asking reimbursement for Burling's trip, the cost of which he put at $1500. Thus with a single stone he hoped to kill not two birds but three. His finesse was not entirely successful. Burling made the trip and returned safely with information about the route. Iturrigary thanked him for his pains but refused payment saying he already knew about Burr's plans. Jefferson, however, obliged with the $1500.

On November 25 the General arrived in New Orleans. He acted vigorously in calling out the militia, repairing the fortifications, and impressing seamen. Then he set in motion a veritable reign of terror. When Bollman delivered his letter from Burr, Wilkinson seized him and threw him into jail. He tried to frighten Governor Claiborne into declaring martial law by asserting that if drastic measures were not taken to meet the danger "the fair fabric of our independence, purchased by the best blood of the country, will be prostrated and the Goddess of Liberty will take her flight from the globe forever."

Following their exoneration by the Kentucky grand jury Burr and Adair proceeded to Nashville where they parted company. Burr boarded his flatboats while Adair set out on horseback for New Orleans. Many believed Adair was second in command to Burr. Oblivious of their past intimacy, dating from the Indian campaign, and no doubt in a desperate effort to erase the damning fact that he had introduced Adair to Burr, Wilkinson had Adair arrested on his arrival in New Orleans. Then he shipped Adair, Bollman, Swartwout, and Ogden under arrest by sea, with Baltimore and Washington as their destinations, to be dealt with by the Government. He set up a system of secret police to search for evidence, confiscated correspondence, and arranged with the postmaster to rifle the mails.

When Governor Claiborne refused to be bullied into declaring martial law Wilkinson declared it himself. But when he tried to force the Louisiana Legislature to suspend the writ of habeas corpus the members rebelled, protesting that such action would be a violation of the Federal Constitution.

As it grew apparent that the threat of invasion had been greatly exaggerated and that the imminent peril of the city was largely a figment of Wilkinson's fevered imagination, the New Orleans public rose in revolt against this assumption of power and disregard of their rights.

In Washington President Jefferson was receiving news of Wilkinson's operations and measuring the nation's reactions. He grew alarmed. In a carefully worded letter to the General he alluded to Wilkinson's mistaken notion that 7000 men were descending the Mississippi with Burr for an assault on New Orleans. This total, Jefferson surmised, must have been based on the estimate of the number of men who could be raised in the western country for an invasion of Mexico under the authority of the Government. But, suggested the President, evidently the General had not taken into account that the instant his proclamation reached the West and made it known that the Government did not sanction the expedition, all honest men deserted Burr and left him with only a handful.

The President then tactfully cautioned the General against making wholesale arrests. His sending Bollman and Swartwout to Washington, he said, was supported by public opinion. So would be the sending of Burr, Blennerhassett, and Comfort Tyler, if they were apprehended. "I hope," added the President, "you will not extend this deportation to persons against whom there is only suspicion, or shades of offense not strongly marked. I fear public sentiment would desert you, because seeing no danger here, violations of law are felt with strength. I have thought it just to give you these views of the sentiment here, as they may enlighten your path."

No doubt, continued Mr. Jefferson, Wilkinson had seen the malicious insinuations in the newspapers against him. But the

President of the United States protested that he still had faith:
"I can assure you that your conduct, as now known, has placed
you on ground extremely favorable with the public."

Shortly thereafter a Major Bruff of the Artillery arrived in
Washington from St. Louis. He went straight to Secretary of
War Dearborn and directly accused Wilkinson of spying for
the Spaniards and committing treason with Burr. Dearborn
heard Bruff out and then replied calmly that there had been a
time when the General had not stood well with the Executive,
but his energetic measures at New Orleans had regained him
executive confidence and the President would sustain him.
Bruff then appealed to Attorney General Caesar Rodney who
gave him a realistic and revealing answer. "What would be the
result," Rodney asked, "if all your charges against General
Wilkinson should be proven? Why just what the Federalist and
all the enemies of the present administration wish—it would
turn the indignation of the people from Burr on Wilkinson.
Burr would escape and Wilkinson take his place."

There could not have been a clearer exposition of the predicament in which Jefferson found himself. He had declared
Wilkinson to be the savior of the nation. To confess now that
Wilkinson was a knave would convict himself of gross negli-
gence in entrusting the safety of the western country to such
a man.

As the time for Wilkinson's presence in Richmond approached, and as he foresaw the attack that was sure to be
made on his integrity, the General recognized the importance
of clearing himself of the charges of being a secret agent of
Spain. He therefore appealed directly to his old friend Governor Folch of West Florida, telling him he was being slandered because of certain alleged Spanish intrigues of a criminal
nature and asking him to state whether he, Wilkinson, had ever
received a pension from the Spanish government.

The Spanish government may on occasion have been remiss
about paying the pension in full and on time, but Folch now
met nobly every obligation his government owed the General.
In a private letter to Wilkinson whom he addressed as "my dear

friend" he assured him he had sent all the documents that pertained to "the ancient history" to Havana, "persuaded that before the United States are in a situation to conquer that capital, you and I and Jefferson, Madison and all the secretaries . . . will have made many days' journey into the other world." Folch reminded Wilkinson that he had been in Louisiana since 1783 and had enjoyed confidential relations with his uncle, Governor Miro, and declared that no document showing Wilkinson to have been a secret agent in the pay of Spain existed in the records. Then in a public letter he came out handsomely with the statement that "his [Wilkinson's] qualities as an honest man and one faithful to his country entitle him to your particular attention and regard and we judge him to be worthy of the commission he holds."

Such was Folch's exoneration of Wilkinson when only a few weeks before, as Burr and his men were traveling down the Mississippi toward Spanish territory, Yrujo, Spanish minister to the United States, was assuring Don Cevallos, Spanish Foreign Minister, that the governors of the Floridas were being informed of what was going on through Folch's connection with Wilkinson.

In assuring Wilkinson that his conduct had "placed him on ground favorable with the public" Mr. Jefferson could not have included that sizable portion of it that just then regarded Wilkinson as a brother in crime with Burr, who at the last minute had lost his nerve and betrayed his partner in a valiant attempt to save himself.

Thus was the stage set for the entry of the Government's star witness.

Chapter X

DISTRICT ATTORNEY HAY had asked that Burr be confined or that his bail be raised for fear he would run away rather than face his former friend and present accuser, General James Wilkinson. On the other hand, there were quite as many people who harbored the belief that General Wilkinson would not dare to come face to face with Burr.

Among the latter was John Randolph of Roanoke who, at the time, was keeping up a lively correspondence with Joseph H. Nicholson, a former colleague in the House of Representatives and now a Federal judge in Baltimore. As late as May 31, while still waiting impatiently for the appearance of the dilatory star witness, Randolph wrote to his friend: "There are, I am told, upwards of forty witnesses in town, one of whom (General Jackson of Tennessee) does not scruple to say that W [Wilkinson] is a pensioner of Spain to his knowledge and that he will not dare to show his face here."

But just as Colonel Burr upset Hay's prediction by announcing his presence whenever his name was called, so General Wilkinson disappointed his critics by at last showing up. Having traveled from New Orleans by sea he landed at Hampton, Virginia. On June 10 his arrival in Richmond by stage was announced. He was reported to be exhausted from his journey, but his appearance did not bear out that impression. As befitted the senior officer of the United States Army, he exhibited himself to the public resplendent in his major general's uniform. To add to the impressiveness of his entry on the scene he was constantly attended in public by his military aides, including his son, Lieutenant James Wilkinson, Lieutenant Edmund Pendleton Gaines, who had received Burr as a prisoner in Alabama, and Lieutenants Murray and Smith. Gaines in later years was to achieve distinction in the War of 1812 and eventually attain command of a department of the United States Army. Still another member of the Wilkinson party was Mr. John Graham, President Jefferson's special agent who had trailed Burr after the issuance of the presidential proclamation. This group, augmented by their servants, produced quite a spectacular array.

On Monday, June 15, the long-awaited personal encounter between Burr and Wilkinson took place. It was a dramatic moment worth recording for posterity, and several first-hand accounts were duly put on paper immediately after the event and thus preserved. General Wilkinson himself was the author of one of them. His was written especially for the eye of the President and it was executed in the General's customarily vivid manner. Colonel Burr was already in the courtroom when Wilkinson entered. Said the General in his letter to Jefferson: "I was introduced to a position within the bar very near my adversary. I saluted the bench and in spite of myself my eyes darted a flash of indignation at the little traitor, on whom they continued fixed until I was called to the Book—here, Sir, I found my expectations verified—this lion-hearted, eagle-eyed Hero, jerking under the weight of conscious guilt, with haggard eyes in an effort to meet the indignant salutation of outraged honor; but it was in vain, his audacity failed him. He averted his face, grew pale, and affected passion to conceal his perturbation."

Altogether different was the impression made by the incident on Washington Irving who was among the spectators in the courtroom that morning. Allowance must, no doubt, be made for the fact that Irving counted himself as being in the Burr camp and was altogether sympathetic with the Colonel in his misfortune. According to Irving, Burr, his back to the entrance, was facing the judge and conversing with his counsel when the General arrived. "Wilkinson," said Irving, "strutted into Court, and took his stand on a parallel line with Burr on his right hand. Here he stood for a moment swelling like a turkey-cock, and bracing himself up for the encounter of Burr's eye.

"The latter did not take any notice of him until the judge directed the clerk to swear General Wilkinson. At the mention of his name Burr turned his head, looked him full in the face with one of his piercing regards, swept his eye over his whole person from head to foot, as if to scan its dimensions, and then coolly resumed his former position and went on conversing with his counsel as tranquilly as ever. The whole look was over in an instant, but it was an admirable one. There was no appearance of study or constraint in it; no affectation of disdain or defiance; a slight expression of contempt played over his countenance, such as you would show on regarding any person to whom you are indifferent, but whom you considered mean and contemptible."

In the next issue of the *Enquirer*, Editor Ritchie, under his nom de plume of the "Resident of Richmond Hill," presented a third version of the encounter. He, of course, championed the Government's star witness, as the mouthpiece of the Jefferson Administration would have been expected to do.

"He [Wilkinson]," wrote Ritchie, "has met Colonel Burr in the presence of the court and a gaping crowd, but who can say that his countenance was flushed and apprehensive or sicklied o'er with the pale cast of fear and guilt? That was a deep mortification to some; had he but fainted or betrayed the least timidity, it would have been a luscious conquest of federalism."

Still another witness of the scene who, in spite of the heat of that partisan battle, somehow managed to maintain a neutral attitude, reported that the meeting had been anticipated for so long by the two principals and had been so often rehearsed in their imaginations that the actual performance of neither party was convincing. Such is the evidence which posterity is invited to hear and weigh, and from it arrive at a decision as to which of the two principals came off the better.

The "Resident from Richmond Hill," having dealt with the meeting of Burr and Wilkinson, could not resist the opportunity of reporting his impressions of Luther Martin, lawyer for the defense. Said he: "As I have mentioned the bar, permit me to introduce a strange lawyer from a neighboring State whose character towers to the highest sphere of jurisprudence. My expectations were at first as extravagant as his character. I marked him in my mind's eye as a happy standard by which I might form some estimate of the Virginia bar. But pardon me ye critics and eulogists of Mr. M. . . . if I cannot join in the forensic paean, if instead of placing him in the zenith I put him in the nadir."

General Wilkinson's presence in court was brief. The Grand Jury, which had been waiting so long, was impatient to hear him. Grand jury proceedings are customarily regarded as sacred and what goes on behind closed doors is supposedly held in the strictest confidence. But the Grand Jury in the Burr case, like so many other features of that strange performance, refused to conform to the normal pattern. At least one serious leak led to a controversy in the press. In his continued correspondence with Judge Nicholson the jury's foreman set down some salty observations. Nor was the star witness silent. His experience gave him another chance to unburden himself to his patron in Washington.

Wilkinson brought with him into the jury room the original of the famous letter in cipher which he had received from Burr by the hand of Samuel Swartwout. It was a complicated cipher which baffled the jury, with one exception. That exception was John Randolph of Roanoke who gave a demonstration of his remarkable intellect by mastering the key at once and explaining the solution to his less astute fellow jurymen.

The General's reception was less than cordial. To a man who claimed to have saved his country through his bold and patriotic actions the militant attitude of the Grand Jury was painful indeed. The General made his lament to Jefferson: "I dreamt

not of the importance attached to my presence before I reached
Hampton . . . for I had anticipated that a deluge of testimony
would have been poured forth from all quarters to overwhelm
him [Burr] with guilt and dishonor." That, perhaps, to excuse
his having kept the Grand Jury waiting. "Sadly, indeed, was
I mistaken, and to my astonishment I found the traitor vindicated and myself condemned by a mass of wealth, character,
influence and talents. Merciful God, what a spectacle did I
behold—integrity and truth perverted and trampled under foot
by turpitude and guilt, patriotism appalled and usurpation tri-
umphant. Did I ever expect it would depend on my humble
self to stop the current of such a polluted stream? Never,
never."

Why the Grand Jury did not overwhelm Wilkinson with
manifestations of appreciation and gratitude is revealed by
John Randolph in a letter to Nicholson reporting on the indictments: "But," said Randolph, "the mammoth of iniquity
escaped. Not that any man pretended to think him innocent,
but upon certain drawn distinctions that I will not pester you
with.

"Wilkinson is the only man that I ever saw who was from
the bark to the very core a villain. I cannot enter upon it here.
Suffice it to say that I have seen it—so that it is not susceptible
of misconstruction. . . . Perhaps you never saw human nature
in so degraded a situation as in the person of W. before the
G. J., & yet this man stands on the very summit and pinnacle
of executive favor—whilst Jas. M—e [James Monroe] denounced. . . ." Just then Monroe stood in Randolph's good
graces. But like so many others he soon was to incur that in-
constant gentleman's displeasure.

A few days later Randolph wrote again: "W— is the most
finished scoundrel that ever lived. A ream of paper would not
contain all the proofs—but what of that? He is 'the man whom
the king delighteth to honor' & all who are in search of promotion find it to their interest to shut their eyes and ears to
the evidence of the guilt—among them I could name some,
whom I blush to think upon."

Randolph then described in detail the scratches with a penknife and restorations in the Burr letter which he claimed were made in Wilkinson's own handwriting. He concludes: "Let me know what the opinion is with you of this redoubtable thief taker (set a thief etc.) who commands our armies."

In another of his emotional letters to the President, Wilkinson confessed his perplexity at the direction the case had taken: "You are doubtless well aware," he wrote, "of the proceedings here in the case of Burr. To me they are incomprehensible as I am no jurist. The Grand Jury actually made an attempt to present me for suspicion [Wilkinson meant "misprision"] of treason on the ground of having failed to report Dayton to you. I feel myself between Scylla and Charybdis. The jury would dishonor me for failing in my duty, and Burr and his conspirators for performing it."

The jury's treatment of Wilkinson provided the subject for a bitter dispute that ran for days in the pages of the *Enquirer*. Under the heading "Drowning Men Catch At Straws," Editor Ritchie set forth that he was authorized to contradict the slander uttered in Davis's *Virginia Gazette and Daily Advertiser* (The *Enquirer*'s Federalist rival) that a motion had been made before the Grand Jury to present the General for high treason and that on the question the jury had divided equally.

The *Enquirer* traced the story to "Mumford Beverly Esq., an unworthy member of the jury, of whose attachment to monarchy and sympathy for Burr no doubts are admitted." A few days later Mr. John Brockenbrough, cashier of the Bank of Virginia and a juryman, entered the controversy. Mr. Brockenbrough said he felt no disposition to interfere in the controversy between General Wilkinson and his friends and Mr. Beverly, but he deemed it his duty to state the facts. He said he had not voted for presenting General Wilkinson for high treason, for no such vote was taken, to his knowledge.

A whole month was allowed to elapse before juryman William Daniel Jr. at last straightened out the matter. The motion was not to present Wilkinson for "high treason," but for "misprision of treason." And, said Mr. Daniel, the jury had been seven for and nine against.

In view of the battering he had received from the Grand

Jury in his gallant effort to serve the Administration, the poor, maltreated General was gravely in need of sympathy and moral support. And he got it. To his lamentation the President replied: "Your enemies have filled the public ear with slanders and your mind with trouble on that account. The establishment of their guilt will let the world see what they ought to think of their clamors; it will dissipate the doubts of those who doubted for want of knowledge and will place you on higher ground in the public estimation and public confidence." Then wholeheartedly and without reservation Jefferson declared: "No one is more sensible than myself of the injustice which has been aimed at you. Accept, I pray you, my salutations and assurances of respect and esteem."

Surely no President of the United States ever expressed gratitude in such extravagant terms to a subordinate who deserved it less. Necessity makes strange bedfellows.

While the Grand Jury was behind closed doors examining witnesses, stagnation settled on the courtroom. Again there was need for diversion to while away the time. The ever-resourceful Burr, seldom wanting for an idea, supplied it. He moved that an attachment be issued against General Wilkinson for contempt in obstructing the administration of justice by rifling the mails, imprisoning witnesses, and extorting testimony by torture. The allusions were to his behavior in New Orleans.

The motion at least afforded opportunity for several witnesses to pour out lurid stories of their experiences at the hands of the tyrant. It caused Wilkinson personal embarrassment—if that were possible—by bringing him back into court, and gave counsel on both sides a chance to disport themselves in prolonged argument.

On June 24, while these arguments were being heard, the Grand Jury, led by its foreman, John Randolph, filed majestically into the courtroom and took seats in the jury box. Argument on Burr's motion was immediately suspended. A profound silence fell over the assemblage and every ear was strained as Mr. Randolph, addressing the bench, announced that the jury had agreed upon several indictments. He then handed the official document to the clerk who read aloud the endorsements:

"An indictment against Aaron Burr for treason."

"An indictment against Aaron Burr for misdemeanor."

"An indictment against Harman Blennerhassett for treason."

"An indictment against Harman Blennerhassett for misdemeanor."

Burr, according to those present, on hearing the indictment read, displayed no emotion. He accepted the action of the Grand Jury as calmly as he had accepted all his misfortunes. There seems to have been no justification for the statement in one of the local papers next day that the prisoner was thrown into a state of consternation and dismay. Such behavior would have been so out of keeping with the man's character that the report can be safely attributed to Republican propaganda.

After the Grand Jury had withdrawn, Judge Marshall announced that he was now under the necessity of committing Burr. So, late in the afternoon, the former Vice-President of the United States had to undergo the humiliation of being conducted by the marshal through a concourse of hundreds of curious people to the city jail, notorious for its filth and vermin. There for the night he shared a room with a man and woman and was in close proximity to the other prisoners.

Next day the Grand Jury indicted for treason and misdemeanor ex-Senator Jonathan Dayton of New Jersey, Senator John Smith of Ohio, Comfort Tyler, Israel Smith, and Davis Floyd.

Dayton went out of office on the same day Burr ceased to be Vice-President. After that they were known to be closely associated. Some people believed that the treasonable projects on which they were supposed to be engaged were as much the handiwork of Dayton as of Burr. It was Dayton's nephew, Peter Ogden, who carried a letter to Wilkinson along with Samuel Swartwout who carried the letter from Burr.

Senator Smith had been suspected of being engaged in the plot from the time Burr stopped with him at Cincinnati in the

summer of 1805. When invited by the Kentucky Grand Jury
to testify to the charges brought by Daveiss he had discreetly
disappeared.

Comfort Tyler, Israel Smith, and Davis Floyd were minor
leaders of the expedition. Tyler, who came from Onandaga,
New York, had served with Burr in the New York Assembly
and there fell under his spell. Israel Smith also was a New
Yorker and Davis Floyd was from Indiana Territory. They
were no doubt indicted because they were present on Blennerhassett Island and took part in any overt act which might have
taken place there and on the proof of which the charge of
treason depended.

Burr's first thought was for his daughter Theodosia. She
must be spared anxiety and mortification. From his cell in jail
he penned her a hurried letter in which he gave no inkling of
his disgusting surroundings. The indictment for treason, he explained, was founded on the allegation that Col. Comfort Tyler, with 20 or 30 men, had stopped at Blennerhassett Island
on the way down the Ohio and ". . . that though these men
were not armed, and had no military array or organization,
and though they did neither use force nor threaten it, yet having set out with a view of taking temporary possession of New
Orleans on their way to Mexico, that such intent was treasonable, and therefore a war was levied on Blennerhassett Island
by construction."

The Colonel went on to say that though he was at that time
in Frankfort, Kentucky, on his way to Tennessee, nevertheless,
having advised the measure, he was by construction of law
present at the island and levied war there. "In fact the indictment charges that Aaron Burr was on that day present at the
island, though not a man of the jury supposed this to be true."

Of the 50 witnesses who were examined by the Grand Jury,
said Burr, "it may be safely alleged that 30 at least have been
perjured." He closed his letter with a characteristically stoical
injunction: "I beg and expect it of you that you will conduct
yourself as becomes my daughter, and that you manifest no
signs of weakness or alarm." Was he thinking of that long line

of Puritan ancestors stretching back through New England to
the old England? He need have no concern on the score of
Theodosia's behavior. A word from her father was the equivalent of a command. She had never failed him yet.

After Burr had spent two uncomfortable nights in the city
jail his counsel complained bitterly to the Chief Justice. They
warned that the unsanitary conditions in the jail would break
down his health. The lack of privacy, they claimed, would interfere seriously with the consultations with his lawyers and
impair his defense. Moved by these appeals, Judge Marshall
consented that the prisoner should occupy a room in a house
which had been rented by Luther Martin across the street from
the Swan Tavern. Consent was given on condition that suitable shutters and door fastenings be installed to insure the security of the prisoner and that a guard of seven men be kept
constantly on duty.

These terms were accepted. The installations were inspected
and declared secure by none other than Benjamin H. Latrobe,
the country's leading architect and at the moment President
Jefferson's Surveyor of Public Buildings, who was then busily
employed in redesigning the national Capitol. Latrobe had been
approached by Burr with a proposal to take part in building a
canal around the falls of the Ohio at Cincinnati and was among
the many persons hauled in by the Government to give testimony.

Burr and the architect were to have another relationship of
which neither of them had dreamed. Latrobe had but recently
completed a design for a penitentiary at Richmond, for the
State of Virginia, drawn up according to the specifications of
Jefferson. The building had been erected and it met all the very
latest requirements set forth by the penologists. In addition to
its functional excellence it was a noble structure characteristic
of Latrobe's imagination and genius. It occupied a commanding
position overlooking the James River on a lofty hill next door
to the one on which stood the Gray House of Robert Gamble.
That, too, it will be recalled, was the work of Latrobe. It now
housed Colonel Gamble and his wife, his two daughters, and

his sons-in-law, Governor William Cabell and William Wirt.

Since the imprisonment of Burr in Mr. Martin's house had brought forth charges of favoritism, Governor Cabell hit on a plan to save Judge Marshall embarrassment by graciously offering the court quarters for Burr in the penitentiary. The offer was accepted by his counsel on the understanding that, as soon as the trial commenced, the prisoner should be returned to the Martin house in town.

So it was that Colonel Burr was transferred to the penitentiary. If in fact, as some alleged, he had plotted to make himself an emperor, the structure in which he was now imprisoned provided a romantic setting. The massive walls and the sturdy tower needed only a banner floating over them to give every appearance of a castle or other imperial stronghold. It was the nearest thing to regal quarters he would ever occupy.

This important housekeeping matter attended to, the prisoner was arraigned and pleaded "not guilty" to the charges. The Court ordered the United States Marshal to summon a panel of 48 men to report on August 3. From these a jury was to be picked for the trial.

The time had come for another intermission. With the intermission came the need for further divertissement. Being secured in prison, Colonel Burr was in an awkward position to supply it. This time the local populace and the visitors to the town who had come to take part in the trial were to be relieved of their boredom by the navy of His Britannic Majesty, King George III.

Chapter XI

ON THE AFTERNOON of June 22, a few miles outside the Virginia Capes, the British frigate *Leopard* fired on the U.S. frigate *Chesapeake*, killing three men, severely wounding eight, and slightly wounding ten. Among the slightly wounded was Commodore James Barron, ranking officer on the *Chesapeake*. The American frigate, taken by surprise and totally unprepared for action, fired one shot of protest and struck her colors. A party from the *Leopard* then boarded the *Chesapeake*, subjected it to the indignity of mustering its crew, and removed from it four men alleged to be deserters from a British man-of-war.

The issue of impressment was then at its height. The British Navy, short of manpower, charged that many of its men were deserting to the American merchant marine to enjoy better pay and working conditions. It was not at all unusual for British men-of-war to hail American merchantmen on the high seas and search them for deserters. Nor were the British too careful about the men they took off, frequently including American citizens among them. This practice had been bitterly resented by a large part of the American public, but, while complaints had been made to the British Government, the abuse had not yet been considered a cause for war.

The incident of the *Leopard* and the *Chesapeake*, however, was different. This was the first time a British man-of-war had

thus dealt with an American man-of-war. It therefore assumed
the proportions of a national insult.

In spite of the primitive communications of the times, the
bad news traveled with astonishing speed. Three days after the
clash between the two ships word of it reached Washington.
It spread rapidly to the cities up and down the coast. As it
spread public indignation rose to fever heat. Political animosities were for the time being forgotten as the public seethed
with resentment at this latest outrage at the hands of the British Navy. The bitterness of the days of the Revolution against
King George III, who, though old and broken mentally, was
still on the throne, was revived. President Jefferson later remarked that at that moment he held the issue of peace and war
in the hollow of his hand.

The Richmond community shared wholeheartedly in this
tidal wave of indignation. The sensational news from Norfolk
reached the city almost simultaneously with the Grand Jury's
indictment of Burr and Blennerhassett and their alleged fellow
conspirators. Momentarily the trial yielded first place in the
public consciousness to this threat against national sovereignty
from abroad.

In its issue of Saturday, June 27, the *Enquirer* published a
dispatch from Norfolk, dated three days earlier, which revealed
the intensity of public feeling there and clarified the reports
and rumors that had reached Richmond by presenting an orderly account of what had actually happened.

"We are now to present our readers," said the *Enquirer*,
"the details of the most unexampled outrage, on the perpetra-
tion of which the blood of our countrymen has been shed by
the hand of violence, and the honor and independence of our
nation insulted beyond the possibility of further forbearance."
There followed a vivid account of the attack.

Most of the young male population of Richmond was organized into uniformed militia companies among which there was
a strong and healthy rivalry. They seized upon this opportunity
to demonstrate their patriotism and willingness to strike a blow
in preserving the nation's honor. The Richmond Light Infantry

Blues assembled at the Bell Tavern and adopted resolutions declaring that "Members of this company pledge their fortunes and their lives." The Manchester Cavalry, meeting across the river at Brooks Tavern, resolved that "We render our services to the Government." The smart Richmond Troop of Cavalry, calling its members to the Eagle Tavern, appointed a committee to draft a suitable address to the President of the United States making a tender of its services.

The demonstrations of loyalty were not confined to the military. On July 1 a great mass meeting of the citizens of Richmond and Manchester and their vicinities was assembled to take under consideration the "late hostile attack upon the *Chesapeake*." Judge Spencer Roane, of the Virginia Court of Appeals, was in the chair. Editor Thomas Ritchie acted as secretary. John Gamble, Colonel Robert Gamble's son; Peyton Randolph, Edmund's son; the venerable mayor Dr. Foushee; William Wirt; and District Attorney Hay were among the speakers who swayed the crowd. At the conclusion of the meeting a letter was addressed to the President of the United States asserting that "While we are sensible of the evils which must result from war, we are prepared to encounter them in defense of our dearest rights."

Not content with the *Leopard* having humiliated the United States Navy by its attack on the *Chesapeake*, the commander of the British squadron, which included the offending frigate now anchored in Lynnhaven Bay, poured salt on the wound by addressing threatening remarks to the authorities of Norfolk. Governor William Cabell interpreted this as a threat and an insult to the sovereign State of Virginia. He promptly called his council together and, after consultation with it, issued an order to the Virginia militia to march to Lynnhaven Bay and there oppose any offensive action the British might take.

Among the militia contingents were some from Richmond and there were few dry eyes as they marched off down Main Street to what many believed would soon be war.

One interested spectator at the trial up to this point found his enthusiasm shifting from the court to the military. Winfield

Scott, though not then a member of the militia, mounted his horse and rode post-haste thirty miles through the night to his home town of Petersburg to volunteer his services. They were accepted, but the quartermaster was hard put to it to find a uniform large enough for the youth's massive frame. Somehow the problem was solved and Scott accompanied the Petersburg troops to Norfolk. This was his first taste of military life and it got into his blood. From then on the army, not the bar, was his vocation.

Still another man to succumb to the military contagion was William Wirt. To his friend Dabney Carr he wrote an impassioned letter announcing his intention to hand his wife back to her father for the time being and join the army. Wirt formed an ambitious plan for creating a legion of four regiments; he was to be the colonel of one, Carr colonel of another. For a few days his letters re-echoed the idea. But the plan aroused opposition and, as the war fever abated, the proposal died. Thereafter Wirt was as completely wedded to the law as Winfield Scott was to the military. Wirt's brief dabbling in the military was to serve as a source of ridicule among his contemporaries.

In the very middle of the excitement over the *Leopard-Chesapeake* affair came July 4. Even under ordinary circumstances the anniversary of the signing of the Declaration of Independence was regularly observed by the Richmond community with appropriate ceremonies as a patriotic celebration. The crisis acted as an extra stimulus on this occasion.

At daybreak the populace was awakened by the firing of a single gun. At sunrise there followed a salute of seventeen guns. Those units of the military which had not gone to Norfolk played a conspicuous part in the ceremonies. At 9 A.M. a troop of light horse, three volunteer companies of light infantry, and several more militia companies assembled on the parade ground. From there they marched to the Capitol Square with bands playing and colors flying. Meanwhile, in the House of Delegates, where Judge Marshall's court had so recently adjourned, the more sedate people of the community were listening to orations from leading citizens of the town, then a popular form of entertainment.

At 2 P.M. the military and civilians joined forces in the Capitol Square. There, according to regular custom, the military formed a great circle and from the center Mayor Foushee solemnly read the Declaration of Independence. At its conclusion three cheers were given, the band struck up "Yankee Doodle" and followed it by "Hail, Columbia," while soldiers and civilians joined in the chorus.

A silence then fell over the crowd as Shelton Jones, Esquire, distinguished for his eloquence, mounted the platform and delivered a funeral oration in memory of the seamen who had lost their lives on the *Chesapeake*. During the oration the troops stood at attention with arms reversed and, as the orator concluded his address, the solemnity of the occasion was emphasized by the roll of muffled drums and the firing of minute guns.

These serious ceremonies duly performed, the public now turned to the lighter features of the celebration. The militia companies repaired to the various places of entertainment previously designated for them while many of the civilians assembled in the Capitol for the drinking of toasts. Word had gone out that in keeping with the theme of independence native drinks—and no others—were to be the order of the day. At the Capitol the official count showed that seventeen standing toasts were drunk, the first having been proposed by Governor Cabell.

There is no mention of the Chief Justice having been present at the celebration at the Capitol. But Richmond was a busy place that day and the festivities were by no means confined to one spot. His absence from the Capitol might have been traced to another and more exclusive assemblage at an inviting spot several miles to the west of the town known as Buchanan's Spring. This was a shady picnic spot on the property of the Rev. John Buchanan. It was the regular meeting place of the social organization known as the Barbecue Club, of which Judge Marshall was an enthusiastic member. The club, composed of the leading citizens of the town, had already been in existence some twenty years and it met regularly for sumptuous dinners at which individual members took turns at being host. The Fourth of July was always the occasion of a meeting of the club.

The dinner, laid out on a table under an open shed, had been prepared by Jasper Crouch, Richmond's most popular caterer. Crouch enjoyed eating food as much as he did preparing it and, according to contemporary accounts, he had by this time "acquired gout and the rotundity of an alderman." The custom of the club forbade either dessert or wine. The ample meal was washed down with toddy, punch, and mint julep. A diversion greatly enjoyed by members of the club was pitching quoits, at which the Chief Justice excelled. Tradition has it that his quoits were made especially for him and were heavier than those used by other members.

One celebrity who, perforce, was unable to join the general public in these festivities was Colonel Burr. He was now a prisoner in the penitentiary; and, if his own word is to be believed, every effort both official and unofficial was being exerted to make his stay there as comfortable as possible. To Theodosia he wrote describing the considerate behavior of his jailer:

"Jailer: 'I hope, Sir, that it would not be disagreeable to you if I should lock this door after dark?'

"Burr: 'By no means, I should prefer it to keep out intruders.'

"Jailer: 'It is our custom, Sir, to extinguish all lights at 9 o'clock. I hope, Sir, you will have no objection to conform to that.'

"Burr: 'That, Sir, I am sorry to say, is impossible, for I never go to bed till 12, and always burn 2 candles.'

"Jailer: 'Very well, Sir, just as you please. I should have been glad if it had been otherwise, but, as you please, Sir.'"

A few days later Burr wrote Theodosia again: "My friends and acquaintances of both sexes are permittted to visit me without interruption, without inquiring their business, and without the presence of a spy. It is well that I have an ante-chamber, or I should often be gené with visitors."

Alluding to the possibility of Theodosia joining him in Richmond, he added: "If you come I can give you a bedroom and parlor on this floor. The bedroom has three large closets, and it is a much more commodious one than you ever had in your life." Once more he admonished her to observe the stoical role he expected her to play: "Remember, no agitations, no complaints, no fears or anxieties on the road, or I renounce thee."

Among Richmond's smart society it became the fashion to prepare dainty dishes for the distinguished and charming prisoner now suffering persecution at the hands of the irascible tyrant in the White House. The Colonel was overwhelmed with wine jelly, a favorite Richmond sweet. Lemons, pineapples, and other rare and exotic fruits were showered upon him. Admirers brought him fresh butter; and to preserve it in the torrid heat of a Richmond summer, an icebox was installed and generously stocked by the owners of icehouses. In short, his friends did all they could during the weeks he was behind the bars to relieve the ennui of his confinement and to supply him with all the luxuries his fastidious nature craved.

The ladies were foremost in their attentions. This was in contrast to the behavior of some of the men. In a letter to a friend, Washington Irving reported that it had almost been considered culpable to evince toward Burr the least sympathy or support. He had, he said, seen many a "hollow-hearted caitiff," who basked in the sunshine of Burr's bounty when he was in power, and who now skulked from his side and mingled among the most glamorous of his enemies. But this, heaven be praised, was not the attitude of the ladies.

"The ladies alone," observed Irving, "have felt, or at least had candor and independence sufficient to express these feelings which do honor to humanity. They have been uniform in their expressions of compassion for his misfortunes, and a hope of his acquittal; not a lady, I believe, in Richmond, whatever may be her husband's sentiments on this subject, who would not rejoice on seeing Col. Burr at liberty. It may be said that Col. Burr has ever been a favorite with the sex; but I am not inclined to account for it in so illiberal a manner; it results from

that merciful, that heavy disposition, implanted in the female
bosom, which ever inclines in favor of the accused and the
unfortunate."

Irving might have observed that the actions of some of the
ladies, whose husbands were in some manner connected with
the trial, could well have caused those husbands embarrassment.
It was fortunate for them that Richmond viewed the personal
entanglements with a tolerance that has seldom been granted in
other criminal cases.

Irving could, for example, have been referring to Mrs. Robert Gamble. The former Catherine Grattan, who had braved
Indians and panthers and other perils of the frontier in her
youth, was not now to be overawed by a son-in-law who was
one of the leading lawyers for the prosecution. Let William
Wirt employ his eloquence to get Aaron Burr hanged. Nevertheless Mrs. Gamble felt free to send refreshments from her
kitchen to the prisoner. After all, were they not neighbors?
The Gray House and the penitentiary occupied adjoining
promontories. They shared equally the architectural genius of
Benjamin Henry Latrobe. Why should not Catherine Grattan
Gamble welcome Burr with all the courtesies customarily extended by Richmonders to a new resident with the proper social background?

Irving's description of Burr in prison was nothing like so
glowing as that of Burr himself. The only reason for immuring
the Colonel in that abode of "thieves, cut-throats and incendi-
aries," commented Irving, was that it would save the United
States a couple of hundred dollars, which would have been the
charge for guarding him at his lodgings.

Contrary to Burr's statement that his friends had ready access to him, Irving reported that, "I found great difficulty gaining admission to him for a few moments. The keeper had orders to admit no one but his counsel and his witnesses—strange
measures these!

"That it is not sufficient that a man against whom no certainty of crime is proved, should be confined by bolts, and bars
and massy walls in a criminal prison; but he is likewise to be

cut off from all intercourse with society, deprived of all the kind offices of friendship, and made to suffer all the penalties and deprivations of a condemned criminal. I was permitted to enter for a few moments, as a special favor, contrary to orders." Could it have been that the Colonel was afraid the enthusiastic young man might stay too long?

Irving thought the Colonel seemed in lower spirits than formerly. He was composed and collected as usual, but there was not the same cheerfulness that Irving had hitherto remarked. The Colonel told him that it was with difficulty that his very servant was allowed occasionally to see him. "He had a bad cold, which I suppose was occasioned by the dampness of his chamber which had lately been whitewashed." It was with a heavy heart that Irving left him.

The Colonel's and Irving's accounts of the imprisonment could hardly be more contradictory. But then Burr was trying to relieve Theodosia's anxieties, whereas Irving's purpose in being in Richmond was to use his talents to turn public opinion in Burr's favor.

Irving's obligation to Burr's friends for enabling him to be present at the trial was not a small one. The young man at this stage of his life delighted in mingling with the great and the near-great and he had had a rare opportunity to do so in Richmond.

To his brother-in-law James Paulding, associate editor of *Salmagundi*, he wrote enthusiastically of his experience: "I have been treated in the most polite and hospitable manner by the most distinguished persons of the place—those friendly to Burr and those opposed to him, and have intimate acquaintances among his bitterest enemies. I am absolutely enchanted with Richmond, and like it more and more every day. The society is polished, sociable and extremely hospitable, and here is a great variety of distinguished characters assembled on this occasion, which gives a strong degree of interest to passing incidents."

But there must be an end to all good things. Irving had his magazine in New York to think about. No telling how long

the trial would take. He had been in Richmond two months
and the Court had done no more than get through the preliminaries. So before the actual business of trying Burr began,
Irving had to set out on his return home. On the way he
stopped off in Washington and from there wrote a letter to his
confidante, Miss Mary Fairlee, a charming young person who
then was the reigning belle in New York. To her he confided
that, as much as he enjoyed Richmond society, he had been
faced by a serious personal problem. It was of a sort that was
likely to happen to a handsome and eligible young man on his
first appearance in a community. He was pursued by designing
young women.

"By some lucky means or other," Irving informed Miss Fairlee, "I got the character, among three or four novel-read damsels, of being an *interesting young man* [the italics are Irving's];
now of all characters in the world, believe me, this is the most
intolerable for any young man, who has a will of his own to
support, particularly in warm weather. The tender-hearted fair
ones think you absolutely at their command; they conclude
that you must, of course, be fond of moonlight walks, and rides
at daybreak, and red-hot strolls in the middle of the day (Fahr-
enheit's Thermom. 98½ in the shade) and 'melting hot-hissing
hot' tea parties, and what is worse, they expect you to talk
sentiment and act Romeo, and Sir Charles and King Pepin all
the while! 'Twas too much for me; had I been in love with any
one of them, I believe I could have played the dying swain, as
eloquently and foolishly as most men; but not having the good
luck to be inspired by the tender passion, I found the slavery
unsupportable; so I forthwith set about ruining my character
as speedily as possible.

"I forgot to go to tea parties; I overslept myself of a morning. I protested against the moon and derided that blessed
planet most villainously. In a word I was soon given up as a
young man of most preposterous and incorrigible opinions, and
was left to do e'en just as I pleased. Yet, believe me, I did, notwithstanding, admire the fair damsels of Richmond exceedingly; and, to be candid at once, the character of the whole sex,

though it has ever ranked high in my estimation, is still more exalted than ever."

Bless the young man! The fair damsels would have been flattered at his general impressions of them, even though not one of them had succeeded in winning his heart. They may have reflected that, had they encountered him when Richmond weather was more on their side they might have made greater headway. If Miss Fairlee was as sentimentally inclined as the young ladies in Richmond she must have felt reassured by this evidence that the handsome young Washington Irving would return home to New York as detached and uninvolved as though he had never been exposed to the wiles of designing southern belles. On the other hand, after reading the letter and reflecting on the character it unconsciously revealed, might she not have concluded that Irving's imperviousness to the assaults of impressionable females knew no sectional bounds?

During the first week in June the *Enquirer* in its columns had hailed the arrival in Richmond of the "celebrated Cowper." The *Enquirer* hoped that the manager of the new brick theater on the edge of Shockoe Hill would not fail to avail himself of the opportunity of gratifying the public by engaging him for a few evenings at least.

The "celebrated Cowper" was without doubt Thomas Abthorpe Cooper, a handsome and talented young Irish actor. No doubt Cooper, too, had been attracted to Richmond by the gathering of celebrities there and had concluded that the list would not be complete without the presence of the leading actor of the day.

Richmond in the summer of 1807 not only attracted the leading actor of the day; it attracted also an artist recently arrived from France who was making a name for himself in the cities of the coast through his ingenious manner of making likenesses. On Friday, July 17, the *Enquirer* carried on its front page a paid notice under the heading "Likenesses Taken and Engraved." It stated that the subscriber, as an advertiser was politely known in those days, begged leave to inform the ladies and gentlemen of the city of Richmond that "he takes and en-

graves Likenesses in a style never introduced before in this
country."

The subscriber respectfully solicited the same favor and patronage he had met with in the largest cities in the United
States. Samples of his work, said the announcement, could be
seen at the subscriber's lodgings in Mrs. Harris's house nearly
opposite the Custom House. To stir the Richmonders to prompt
action he closed his public notice by stating that in order not
to disappoint those who might desire to "set for their likenesses," he begged leave to suggest that his stay in the city
would be short. The notice was signed, "St. Mémin."

The subscriber, to give him his full name, was Charles Bal-
thazer Julien Ferret de Saint-Mémin. Born in Dijon, France, of
an aristocratic family, he fled the French Revolution and arrived in New York in 1793. He proceeded at once to tour the
cities of the East. He visited Philadelphia, Baltimore, and Annapolis successively. Wherever he went he left behind him a
trail of his crayon portraits. They were done in black and white
crayon on pink paper with the aid of a device invented by the
gentleman himself and known as a "physionotrace." The pro-
file of the subject was thrown as a shadow on the paper and
there traced with mathematical exactness. Saint-Mémin was an
artist as well as a technician. The portrait executed life size was
framed in black and gold and the whole presented a lifelike
and satisfying effect.

But that was not all. In addition to every life-size portrait, the
artist made a small copper plate about two inches in diameter
from which were struck off a dozen engravings. The sitter received the framed portrait, the engravings, and the plate. Saint-
Mémin's usual price was $25 for gentlemen and—somewhat un-
gallantly—$35 for ladies. Though high according to contempo-
rary values the price was not exorbitant as portraits go.

Saint-Mémin's reputation preceded him to Richmond. Shrewd
man that he was, he no doubt counted on the trial to provide
a healthy lot of potential customers. If so, he was not disappointed. He did the Chief Justice. He did John Wickham, and
Mrs. Wickham too. He did William Wirt, and the Cabells, the

Gambles and the Mayos, and others prominent in Richmond society.

Modern art critics are inclined to turn up their noses at Saint-Mémin's work because of its mechanical quality. Yet from the standpoint of social prestige the money paid out for it could not have been better spent. No doubt there were many men and women in Richmond who thought of engaging Saint-Mémin. They may then have reflected that $25 or $35 was a goodly sum. They would have been unusual if they had not had more pressing demands than portraits—perhaps new parlor furniture, or a great four poster bed in the heavy empire style just coming into vogue. Perhaps they reflected that at least part of that sum might be needed to pay the fees for their children at the dancing class going on at the Haymarket Gardens. What better and more direct way to obtain social prestige than by sending children to a dancing class? Or a room may have needed papering or a leaking roof called for attention.

Whatever the practical, common-sense reason, there were many who failed to seize the opportunity presented them by Saint-Mémin. They could not know that a hundred years or so after they had gone to their reward their portraits, in black and white crayon on pink paper, hanging on a wall in New York, Philadelphia, Baltimore, Annapolis, or Richmond, and duly authenticated as an ancestor, entitled its owner to a place in the most exclusive social circles.

In a country where a coronet is not worn a "Saint-Mémin" comes closest to being the equivalent symbol of nobility. Anyone who unguardedly inquires "what is a Saint-Mémin?" could offer no better proof of not belonging. The moral of the Saint-Mémin episode is that whenever an offer to be extravagant appears, take it. No telling what social prestige it may bring one's descendants.

No, following the indictment of Burr and the others, and the adjournment of court, and while waiting for it to convene again on August 3, Richmond was far from dull.

Chapter XII

As the day for his trial approached Burr felt the need for Theodosia. His daughter was now in Charleston with her husband and little boy. But Burr was not the kind to yield to sentimentality. His appeal was quite impersonal; it might have been made to any stranger. It was based on logical reasons and did not for once intimate that in this crisis of his life he needed the affection and understanding which only Theodosia could give him.

"I want," he wrote toward the close of July, "an independent and discerning witness to my conduct and to that of government. The scene which has passed and those about to be transacted will exceed any reasonable credulity, and hereafter will be deemed fables, unless attested by very high authority."

If there was any doubt in his mind as to the outcome he evidently was determined not to let Theodosia know it. In his letter he breathed nothing but self-confidence. "I repeat what has heretofore been written, that I should never invite anyone, much less those so dear to me, to witness my disgrace. I may be immured in dungeons, chained, murdered in legal form, but I cannot be humiliated or disgraced. If absent you will suffer great solicitude. In my presence you will feel none, whatever may be the malice or the power of my enemies and in both they abound."

It was as though Burr had trained his daughter from her

birth with this critical moment in view. And the training had been carried out with all the puritan vigor that ran in the blood of the Burrs and the Edwardses. The child was the first born to the Colonel and his wife, the widow Theodosia Bartow Prevost. The event took place in 1783 while the Burrs were still living in Albany. The infant was named for her mother though Theodosia Prevost Burr professed that she wanted to name it for Aaron's sister Sally.

Soon after the baby's arrival the mother wrote to Sally's husband, Tapping Reeve, announcing the event: "Providence smiled upon óur wishes and on the 21st of June blest us with a lovely daughter . . . and you will believe me, Reeve, when I tell you the dear little girl has the eyes of your Sally, and promises to be as handsome. I would also have given her her name; but Burr insisted on calling her Theo—assure my sister for me that I submitted with the greatest regret."

The baby was barely five months old when the family moved to New York City, and there the child grew up. Soon after, another daughter was born to the Burrs, but she died in a few years and little is known about her. Early in little Theo's life she exhibited a marked devotion to her father. At the age of four years Mrs. Burr was reporting, "Our sweet prattler exclaims at every noise, 'There's dear papa' and runs to meet him." It was said that her attachment for her father was not of a common nature and that when he was away she could not hear him spoken of without an apparent melancholy.

Such accounts sound suspiciously like an effort on Mrs. Burr's part to flatter the Colonel into forgiving her for having presented him with two daughters and no sons. They might be dismissed as such had not their truth been clearly demonstrated by later events. By this time the once delicate baby had grown into a plump, gay little girl with rosy cheeks and a winning smile.

Little Theo's upbringing became almost immediately the special care of the Colonel. The way he went about it suggests that subconsciously at least he was trying to make amends for her not being a boy. Wherever business might take him and however occupied he might be with his law practice and politics and other personal matters, his thoughts were never far away from his daughter and her training.

Burr was years ahead of his time in his acceptance of revolutionary theories on the education of women. Someone had put in his hands a book by the pioneer feminist Mary Woolstonecraft entitled *Vindication of the Rights of Women*. He had been greatly impressed by it. Writing to his wife he said: "I had heard it spoken of with a coldness little calculated to excite attention; but as I read with avidity and prepossession everything written by a lady, I made haste to procure it, and spent last night, almost the whole of it, in reading it. Be assured that your sex has in her an able advocate. It is, in my opinion, a work of genius."

The burden of Miss Woolstonecraft's argument was that women are as capable of receiving an education as are men, if not more so. Burr embraced the theory; or else he was determined to test it. Forthwith he proceeded to put it into practice in the education of his own daughter. To his wife he remarked: "But I yet hope, by her, to convince the world what neither sex appears to believe, that women have souls." So obsessed was he with this idea that he later confided to his wife: "If I could foresee that Theo would become a mere fashionable woman with all the attendant frivolity and vacuity of mind, adorned with whatever grace or allurement, I would earnestly pray God to take her forthwith hence." Strange sentiments coming from a man who in his usual contacts with women was reputed to be attracted chiefly by their physical attributes.

In his determination to give his daughter the same education he would have given a son the Colonel spared no expense in employing tutors. At this period, with a flourishing law practice, he was probably better off financially than at any time in his life. Two or more hours both in the afternoon and evening were reserved for the child's instruction. And Theo proved an excellent student, thriving under what surely would have broken down the health of an ordinary child. By the age of ten years she was reading Horace, Terence, and Lucian and preparing to begin Homer and Vergil. Exercises in Greek grammar shared a place with the study of Gibbon. Her curriculum included as well philosophy and political economy, French and German.

The Colonel's solicitude did not confine itself to Theo's mind. It extended to her deportment, speech, expression, and dress as well. Nor was her musical education neglected. Under competent instruction she mastered the two popular instruments of the day—the pianoforte and the harp. Besides all this, in the hours set aside for recreation she was taught to ride, skate, and dance. Not even a princess being prepared to sit some day on a throne could have been subjected to a more well-rounded program of education than that which Colonel Burr bestowed on Theodosia.

Colonel Burr's prosperity was more apparent than real. Possessed of extravagant tastes and a flair for lavish entertainment, he was condemned forever to live beyond his means. In addition to his house in the city he purchased an estate outside which he named Richmond Hill. It comprised a commodious dwelling house, a stable, a dairy, numerous other appurtenances, and abundant ground.

Theodosia was barely ten years old when her mother, after an illness of several months, died of cancer. Since there was no one else for the Colonel to call on, at that tender age Theodosia assumed the exacting duties of acting as hostess for her father. This was no insignificant task as the Colonel delighted in extending the hospitality of his house to distinguished visitors who were constantly arriving in New York. Theodosia presided at table with dignity and poise and without self-consciousness in the presence of such notables as Talleyrand, Louis Philippe, and Jerome Bonaparte.

It is not surprising that her fame spread throughout the city and beyond it. An English traveler who had the privilege of being received at Richmond Hill noted in his diary that this precocious young lady was "elegant without ostentation, learned without pedantry" and "educated with uncommon care." He found her speaking French and Italian with facility and "perfectly conversant with the writers of the Augustan Age."

The Colonel schooled his daughter, too, in fortitude and stoicism, two qualities which he regarded as being among the higher virtues, and which he practiced so industriously himself. There was a tradition that even while she was little more than a child he required her to sleep alone in a remote part of the house the better to exercise her courage.

Yet in spite of this exacting routine, the prodigy lost none of her feminine charm. The English visitor at Richmond Hill observed that she "danced with more grace than any young lady in New York." Theodosia is reputed to have had a number of suitors. When she had become famous many were attributed to her with whom she was barely if at all acquainted. Washington Irving's name, for example, was linked with hers, though there is no convincing evidence that they ever met.

It was to be assumed that so gifted a young woman would be hard to please and that she was not likely to be won by an ordinary man. However, Theodosia proved not to be unconquerable. At the age of seventeen years she was writing to young Joseph Alston in Charleston, South Carolina: "I shall be happy to see you whenever you choose; that, I suppose, is equivalent to very soon. . . . My father laughs at my impatience to hear from you, and says I am in love. . . . I had not intended to marry this twelvemonth . . . but to your solicitation I yield my judgment."

Joseph Alston was in every way eligible. He was the son of Colonel William Alston, a South Carolina planter, whose wealth ran to land and slaves. He had read law and, at the age of 22 years, was the owner of two estates in South Carolina as well as a mansion on the Hudson River above New York. He already had displayed talent that promised to carry him far in his profession and in the public affairs of his state.

The young people, very much in love with each other, were married at Albany in February, 1801. After a honeymoon spent at Richmond Hill they journeyed to Washington to be present when the Colonel was inaugurated as Vice-President of the

United States. From there Alston took his wife to Charleston where her personality earned for her the same popularity she enjoyed in New York.

Theodosia seems not to have been altogether happy with her in-laws. A letter is attributed to her in which she remarked: "We travel in company with the two Alstons. Pray teach me how to write two A's without producing something like an ass." This is one of the few unkind comments that has been credited to her. It suggests that the Alstons must indeed have been trying. On the other hand, how could ordinary elderly folk entertain a young woman who had been accustomed to the stimulating company of Aaron Burr?

In the spring of the year following their marriage a son was born to the Alstons. They named him Aaron Burr Alston. The Colonel was delighted. The boy was not yet two years old when his grandfather began planning for him the same exacting educational program he had imposed on his mother. "You do not say whether the boy knows his letters," he wrote to Theo. "I am sure he may be taught them. He may read and write before he is three years old. This, with speaking French, would make him a tolerably accomplished lad of that age, worthy of his blood."

Most remarkable of all Theodosia's qualities was the genius she displayed in bestowing her affection equally upon her father and her husband without arousing the jealousy of either of them or bringing on herself charges of favoritism or neglect. In no case was the Colonel's spell cast more magically than over his daughter. In her eyes he could do no wrong. Let others accuse him of political chicanery, let them question his integrity, let the public of New Jersey and New York condemn him as a murderer. Let the Government of the United States charge him with treason and its President declare that his guilt was beyond question. In the face of it all Theodosia remained steadfast, her faith unshaken. Though it must have been a mortification to her pride to know that he was in prison, she did not blame him but attributed this base treatment to the machinations of his enemies.

Toward her husband Theodosia's demonstrations of affection were eloquent. During their engagement she wrote him with all the girlish enthusiasm of her seventeen years: "Where you are, there is my country, and in you are centered all my wishes." And again, on an occasion when they were separated from each other: "Every moment I feel that I have lost so much of your society which can never be regained."

The birth of little Aaron left the mother weak and subject to physical disorders that she was never entirely to be free of. For a time she despaired of her life and in one of her melancholy moods she wrote Alston: "Death is not welcome. I confess it is ever dreaded. You have made me too fond of life. Adieu, then, thou kind, thou tender husband. Adieu! friend of my heart. May Heaven prosper you and may we meet hereafter."

In the fateful summer of 1806 when Colonel Burr departed from the East "never to return," he was joined in the western country by the Alstons—Theodosia, Joseph, and little Aaron. The Alstons were for a time guests of the Blennerhassetts on their island in the Ohio River. There Theodosia won the undying affection of Margaret Blennerhassett and the admiration of her husband Harman. Although the Alstons were not present at the time of the alleged "overt act," their visit a short time before served to increase the public's suspicion of Alston's implication in the plot. His name, it will be recalled, was mentioned in Burr's letter to Wilkinson of July 29.

The circumstance caused Alston intense embarrassment. He had become accustomed to the annoyance of receiving requests for loans from his father-in-law, but that was a small matter compared with the Colonel's use of his name in so damaging a document as the cipher letter to Wilkinson. In his perplexity Alston unburdened himself in a letter to his friend Charles Pinckney, then Governor of South Carolina.

"I have," he said, "received and read the President's message with deep mortification and concern; but the letter annexed to it, stated to be a communication in cypher from Col. Burr to Gen. Wilkinson, exacted my unfeigned astonishment.

"I solemnly avow that, when that letter was written, I had never heard, directly or indirectly from Col. Burr or any other person, of the meditated attack on that place, or any other part of the United States, than I have at this moment to suspect that our militia will be forthwith ordered on an expedition against Gibraltar. On the other hand, I had long had strong grounds for believing that Col. Burr was engaged by other objects, of a very different nature from those attributed to him, and which I confess the best sentiments of my heart approved. I need not add that those objects involved not the interests of my country.

"Without adverting to that integrity of principle, which even my enemies I trust have allowed me, can it be supposed that a man situated as I am—descended from a family which has never known dishonor, happy in the affection and esteem of a large number of relations and friends, possessed of ample fortune, and standing high in the confidence of his fellow-citizens —could harbor for an instant, a thought injurious to the country which was the scene of those blesssings?

"Whatever may be thought of the *heart* of Mr. Burr, his *talents* are great beyond question, and to reconcile with such talents the chimerical project of dismembering the union, or wresting from it any part of its territory is difficult indeed. . . . He imagined perhaps—which, by the way, he had no right to do—that his influence would be sufficiently great to induce my assent and thought, therefore he might as well consider it already obtained; or which is more probable, he might have imagined that by the apparent concern of a number of persons from different States, a stronger impression would be made on his correspondent."

Alston's letter, of course, soon became public property. Could a young man have found himself in a more embarrassing position? His good name had been dangerously compromised. Alston rightly felt he should clear himself of the suspicions which mention of his name in the letter naturally aroused. But how could he do that without casting reflections on his father-in-law? And how could he cast reflections on his father-in-law without showing disloyalty to Theodosia?

The effort was not altogether successful. The first paragraph of the letter was favorable to the Colonel in that it repudiated any idea that he was contemplating an attack on New Orleans or on any other part of the United States. It was as much a defense of the Colonel as it was of himself. But the closing passages did not express sentiments which were flattering or with which Colonel Burr could be greatly pleased.

The distinction made between Burr's "heart" and his "talents" intimated that while the moral issue involved in a conspiracy against the Government would not have restrained him, his intelligence would have told him the idea of dividing the Union was impractical. Then Alston had gone on to state frankly that Burr had no right to use his name without his consent and to suggest that it had been only a cheap trick to impress Wilkinson. It definitely was not the sort of letter to help preserve peace in the family.

On the other hand, when the Government was stretching forth its mighty hand to grasp Burr certainly was no time for discord between him and his son-in-law. It was reported in some quarters that when Burr heard about the letter there was a scene between the two men. If so, wisdom and necessity triumphed over ill temper. Whatever their innermost feelings may have been, Burr and Alston presented to the world a solid front.

So the Colonel wanted Theodosia at his side. She was not well, but well or not there could be only one response to his request. The Alstons soon were on their way from Charleston to Richmond, taking little Aaron with them. The Colonel had time for one last letter: "I am informed that some good natured people here have provided you a house, and furnished it, a few steps from my 'town house' [he was referring to Luther Martin's]. I had also made a temporary provision for you in my town house whither I shall remove on Sunday; but I will not, if I can possibly avoid it, move before your arrival, having a great desire to receive you in this 'mansion.' Pray, therefore, drive directly here." It took more than confinement in the penitentiary to dampen Burr's naturally ebullient spirits.

The Alstons duly arrived in Richmond and drove directly to the penitentiary. They spent their first night there, then moved to the house the "good natured" Richmonders had offered them. From there Theodosia could supervise the menage of her father and Luther Martin in Martin's house nearby. Her sojourn in Richmond witnessed a repetition of her triumphs elsewhere. The Federalist upper crust found her to be a welcome addition to their exclusive and accomplished society. She went about making friends everywhere until observers came to the conclusion that by her mere presence in Richmond she did more to further the cause of the defense than all of Burr's brilliant array of counsel. Long after the actors in the drama had gone to their various rewards Theodosia's stay in Richmond and the impression her exceptional personality made on the community was established as a part of local legend. She could scarcely have been treated with greater deference had she really been the empress with whose attempted creation Aaron Burr was charged.

Chapter XIII

DUDLEY WOODBRIDGE, who was his partner, said of Harman Blennerhassett that he had every sort of sense except common sense. That is the simplest explanation why this Irish gentleman found himself in the summer of 1807 in the State Penitentiary in Richmond, facing a charge of treason against the United States.

Harman Blennerhassett was born quite by chance, in Hampshire, England, while his parents were there on a visit from Ireland. He was the youngest son of a family described as distinguished. As a boy he attended the famous Westminster School in London and from there went on to Trinity College, Dublin, where he was graduated with honors. He chose law as his profession and at the age of 25 years was admitted to the bar. Through the death of his elder brother he unexpectedly succeeded to the family estates, which were considerable.

Harman's sister Katherine married Captain Robert Agnew, Lieutenant-Governor of the Isle of Man. They had a daughter Margaret who, on reaching her teens, was sent to school in England. While Harman was on a visit to the Agnews he was entrusted with the pleasant mission of crossing to the mainland to bring his niece home. Harman at this time was 31 years old and Margaret 18. In the course of the trip he became completely infatuated with her and proposed marriage. No doubt dazzled by this man of the world thirteen years her senior, Margaret accepted him. When the newly married uncle and niece arrived on the Isle of Man and Harman introduced Margaret to her parents as his wife the Agnews were furious. In their anger and humiliation they disinherited Margaret and repudiated Harman. In fact the Agnews and their friends made the situation so unpleasant that the Blennerhassetts concluded their only recourse was to leave home and seek asylum in the United States.

Blennerhassett sold his estates, which brought him $100,000, a tidy sum in those days, and he and Margaret sailed for New York where they arrived in 1796. As though this were not enough to rid them of the curse that had descended on their romantic adventure, they did not linger long in the East but set out to look for a permanent home on the frontier.

Reaching Pittsburgh in the fall of the year, they bought a keelboat and dropped down the Ohio River. The valley of the Ohio was then a wilderness save for a few small settlements at favorable spots along the stream. One of these was Marietta where the Blennerhassetts found a society of refined and cultivated people who received them cordially. There they remained throughout the winter while they reconnoitered the neighborhood for a suitable site for an estate.

At last they found what pleased them on an island in the river two miles below the present Parkersburg, West Virginia, at the mouth of the Little Kanawha. This island they purchased. It consisted of 170 acres, which lay in Wood County, Virginia, a significant circumstance in the light of later developments. There the Blennerhassetts spent $30,000 erecting a spacious two-story dwelling with wings and numerous appurtenances. In keeping with the custom of the time, they also purchased slaves to serve the household and work the land.

In this American wilderness they brought into being an establishment such as might have been found in England or on the continent of Europe. The spacious mansion was painted white and the fields surrounding it were neatly inclosed in white post fences. Attached to the house was a formal garden with shrubbery and hedges in the English style and espaliers of

peach, apricot, quince, and pear. With stables, barns, overseers'
houses, and quarters for the slaves the settlement made an impressive sight indeed.

No less impressive was the interior of the mansion which was
richly furnished from top to bottom. Costly paintings adorned
the walls and handsome imported rugs covered the floors.

Margaret Blennerhassett was above average height, well
proportioned and graceful. Her eyes were blue and her hair
dark brown and, in keeping with the prevailing mode, she wore
it in a turban. In England she had enjoyed the benefits of the
best education that was to be had by a young woman. She
spoke French and Italian fluently and was well versed in Shakespeare's plays, which she liked to recite. She herself wrote po-
etry. In spite of these intellectual qualities she delighted also in
the rugged out-of-doors life the island afforded. She rode horseback and not infrequently took long walks on the mainland of
from ten to twenty miles in a day. Withal she was a good
housekeeper and kept an excellent table.

Nature had been less kind to Harman. He was a spare man,
standing six feet tall, and his distinguishing feature was a long
nose. He was so near-sighted that he was helpless without his
eyeglasses, and it was jocularly reported that on the rare occasions when he went hunting he had to take his wife and a
servant along to aim the gun! Unlike his wife he was not partial
to outdoor exercise, preferring to spend his time with books
and engaging in scientific experiments. He was interested in
chemistry, electricity, and astronomy. In fact he came to know
too much about electricity and its dangerous properties. A
thunderstorm so played on his nerves that he had to close the
doors and windows and get into bed. In addition to his scholarly talents Blennerhassett was an accomplished musician, playing both the violin and the 'cello.

The Blennerhassetts had two sons whom they named Dom-
inic and Harman. What with their children, their servants,
their livestock, their well-appointed house and grounds, and
their deep affection for each other they seemed at last, after a
somewhat inauspicious start, to have achieved domestic bliss.

But, under the surface disturbing forces were at work. After eight long years, life on the island was growing monotonous and the proprietor and his family restless. Even more disturbing, the plantation failed to clear expenses and Blennerhassett saw his fortune gradually wasting away.

Such was the situation when Aaron Burr, on his first trip to the West in 1805, passed down the Ohio River from Pittsburgh in his houseboat. He mentioned in one of his letters to Theodosia at this time that whenever he came upon a likely looking house along the river he would dispatch a note to the owner stating that Mr. Burr, the former Vice-President of the United States, was in the neighborhood and would like to call. He boasted that not once was such a request refused. Naturally Blennerhassett Island did not escape his keen eye and he was duly impressed with its magnificence. He sent his customary note and his request to call was readily granted.

The master was away but the Colonel was cordially received by Mrs. Blennerhassett. It must have been a surprise to Burr to discover in this remote frontier a woman of Margaret Blennerhassett's breeding and cultivation, which were of a quality little inferior even to Theodosia's. And surely so polished a man as Burr, and one so capable of making himself fascinating to women, must have been a welcome sight to Margaret who seldom had an opportunity to entertain such congenial company. Burr probably did not discern the financial problem that hung over the Blennerhassetts. On the contrary, the elaborate appurtenances of the estate may readily have misled him into estimating their fortune at a figure much greater than it was in fact. At any rate, his attitude toward the Blennerhassetts indicated that he considered their acquaintance well worth pursuing.

Burr must at some time on this first trip to the West also have encountered Harman, for a correspondence sprang up between them in the course of which Burr suggested several plans by which Blennerhassett might improve his fortune, and the latter asked Burr's opinion as to the advisability of his moving to Louisiana.

The Colonel was not above using flattery to ingratiate himself with the Irishman. "Your talents and acquirements," he wrote, "seem to have destined you for something more than vegetable life, and since the first hour of our acquaintance I have considered your seclusion as a fraud on society." How Blennerhassett's ears must have burned on reading that high praise from a man of the Colonel's standing in the great world.

During the last days of August in the following year Colonel Burr landed once more on Blennerhassett Island. This time he was accompanied by a Col. Julien de Pestre, a French émigré who had served both in the French and English armies. De Pestre now held the imposing office of Burr's chief-of-staff. In attendance also was one Charles Willie, a young German acting in the capacity of Burr's secretary. The fourth member of the party was Dudley Woodbridge, Blennerhassett's partner, whom they had picked up at Marietta.

The party was most kindly welcomed by Blennerhassett and spent the night in his house. Next day the Colonel returned to Marietta where he contracted with Woodbridge for 100 barrels of pork. He also ordered from a local boatyard on the Muskingum River fifteen barges of impressive dimensions. They were to be from forty to fifty feet long and have a ten-foot beam. One of them was to be specially equipped for the Blennerhassett family. The whole flotilla, when completed, was estimated to be adequate for the transportation of 500 men and their necessary equipment and provisions. These matters attended to, Burr continued down the river to Cincinnati.

What Burr discussed with Blennerhassett on the night he spent on the island was not recorded, but a hint is found in four articles which were published a few days later in the Ohio *Gazette*. Bearing the signature "Querist" they were the work of Harman Blennerhassett. In them he set forth arguments as to why it would be to the advantage of the western states to separate from the Union. He dwelt upon the fact that the money now paid to the Federal Government in taxes, and from which the westerners derived little return, could serve a better purpose if kept in the West and used for local improvements.

In one of the papers Querist was careful to remark: "But I wish it understood that I have no intention of recommending either the mode or the time in which it should be effected." In other words, the articles were no more than a means of sounding out the western inhabitants to see what their reaction to the suggestion would be. Not too many years before secession had been openly discussed in the West and it had attracted a number of prominent citizens. But now both Kentucky and Tennessee were glorying in their newly acquired statehood, the transfer of New Orleans to the United States had removed that barrier to commerce, and other grievances of the frontier people had been corrected. In consequence, the desire to separate from the Union had greatly diminished if it had not entirely disappeared. So much for what Blennerhassett wrote. If the later testimony of witnesses is to be believed, he also engaged in some indiscreet talking, as did Burr in Cincinnati.

From Cincinnati Burr proceeded on horseback to Nashville, Tennessee, stopping at Lexington, Kentucky, on the way. At Nashville he met Andrew Jackson, and it was on this visit he engaged with Jackson and John Coffee for the building of five more boats and the assembling of supplies.

Meanwhile Theodosia and her son arrived on Blennerhassett Island, and here, in October, they were joined by Joseph Alston. It was not long before Margaret Blennerhassett developed an admiration for Theodosia that bordered on idolatry. It could hardly have been otherwise. Imagine the many interests these two exceptionally well-educated women found they had in common. It must have been distressing to both of them when the visit came to an end. The Alstons said goodby to Margaret and, accompanied by Harman, set out to join Colonel Burr in Lexington, Kentucky.

The building of the boats and the collecting of supplies soon was known to all the community and lent force to the rumors of a conspiracy. John Graham, Secretary of the Orleans Territory, had now been assigned by President Jefferson to pick up Burr's trail and to report back on his findings. He reached Marietta on his quest in the middle of November. There he met

Blennerhassett who by now had returned home from Kentucky. As previously mentioned, Blennerhassett, supposing Graham to be one of Burr's adherents, talked to him freely. He confided to him that he thought the West would profit by getting out of the Union. He said Burr was of the same opinion but added that the reaction to the articles by Querist indicated that the public was not yet ripe for the move.

In the Pittsburgh area Burr's lieutenant, Comfort Tyler, was assembling supplies and enlisting recruits. Reports were gaining currency that as many as a thousand young men had responded favorably to the appeal for volunteers. But when the time came for departure the party consisted of not more than thirty men distributed among four boats. The immediate objective of Tyler's contingent was Blennerhassett Island. There the flotilla arrived on December 7.

While Graham was in Marietta he learned that a committee of citizens, stirred by the President's proclamation, had been organized in Wood County, Virginia, opposite the island, to oppose any illegal scheme that might be in the making. On November 21 Graham met with this group at the courthouse near Parkersburg, and Col. Hugh Phelps, commander of the Wood County militia, told him he had been urged by Blennerhassett to join the expedition. According to Phelps, Blennerhassett assured him that General Andrew Jackson had promised 1,000 men, that 800 were expected to join the expedition from Kentucky, and from 200 to 300 from Pittsburgh. Alexander Henderson, another Wood County man who was at the meeting, said he was not free to give details, but advised that the United States send a strong military force to New Orleans at once.

It was then that Graham set out in haste to catch Governor Edwin Tiffin of Ohio, who was at Chillicothe, and lay what evidence he had before him. With equal dispatch the Governor sent a message to the Ohio Legislature stating that Blennerhassett had approached two gentlemen of great respectability and invited them to join in an expedition planned by Burr to seize New Orleans by force, take possession of $2,000,000 known to be in the bank there, and also the military stores and two brass cannon belonging to the French.

A new government, the message continued, then would be set up under the protection of a foreign power. This done, overtures would be made to the western states to sever their connection with the Union and attach themselves to the new government in New Orleans. The Governor added that he had been informed that a force of 1,500 men had been recruited in Ohio. His recommendation to the Legislature was that it issue authority for the seizure of the boats that were building on the Muskingum and the provisions collected at Marietta, and for the arrest of any of Burr's agents discovered within the jurisdiction of the Ohio authorities or attempting to pass down the Ohio River.

So it was that a bill containing these authorizations was prepared and hastily passed by the Legislature, and Judge Return Jonathan Meigs and Major General Buell were sent to Marietta with a small body of Ohio militia to carry out the order. Mrs. Blennerhassett, who was on the island, learned of the rising tide of public indignation and dispatched Peter Taylor, her gardener, to Kentucky to find Blennerhassett and Burr and to warn Burr not to return.

On hearing that the Ohio militia under Judge Meigs and General Buell were on the way to the boat yard, Dudley Woodbridge set off for the island to give the alarm. On the way he ran into Blennerhassett, Comfort Tyler, and some of the young men who were going after the boats. But they were too late. The boats had been seized by Meigs and Buell and with them 200 barrels of provisions.

Following this loss, and alarmed by the threatening attitude of the Wood County militia, Blennerhassett and Tyler concluded that the expedition would be jeopardized by remaining longer on the island. They decided, therefore, to slip away during the night on Tyler's four boats, leaving Mrs. Blennerhassett and the two boys on the island with instructions to follow later when arrangements could be made.

The weather was enough to take the heart out of the conspirators. It had snowed during the day; then the snow was followed by rain and the ground near the river bank was a sea of mud. Regardless of the need for secrecy, a fire was lighted where the members of the expedition might find a little warmth and perhaps a chance to get partially dry. Throughout these trying preliminaries Margaret Blennerhassett exhibited surprising energy in helping with preparations for the departure.

It was 1 A.M. on the morning of December 10 when the four boats put off from the island and began their long journey downstream. The conspirators numbered about thirty in all. It was a sorry war they were waging against the United States, if war it could be called. Their departure was made none too soon. A few hours later Colonel Phelps arrived at the head of the Wood County militia. These patriots, finding their quarry gone, made free with Blennerhassett's wine, got drunk, insulted Mrs. Blennerhassett, and vented their wrath against the owner of the house by smashing windows, breaking up pictures and furniture, and committing other disgraceful acts of vandalism.

The Ohio authorities set a guard on the river at Cincinnati to halt any expedition as it came down, but the little flotilla passed during the night and was not detected. Six days after leaving the island it arrived at Jeffersonville, Indiana, opposite Louisville. There it found and joined forces with Davis Floyd, another Burr lieutenant, and his detachment of two boats.

Meanwhile Burr had appeared before the two grand juries in Kentucky and had been discharged by both of them without being indicted. He had faced up to Andrew Jackson's suspicions and convinced that gentleman of his innocence of any wrongdoing against the United States. In the boats built for him by Jackson and John Coffee he set out from Nashville down the Cumberland River to rendezvous with his forces on the Ohio. Burr had sent word to Blennerhassett by Jackson's nephew that he would join him at the mouth of the Cumberland on December 28. He actually arrived one day ahead— the historic meeting took place on December 27. The flotilla had now grown to ten boats and a company of not more than 100 men.

The rank and file were in need of inspiration by this time and it seemed appropriate for the leader to say a few words to them. So they were marshaled on Cumberland Island for that purpose. But if they expected to get any information from their leader they were disappointed. With his customary air of mystery Burr merely announced that he could not at that time tell them what their destination would be, and that he must wait for a more appropriate occasion.

From there the flotilla continued on its journey down the Ohio River. At Fort Massac, the army post above the confluence of the Ohio and the Mississippi where Burr and Wilkinson had conferred in the summer of 1805, Burr presented himself to the commander, Captain Daniel Bissell, who greeted him warmly and extended to him all the courtesies of the post. The party had completed its visit and departed when a messenger arrived posthaste from General Jackson warning Bissell of the nature of the expedition and urging him to halt it. Bissell, having seen the force with his own eyes, sent the messenger back to Jackson with the report that there was nothing to fear from it. From then on Jackson was more than ever convinced that the furore raised by the Administration over the conspiracy was purely political and had no basis in fact.

On January 10 the flotilla reached Bayou Pierre, some thirty miles north of Natchez, in Mississippi Territory. There Burr landed and went to pay a call on a friend, Judge Bruin, who lived nearby. And there, in a newspaper handed him by the Judge, he saw his letter of July 29 to Wilkinson and knew for the first time that he had been deserted and betrayed by the General. At Judge Bruin's, too, he learned of the President's proclamation and that his arrest had been ordered by the acting governor of the territory, Cowles Meade.

According to their later testimony some members of the party proposed resistance to any force that might come to arrest them. But by this time Colonel Burr perceived that matters had gone far enough. It no doubt occurred to him also that resistance to the civil authorities would be most incriminating. Since he was going to base his defense on innocence of any wrongdoing he must act in accordance with that assumption.

Therefore, as any innocent man would have done on learning that charges had been preferred against him and that he was, so to speak, a fugitive from justice, Burr hastened to vindicate himself by seeking out Acting Governor Meade and surrendering at discretion. He was taken to the village of Washington, then the capital of Mississippi Territory, where a grand jury was summoned and the territory's attorney general, one Poindexter, tried to get out an indictment against him. Again, as in Kentucky, the Colonel's bravado stood him in good stead. The grand jury not only refused to indict him but took the territorial officials to task for having arrested Burr and his men without cause.

But the Colonel knew that the respite was only temporary, since the Federal authorities were hot on his trail. So, on February 1, after assuring his followers that he would rejoin them shortly, he assumed a disguise and fled.

Once more Blennerhassett, Tyler, Floyd, and the rank and file of the now pathetic little band, were arrested and placed under guard. But they were treated with humanity and permitted occasionally to walk about with no restraint more binding than their own honor. As soon as the excitement died down they were set free.

After her distressing experience on the island Margaret Blennerhassett, accompanied by the boys, took refuge in Natchez, Mississippi. There she was joined by her husband. Curious to know the condition of his property Harman set out in June to visit it. He had reached Lexington, Kentucky, when on the 25th the news of the proceedings in Richmond caught up with him and he was arrested. He at once called in Henry Clay to defend him but, in spite of that able counsel, the court refused to grant a release.

On July 14 Blennerhassett wrote to his wife that a messenger, after making a rapid journey from Richmond, had brought him intelligence of his indictment with Colonel Burr on the charges of treason and misdemeanor. "I have no idea of attempting an escape," he assured her. "I feel conscious of all want of law or evidence to convict me."

At this point his letter was interrupted by the arrival of a Mr. David Mead who had come to arrest him on the part of the United States. "He is an amiable, kind young man, with whom I shall set out in a few days for Richmond."

Four days later, from jail, Blennerhassett wrote again asking Mrs. Blennerhassett to look for the copy of the first letter he had written to Burr which he thought he might need for his defense. He also asked her for any letters she could find from Burr to her. Nor was his present predicament to interfere with his artistic pursuits if he could help it. He directed Margaret to forward also "the morocco case, containing my music and the two sheets of manuscript I lent Mrs. Wallace, with my spectacles."

At last Blennerhassett's slow mind was beginning to perceive the manner in which he had been exploited by Colonel Burr. To his wife he confided: "I am extremely sorry to find the injury to private individuals of this country in consequence of a baseless authority for Burr's financial operations here last autumn far exceeding my greatest suspicions. If it be shown that he had not funds and friends pledged to him to warrant his drafts, his conduct would appear nefarious enough to displace all the friendships he ever formed."

Burr was aware of the danger to himself that lay in the possible defection of Blennerhassett. As early as May 21 he had written him from Richmond: "I have barely time . . . to assure you and Mrs. Blennerhassett of my devoted attachment and regard, and to express my sympathy for all the vexations you have encountered." From then on he was to exert every effort to keep his alleged co-conspirator in line.

Under the gracious chaperonage of young Mr. David Mead, Blennerhassett made the journey from Lexington to Richmond, where they arrived on August 3. Mead took his prisoner to the Washington Tavern, to the west of the Capitol Square, and there they had an excellent dinner. This over, another deputy marshal appeared to present Blennerhassett with a warrant for high treason. He had a carriage waiting outside and in this Blennerhassett was conveyed to the penitentiary where he was assigned the sumptuous apartments lately vacated by Colonel Burr. Here he was to remain throughout the course of Burr's treason trial. And here he was to find ample time to set down an account of the proceedings. He too was to enjoy the same gracious treatment by the best people of Richmond that had been accorded Colonel Burr.

Chapter XIV

PROMPTLY AT NOON on Monday, August 3, the Circuit Court of the United States for the Fifth Circuit and District of Virginia was opened by the Chief Justice. The midsummer heat had done nothing to discourage the public from attendance, and, as usual, every seat and vantage place was at a premium.

On the bench the Chief Justice in his robes of office sat alone. Judge Griffin is not reported to have been present on this occasion. In the places reserved for the prosecution were District Attorney Hay, Mr. Wirt and Mr. MacRae. Ready to act for the defense were Mr. Randolph, Mr. Wickham, Mr. Martin and Jack Baker. Baker, a jovial fellow, appears to have been retained because of his popularity: he played a small part in the trial.

The clerk called the names of more than 100 witnesses. Then followed another of those legal hitches that by this time had become so characteristic of the trial. Mr. Hay asked for a postponement since, he said, he had been unable to furnish Colonel Burr with a list of the witnesses and their addresses. He reported also that he had found that the list of the venire he had delivered to the accused was inaccurate. So the Chief Justice obligingly granted a postponement of two days, but not before Colonel Burr had attempted to enliven the proceedings by again asking for a *subpoena duces tecum*.

So there was nothing for the disappointed crowd to do but file out of the courtroom to swelter through the afternoon in the taverns and in their homes until the sun had set and darkness had brought some slight relief. Those who were determined to follow the proceedings by this time were beginning to realize that they would have to adapt their habits to the spasmodic stops and starts of the hesitant machinery of justice.

On Wednesday court assembled only to adjourn almost immediately because witnesses were absent. On Friday another assembly was followed by adjournment because counsel for the United States pleaded they were not prepared to proceed. Thus another whole week passed by with nothing tangible accomplished toward either dismissing Colonel Burr with a clean bill of health or consigning him to the gallows.

At last, on Monday, August 10, the proceedings got under way. A touch of novelty was provided by the first appearance in court of Harman Blennerhassett. He had made the trip from the penitentiary to the Capitol in fine style, riding in a carriage drawn by a span of horses and attended by two guards. The crowd outside the courthouse was smaller than he had anticipated, but he found the spacious courtroom well filled. Colonel Burr entered soon afterwards and, on catching sight of Blennerhassett, immediately came to his side, shook him warmly by the hand and, with a welcoming smile, told him how glad he was to see him. It was the first time the alleged conspirators had met since Burr said goodby to his little army at Cole's Creek in February and slipped out into the wilderness. That magic smile and handshake were enough to banish for the moment the resentment Blennerhassett felt over his treatment.

Now commenced the arduous task of picking twelve good men and true from among the prospective jurymen who had answered to their names. In view of the fact that virtually every bit of the most important evidence against the accused, including all the fantastic rumors, had appeared in the press and was common knowledge to the reading public, it was no simple task to find men of intelligence who had not already formed their opinions.

No sooner had Mr. Buckey, the first venireman called up, been questioned than the difficulty became apparent. Asked if he had formed an opinion prior to receiving his subpoena Mr. Buckey replied that he had. Mr. Hay ventured that if the question were put to this man and every other man on the panel no jury could ever be selected in the State of Virginia. If the Court were to adopt that doctrine, he said, why then it would be the equivalent of acquitting the prisoner for want of a jury to try him.

Young Botts bristled at this remark of the District Attorney. He asked for the floor to deplore that in this country and in this case there had been such a general expression of public sentiment. However, until the gentlemen for the prosecution had avowed it Mr. Botts professed he had never doubted that twelve men might be found in Virginia capable of deciding the question with the strictest impartiality.

Judge Marshall here intervened between counsel to point out that asking a man whether he had formed an impression about Colonel Burr was too general. The impression might be so slight that it did not amount to an opinion of guilt, nor go to the extent of believing he deserved capital punishment.

Mr. Botts addressed the venireman. "Have you said that Colonel Burr was guilty of treason?" he asked. "No," was the reply. "I only declared that the man who had acted as Colonel Burr was said to have done, deserved to be hung." "Did you," pursued Mr. Botts, "believe that Colonel Burr was that man?" "I did from what I had heard," admitted Mr. Buckey. The gentleman was rejected.

So it went with venireman after venireman. A typical instance was that of Mr. Jervis Storrs. He was, he said, in the habit of reading the newspapers and could not but examine their statements relative to these transactions. If he could believe General Eaton's assertion that the prisoner had threatened to turn Congress out of doors and assassinate the President, he had said and would still say that Colonel Burr was guilty of treason. If the letter to General Wilkinson was true, Colonel Burr had surely been guilty of something in the West that was hostile to the interests of the United States. On the whole Mr. Storrs expressed a wish not to serve on the jury.

Among the veniremen questioned was Peyton Randolph. He asked to be excused on the ground that he was a lawyer, practicing at the Richmond bar, and as such immune to jury duty. It did not seem to occur to him that he had ample reason for not serving in view of the fact that he was a son of Edmund Randolph, leading counsel for the defense. These Virginia relationships were so hopelessly intertwined that Mr. Hay, on questioning the possibility of getting twelve men in the state who had not made up their minds, might have added a doubt that it would be possible to organize a court, comprising judge, jury, and counsel, where family relationships would not endanger strict impartiality.

This circumstance was abundantly illustrated when out of the list of veniremen Colonel Edward Carrington was called to the stand. He was the Chief Justice's brother-in-law and a devoted friend. But this connection had not stood in the way of his being subpoenaed for jury duty.

On being questioned as to his fitness to serve Colonel Carrington expressed his feelings with complete candor. He had, he admitted, formed an unfavorable opinion of the views of Colonel Burr, but it was not definitive. Some people said that Colonel Burr's object was to invade the Spanish territories; others that it was to dismember the Union. As for himself, said Colonel Carrington, his own opinion had not become fixed.

But there was another subject connected with the trial, on which he had stated an opinion. That was on General Wilkinson's actions in New Orleans. On the basis of what Wilkinson had been told of Burr's activities Colonel Carrington thought the General had behaved in a proper manner and had said so publicly.

Burr himself addressed the venireman. "Have you, Colonel, any prejudice of a more settled kind and ancient date against me?"

"None at all," Colonel Carrington assured him.

"He is elected," declared Burr.

So it was that, with the Chief Justice, the prisoner, and counsel for both sides agreeing, the brother-in-law of the Chief Justice became one of the first four out of that first venire of nearly forty to be elected and sworn.

Thus were concluded the proceedings on August 10. Seven days had passed since the convening of the court and the jury still needed eight members to complete it.

Blennerhassett, who had been a silent witness to these events, returned to his quarters in the penitentiary. The day in court and the intense heat oppressed him. He dined with less appetite than the day before, and tried to get cool by pacing his commodious cell and fanning himself. But it did no good. He soon found himself so weak he had to lie on the floor, and there he slept he knew not how long. At length he awakened on hearing mention of the name of Mrs. Alston. A servant had come from Theodosia bearing a gift of oranges, lemons, and limes. This was not the first time she had showed the same attention. In fact Blennerhassett had not been in prison half an hour before her first gift arrived—tea, sugar, and cakes. Alston had come, too, to offer reassurances on the score of the money Blennerhassett had sunk in the adventure. He had not been too successful in this, since Blennerhassett had formed a dislike for him. In fact it seemed as though Blennerhassett, disarmed by Burr's ingratiating manner, vented his spleen on the unoffending Alston. Alston had brought with him Edmund Randolph who volunteered his professional services in Blennerhassett's defense.

There were other compensations for being behind bars. The prisoner was permitted to hire a servant at $13 a month to wait on him. He was given every liberty inside the prison, except that he could not pass from under its roof by day or out of his room by night. He did, therefore, have to suffer the indignity of being locked in from 8 o'clock in the evening until sunrise.

On the other hand, no objection was made to his stocking up with groceries and liquors. His dinner was provided by a tavern across the road from the penitentiary. He also enjoyed the services of a fellow prisoner who was a skillful barber. "This Vaun," he recorded in his diary, "is only here for 18 years, merely for cutting his wife's throat with precisely the same sort of instrument with which he operates most delicately on mine every other day."

There came also a message from a lady unknown to him who did not wish to have her name mentioned, begging him to accept soups and jellies. Later Blennerhassett learned her identity. No wonder the lady felt a delicacy about having her name mentioned as a benefactor of Burr's alleged accomplice. She was Eliza Carrington, adoring sister-in-law of the Chief Justice and wife of the juryman who was to have an important part in trying Colonel Burr. Washington Irving was no doubt right when he praised Richmond's women for their compassion, their boldness, and their independence. Could he have said as much for their discretion?

Thursday, August 11, was another sweltering day. The Court concerned itself with completing the jury. The proceedings were uneventful save for one brief moment when a venireman named Hamilton Morrison was challenged by the defense.

"I am surprised why they should be in so much terror of me," he observed. "Perhaps my name may be the terror, for my first name is Hamilton."

Colonel Burr was not amused. He stated that the remark was in itself sufficient cause for disqualifying the venireman and the facetious Mr. Morrison was excused.

By now the venire had been exhausted and yet eight seats on the jury still remained empty. Mr. Hay therefore moved that the Court award a new venire, and the Chief Justice granted a panel of forty-eight and ordered an adjournment until Thursday, the 13th, in order to allow time for bringing it together. But when Thursday came Burr objected that the list of the panel he had received contained no addresses. In consequence the adjournment was continued until Saturday. Even then the prospect was discouraging; it was beginning to look as though Mr. Hay was right when he expressed a fear that Colonel Burr would not be tried for want of a jury.

However, it was Colonel Burr who offered a solution to the

problem. He proposed that he be permitted to select eight men out of the new panel. The prosecution, despairing of getting a jury any other way, agreed. And so at last the jury box was filled, twelve days after court had been convened for the trial.

Unlike the Grand Jury, the Petit Jury could not boast a particularly distinguished list of members. Colonel Carrington stood out prominently among them; so much so in fact, that the Chief Justice waved aside whatever scruples he may have had and placed his brother-in-law in the key position in the trial by appointing him foreman.

Though the other eleven jurymen were not destined for immortality they all bore substantial names that meant something in Virginia. They were David Lambert, Richard E. Parker, Hugh Mercer, Christopher Anthony, James Sheppard, Reuben Blakey, Benjamin Graves, Miles Bott, Henry E. Coleman, John M. Sheppard, and Richard Curd.

By the time the jury had been organized it was Saturday again and it hardly seemed worth while to start the trial. So Judge Marshall adjourned the Court for the weekend. Even the heavens seemed relieved that at last progress had been made. A violent thunderstorm on Tuesday night broke the heat wave and made life more bearable.

During the weekend Blennerhassett was the object of what he described as "another advance from female humanity." Mrs. Jean Auguste Marie Chevallié, wife of the French Consul and Judge Peter Lyon's daughter, sent him a message asking if he would accept refreshments of delicacies she might provide. The ladies were outdoing themselves to see which one could qualify as benefactor-in-chief. Mrs. Chevallié's genteel inquiry offset in some degree the annoyance the prisoner was experiencing at the hands of idle visitors to the penitentiary desirous of gratifying their curiosity by surveying his countenance and his quarters. More disturbing than that was a letter from his financial agent in Philadelphia informing him that, because of the attachment served on Blennerhassett's funds, he had been obliged to dishonor all the bills drawn and presented for acceptance since January 20 last. Blennerhassett interpreted the statement as marking the disappearance of the last pecuniary resources of his poor family.

Now at last, after weeks of delay, the stage was finally set. When Court convened on Monday, the completed jury was seated. This day saw the arrival of reinforcements for the defense in the person of Charles Lee. His presence appears to have been designed primarily to lend distinction to Burr's cause by including the magic name of Lee among his defenders. Charles Lee, a brother of "Light Horse Harry," had been Attorney General of the United States in Washington's cabinet. He, too, was a descendant of William Randolph of Turkey Island and his wife Mary Isham. So far as the record of the trial shows, his participation was not in proportion to his eminence as a lawyer.

When the bailiff had called the Court to order the prisoner was directed to stand while the clerk read the indictment. It was the same to which he had pleaded "Not guilty" when the Grand Jury returned a true bill on June 24.

It proclaimed that the Grand Inquest of the United States of America, in and for the Fifth Circuit and the Virginia District, did present that Aaron Burr, late of the city of New York, and the State of New York, attorney at law, residing within the United States and owing allegiance and fidelity to the same, "not having the fear of God before his eyes, nor weighing the duty of his said allegiance, but being moved and seduced by the instigation of the devil," on the 10th of December, 1806, at a certain place called by the name of Blennerhassett Island, "with force and arms, unlawfully, maliciously and traitorously did compass, imagine and intend to raise and levy war, insurrection and rebellion against the said United States."

The indictment, in its noble Tudor phraseology, went on to point out that in order to achieve his purpose Burr, "with a great multitude of persons whose names at present are unknown to the Grand Inquest aforesaid, to a great number, to wit, *to the number of thirty persons and upwards,* armed and arrayed in a warlike manner, that is to say with guns, swords and dirks, and other warlike weapons as well offensive and defensive, being then and there unlawfully, maliciously and traitorously assembled and gathered together," did "falsely, and traitorously and in a warlike and hostile manner array and dispose themselves against the United States."

The indictment added that this force on the same day had left the island "with the wicked and traitorous intention of descending the river and taking possession of the city of New Orleans."

". . . a great multitude of persons . . . to wit, to the number of thirty persons and upwards . . ."

Not since the three famous tailors entitled their manifesto "We, the People of England" had so little been made to sound like so much. Thus the indictment set for the prosecution the exacting task of proving that thirty persons, mostly youths, assembling on an island in the Ohio River for little more than twenty-four hours, constituted levying war against the majesty and might of the United States of America.

To render the charge even more difficult of proof the prosecution admitted at the outset that the alleged arch-traitor, Aaron Burr, was not even present in person at the warlike assemblage!

But was his presence necessary to prove his guilt? In the habeas corpus proceedings in the case of Erich Bollman and Samuel Swartwout the Chief Justice had delivered an opinion indicating that it was not. The prosecution lost no opportunity of reminding him of it. It was on this opinion that it had largely counted on a conviction.

So, in his opening remarks to the jury, Mr. Hay once more quoted from the Chief Justice's opinion: ". . . if war be levied, that is, if a body of men be actually assembled for the purpose of effecting by force a treasonable purpose, all those who perform any part, however minute, *or however remote from the scene of action*, are to be considered as traitors."

Mr. Hay went farther afield. He delved into the English authorities to demonstrate that in Great Britain, under the statute of 25 Edward III, on which the American theory of treason was based, the crime of treason might be committed not only in the physical absence of the principal but also without the bearing of arms.

When Mr. Hay had completed his opening statement, Colonel Burr appealed to the Court to expedite the business by meeting as early as possible and adjourning late. He cited the English custom of sitting from twelve to sixteen hours a day. Learned counsel shuddered at the very thought. Objection was instantly raised on the ground that English courts did not have to contend with the heat of Richmond in midsummer. Tempering justice with mercy, Judge Marshall ruled that the Court would meet at nine o'clock in the morning and sit until four o'clock in the afternoon.

These preliminaries having been attended to, the call came for the first witness for the prosecution and General Eaton was sworn. No sooner had he taken the stand than the defense was on its feet protesting the propriety of hearing Eaton's evidence. They contended that it had to do only with intention. Therefore before it could be admitted an overt act had to be proved. The controverted point led to a long and animated debate which consumed the rest of the afternoon.

As was to be his custom throughout the trial, Judge Marshall adjourned Court before presenting his opinion. With his genius for application he would work far into the night preparing his opinion in order to have it ready when Court convened in the morning. Where he was concerned there was to be no undue haste, no chance for misconstruction. The opinion would be in writing and reflect the logical approach that was characteristic of his legal papers. It was on his acute reasoning rather than profound knowledge of the authorities that the force of his opinions depended.

In the morning, true to his promise, the Chief Justice was ready to deliver his opinion. It was a dissertation on what testimony was and was not relevant to this time. As applied to General Eaton's testimony it permitted that part which related to Burr's design to seize New Orleans and divide by force the western from the Atlantic states. It excluded the more colorful passages which had to do with Burr's alleged plans for the overthrow of the Government in Washington.

With this injunction Eaton was told to go ahead and tell his story in his own way. The hint, however, was made to him that he might well leave out autobiographical material having to do with his services to the nation in Tripoli, which he considered a basis for the nation's gratitude. Eaton, however, did not take the hint, but reviewed his exploits at considerable length before launching into the now familiar story of Burr's advances to him in the prospect of interesting him in the expedition. It had appeared in print so many times that the majority of those present knew the essential details.

When General Eaton at last finished his testimony, cross-examination by the defense was brief and to the point. He was asked if he had not long had a claim against the Government for repayment of the expenses allegedly incurred by him on his Tripoli expedition. He replied that such was the case. And was not the claim for $10,000? Eaton replied that it was. And had it been paid? Yes. When had it been paid? In March last!

What the defense brought out in those few short questions was that, after years of refusal, the Congress that was in the hands of the friends of President Jefferson at last had honored General Eaton's claim. And it had done so just when General Eaton's testimony gave every indication of being essential to the conviction of Aaron Burr.

That was all the defense wanted. It let General Eaton go. Less than a fortnight before Eaton's appearance in court as a witness Blennerhassett wrote in his diary: "The once redoubted Eaton has dwindled down in the eyes of this sarcastic town into a ridiculous mountebank, strutting about the streets under a tremendous hat, with a Turkish sash over colored clothes when he is not tippling in the taverns." That perhaps was a fair expression of the attitude at least of the better people of the town toward this spurious general.

What a contrast to Eaton the next witness presented! In the prevailing atmosphere of suspicion and distrust of actions and motives and testimony, Thomas Truxtun stood forth as the embodiment of truth and honor. Yet no man of his time had less reason to be loyal to the Administration in Washington or more cause to resent the shabby treatment he had received from its hands. His personal circumstances were just the sort that Burr so often undertook to make capital of in the pursuit of his own questionable designs.

Truxtun had had a distinguished career in the United States Navy, advancing to the rank of commodore. In the quasi-war with France he had commanded the U.S. Frigate *Constellation* in its two victorious battles with the French frigates *L'Insurgente* and *La Vengeance*. His professional skill was so well recognized that in 1802 he was chosen to command a squadron which had been fitted out for the war with Tripoli. As the squadron was about to put to sea Truxtun requested that a captain be appointed to command his flagship. It was a reasonable request in keeping with naval custom. But President Jefferson at that time entertained little enthusiasm for the Navy, which he regarded as a symbol of imperialism clashing with his democratic principles. So the Administration refused the request.

Commodore Truxtun, feeling that he had been indifferently treated, wrote an indignant letter of protest to Washington. It may have been too strongly worded and impolitic, yet Truxtun's fine record was deserving of some consideration. But the authorities were annoyed and interpreted the letter as an offer of resignation, which it was not. Acting on this assumption the Administration accepted a resignation which had not been offered, and in so doing lost a capable officer while it opened itself up to a charge of base ingratitude toward a deserving public servant.

Under the circumstances there was nothing for the Commodore to do but retire to his farm in New Jersey, his outstanding professional career having been brought to an abrupt end, and to brood over the injustice that he had every reason to believe had been done him. He was on his farm in the summer of 1803 when Burr, having fought his duel with Hamilton, found it expedient to get away from New York. He and Truxtun were friends and Burr, on his way south, spent a night under Truxtun's roof.

None of these past circumstances concerned Thomas Truxtun as he raised his right hand and solemnly swore to tell "the truth, the whole truth, and nothing but the truth."

During the winter of 1805–06, the Commodore began, he saw much of his friend Burr, who in their conversations frequently mentioned a speculation in western lands. He spoke also of opening a canal or building a bridge on the Ohio River. But Truxtun made it clear that he was not interested.

The topic of conversation then turned to the Government. According to Truxtun, Burr urged him to get the Navy out of his head, declaring it would dwindle to nothing. Finally, some time in July of 1806, Truxtun recalled, Burr told him he wished to see him unwedded from the Navy of the United States and to think no more of "those men at Washington." Burr, according to the Commodore, said he wanted to "see" or "make" him an admiral. Truxtun was not sure of the expression used. Burr then disclosed that he contemplated an expedition to Mexico in the event of a war between the United States and Spain. He asked if Truxtun would take command of a naval force in this undertaking. Truxtun said he inquired whether the Chief Executive of the United States was a party to or concerned in the project. When Burr answered emphatically that he was not, Truxtun replied that in that case he would have nothing to do with it.

Burr, according to Truxtun, confided to him that, in the event of a war with Spain, he proposed to establish an independent government in Mexico, that General Wilkinson of the Army and many officers of the Navy would join him. Truxtun remarked that he did not see how an officer of the United States could join. To this Burr replied that Wilkinson had first projected the expedition and that he, Burr, had matured it. He added that many greater than Wilkinson would take part, and thousands to the westward.

Truxtun testified further that Burr told him that, if there

were no war with Spain, he intended to invite friends to settle on a piece of land on the Washita River for which he was about to complete a contract. Burr estimated that within a year he would have 1,000 families of respectable and fashionable people there.

Such in substance was Commodore Truxtun's testimony. It was worth all the rest, for it was so patently honest that nobody questioned it.

When he had finished Burr inquired of him: "Did you ever hear me express any intention or sentiment respecting a division of the Union?"

"We were very intimate," Truxtun answered. "There seemed to be no reserve on your part. I never heard you speak of a division of the Union."

Burr could not have asked for better testimony from one of his own witnesses. It must have erased from the minds of the jury whatever unfavorable conclusions had been reached as a result of Eaton's insistence that division of the Union was Burr's aim. On the other hand the more astute among them may have made allowances for Burr's habit of saying to each individual just so much as he felt that individual should know.

When Commodore Truxtun had stepped down from the witness stand the prosecution called Peter Taylor, the Blennerhassetts' English gardener. He was a simple country man of limited education, in striking contrast to the distinguished naval officer who preceded him. In introducing him Mr. Hay explained that the witness would directly prove the connection between Burr and Blennerhassett. It appears, too, that the prosecution counted on Taylor as one of the two witnesses to the overt act which the Constitution required to prove guilt of treason.

Taylor's testimony began with the events on the island immediately after receipt of the President's proclamation informing the public of the existence of a plot and cautioning all loyal citizens to have nothing to do with it. Mr. Blennerhassett and Mr. Alston, said Taylor, had gone down the river to join Colonel Burr. On reading the proclamation the people in the vicinity of the island had become alarmed and Mrs. Blennerhassett sent Taylor in search of her husband and Burr to warn Burr not to return to the island because of the public outcry against him.

According to Taylor's story, after going to Chillicothe and Cincinnati, he caught up with Burr in Lexington, Kentucky. Burr inquired news of the island to which Taylor replied that he had been sent by Mrs. Blennerhassett to warn him not to return. Taylor quoted himself as saying: "If you come up our way the people will shoot you." He also testified that he had told the Colonel the people were saying the land settlement was all a fib and that Burr had something else in view.

After further wandering in Kentucky, Taylor testified that he at last came up with Blennerhassett and that they set out together on a return journey to the island. He pictured Blennerhassett as shrouding himself in mystery and, when people at the inns along the way inquired Blennerhassett's name, Taylor was instructed to tell them it was "Tom Jones." Blennerhassett also directed Taylor to call him that.

Taylor said Blennerhassett began to inquire for young men who owned rifles, explaining that he and Burr had bought land and wanted young men to settle on it. To this Taylor replied that he would like to go along if he could take his wife and family with him. But, according to his testimony, Blennerhassett replied that he would have to have further consultation with Burr on that point.

Then, according to the witness, Blennerhassett paused and after a moment's hesitation said: "I will tell you what, Peter, we are going to take Mexico, one of the finest and richest places in the whole world." Taylor went on to say that Blennerhassett told him Burr would be king of Mexico, and Mrs. Alston, Burr's daughter, was to be queen when Burr died.

Taylor said he inquired of Blennerhassett what would happen to the young men when they found out that the expedition was against Mexico, after they had signed up to settle the lands. He quoted the latter as replying: "Oh, by God, I tell you, Peter, every man that will not conform to order and discipline I will stab; you'll see how I'll fix them."

The witness said he then remarked to Blennerhassett that people were spreading the rumor that he wanted to divide the Union. According to Taylor, Blennerhassett explained that he and Burr could not do that themselves. All they could do was to tell the people the consequences of it. Blennerhassett, said Taylor, pointed out that the people in the western states now paid $400,000 a year to the Government in taxes and received no benefit from it. What a fine thing it would be if they could keep the money among themselves on the western side of the mountains, make locks, build bridges, and cut roads.

The District Attorney now took over the witness. He wanted to know if Taylor was not on the island at the time of the assembly. On being answered in the affirmative he asked if the men had guns. Taylor replied that some of them had and that they went hunting. He could not give the exact number that were armed. Further questioning brought out that Taylor did not know whether the weapons were rifles or muskets. He said the only pistols he saw were Blennerhassett's. He added that the men had powder and lead and that some of them were running bullets. He admitted that at no time had he seen Burr on the island and that he understood he was not in that part of the country at the time.

With the conclusion of Peter Taylor's testimony Court adjourned for the day. There was no doubt that much of this testimony was damaging. Some of Taylor's statements of what Blennerhassett said corresponded with the testimony of other witnesses. For example, Blennerhassett's alleged remarks about Burr and himself being unable to divide the Union but only to point out the advantages of such a division, corresponded exactly with what John Graham, the Government's investigator, said Blennerhassett told him. But could Taylor's word be trusted on the matter of the Mexican empire with Burr at its head and Theodosia as his successor? The more melodramatic the evidence the greater the suspicion that the witness had been coached before taking the stand, or that such wild statements were mere figments of his imagination.

When the Court reconvened on the morning of Wednesday,

August 19, the first witness to take the stand was General John Morgan, a sturdy frontiersman who lived with his father, Colonel George Morgan, and his brother Tom on an estate appropriately named Morganza, a few miles from Pittsburgh.

General Morgan, having been sworn, testified that some time in August of 1806, his father received a letter signed by Aaron Burr stating that he and Colonel de Pestre would like to dine with them the following day. His father, said General Morgan, asked his two sons to meet Colonel Burr on the road and this they did about seven miles distant from Morganza.

After a few words of general conversation, continued the witness, Colonel Burr observed that the Union could not possibly last and that a separation of the states must ensue as a natural consequence in four or five years. General Morgan went on to say that, at his father's table during dinner, Colonel Burr again observed that the separation of the Union must inevitably take place in less than five years. To this General Morgan said his father exclaimed "God forbid!" General Morgan testified further that Burr observed that with 200 men he could drive the President and Congress into the Potomac, and that with 400 or 500 he could take possession of the city of New York.

After dinner, said the General, Burr walked with the two brothers for about a mile. In the course of this airing he asked if either of them had a military turn, surely a surprising question to ask a man bearing the title of General! Morgan's testimony ended with an account of a farewell ride with Burr to the town of Washington, about ten miles distant, during which Burr made further inquiries about the local militia.

On cross-examination by Colonel Burr, General Morgan admitted that the letter from Burr to Morgan's father followed one from the elder Morgan to Burr inviting him to Morganza, so that the meeting between Burr and the Morgans had not after all been initiated by Burr.

General Morgan was followed on the witness stand by his father who confirmed in substance the evidence presented by his son. He explained further that he had enjoyed a long acquaintance with Burr and had received many civilities from him. In fact, said Colonel Morgan, when Burr was being persecuted after his duel with Hamilton he had invited Burr to stay with him at Morganza.

Colonel Morgan considered Burr's conversation at dinner so reprehensible that he informed his neighbors, General Neville and Judges Tilghman and Roberts. It was they, he said, who wrote a joint letter of warning to President Jefferson.

General Morgan was recalled to the stand by Burr just long enough to be asked what state of mind his father was in when General Neville and Judge Tilghman visited him. General Morgan replied that his father had recently had a fall which had done him considerable injury. Colonel Burr wanted to know if General Morgan had not made an apology to Judge Tilghman for the state of his father's mind. But the only admission Burr could wring from the witness was that he had said his father was old and infirm and, like other old men, told long stories and was apt to forget his repetitions.

Thomas Morgan, the General's younger brother, on taking the stand quoted Colonel Burr as having said that under the existing government there was no encouragement for talents; that John Randolph of Roanoke had declared on the floor of the Congress that men of talents were dangerous to the Government. He said Burr next asked him whether he, who at the time was studying law, would be interested in a military enterprise. And, said Tom, when he replied that it depended entirely on the object, Burr explained: "I wish you were on your way with me."

The testimony now returned to the Blennerhassett household. The next witness was Jacob Allbright, a stolid Dutchman who, like Peter Taylor, had been in the employ of the Blennerhassetts. He testified that he had been invited to go on the expedition and that he also had been offered a dollar a head for any volunteers he could get from the Dutch colony in New Lancaster, Ohio, from which he came.

But Allbright's most important testimony had to do with the appearance on the scene of the assemblage of Brig. Gen. Edward Tupper, of the Ohio militia, for on it depended proof of the use of force which might be construed as levying war. According to Allbright, General Tupper laid his hand on Blennerhassett and at the same time declared: "Your body is in my hands, in the name of the Commonwealth." Then, continued the witness, seven or eight muskets were leveled at him at which Tupper protested, "Gentlemen, I hope you will not do the like."

To this, said Allbright, one of the men who was about two yards away replied, "I'd as lieve as not." This threat, Allbright testified, changed Tupper's attitude and he wished Blennerhassett good luck. Allbright's testimony was as close to showing an act of violence as that of any of the witnesses.

Recognizing the seriousness of the charge Burr questioned the witness at length in an effort to show that Allbright's testimony had been different on an earlier occasion and, as he expressed it, "to degrade the witness by invalidating his credibility."

Mrs. Blennerhassett, in Natchez, expressed herself as being shocked when she learned of the testimony of their former servants. In a letter to her husband she set forth in strong words her opinion of Peter Taylor and his responsibility for her husband's indictment. "Gracious God!" she exclaimed, "confined in a prison in the dog days, and by the perjury of a wretch not many degrees from a brute!"

Next came the testimony of one Peter Love, still another of Blennerhassett's retainers, a man who had volunteered for the expedition. He placed the number of persons assembled on the island at between twenty and twenty-five. He mentioned men with rifles, two braces of pistols, and a dirk belonging to Blennerhassett. But he weakened the charge of armed force by testifying that General Tupper and Blennerhassett had parted "in the greatest friendship," or so he understood from others. Nor was he of much help to the prosecution when, in reply to a question, he said it was his understanding the expedition's purpose was the settlement of the Washita lands.

On being asked by Mr. Parker, a juror, if he had seen any

bullets run, Love replied that he had, but he could not say how many. "I was a servant in the house," explained Love, "but could not mind my own business and other people's too."

Next to be heard was Dudley Woodbridge, Blennerhassett's business partner and a man of parts. They operated together under the firm name of Dudley Woodbridge & Company. He testified that in September, 1806, Blennerhassett had called on him with Colonel Burr at the company's counting house in Marietta. There, said Woodbridge, Blennerhassett told him Burr wished to buy a quantity of provisions.

The Colonel, said Woodbridge, then inquired the price of provisions and the cost of boats best calculated to carry the provisions up and down the river. Burr left with him a memorandum of the provisions wanted and also put in an order for the boats to be built. The latter were to be of the Schenectady model such as were used on the Mohawk River.

The witness described Burr ordering provisions which included pork, flour, whiskey, bacon, and kiln-dried meal, but the only thing actually purchased was the pork. The boats, said Woodbridge, were built on the Muskingum River about seven miles above Marietta. Only eleven of the fifteen ordered were completed. He then went on to tell about their seizure by the Ohio militia following publication of the President's proclamation. He also told of being on the island the night of December 10, but added nothing new to what other witnesses had testified as to the happenings there.

Then, under the direction of Mr. Hay and with the consent of the Court, Woodbridge proceeded to recount the circumstances leading up to the assembly on the island. Late in August or early in September, he said, Blennerhassett mentioned to him that he had embarked on an enterprise with Colonel Burr; that General Eaton and others were engaged in it and that the prospects were flattering. From Blennerhassett's statements Woodbridge inferred that the object was Mexico, though he admitted that that was not positively stated.

Blennerhassett, said Woodbridge, asked him if he had a disposition to join but he replied that he preferred his present situation to the uncertainties of such an expedition.

"You know Mr. Blennerhassett well," remarked Colonel Burr in commencing the cross-examination. "Was it not ridiculous for him to be engaged in a military enterprise? How far can he distinguish a man from a horse? Ten steps?"

"He is very nearsighted," agreed Woodbridge, "and cannot know you from any of us at the distance you are now from one another. He knows nothing of military affairs. I never understood that he was a military man."

"Is he esteemed a man of vigorous talent?" interposed Mr. Wirt.

"He is," replied Woodbridge, "and a man of literature." Then he delivered his estimate of his partner's limitations: "But it was mentioned among the people in the country that he had every kind of sense but common sense; at least he had a reputation of having more of other than of common sense."

To the question: "What were his favorite pursuits?" Woodbridge mentioned "chemistry and music."

Here Court adjourned for the day. When it convened on the following morning three more eye-witnesses of the events on Blennerhassett Island were heard. Simeon Poole, who was not on the island itself but on the mainland opposite it, saw what looked to him like sentinels and heard what sounded like a watchword. Maurice P. Belknap was on the island and saw men cleaning rifles. He contradicted Poole's testimony by stating that though he was a stranger he had been admitted to the island without being challenged and having to give a watchword. Edmund P. Dane, too, was permitted on the island to wander at will about the Blennerhassett mansion. Though he was a total stranger he said nobody appeared to be greatly alarmed.

The sum total of the evidence suggested that if this were levying war against the United States it was a very tepid manifestation of it.

Meanwhile Colonel Burr and his counsel were chafing over

the direction the testimony was taking. At last they could re-
strain themselves no longer. The evidence that was being heard
they protested was collateral evidence. They insisted that the
prosecution be made without further delay to produce all the
testimony they had relating to overt acts.

Counsel for the prosecution on the other hand maintained
that it was unusual, irregular, and improper thus to restrict the
testimony. The whole evidence, they contended, should be
submitted to the jury whose province it was to decide whether
there had been war or not.

Judge Marshall interposed to say there was no doubt the
Court must hear the objections to the admissibility of evidence. Mr. Wickham urged the gentlemen of the prosecution
to introduce if they could any more testimony they might have
pertaining to what they deemed to be the overt acts. Mr. Hay
objected to this course of procedure. But, he agreed, if the gentlemen of the defense were determined to make their motion
they might proceed.

That motion, proffered by Mr. Wickham, was that until an
overt act had been proved all other evidence was collateral, and
therefore irrelevant and inadmissible.

Since apparently the Government's witnesses to the alleged
overt acts on Blennerhassett Island on the night of December
10, 1806, had been exhausted, if the motion of the defense were
sustained no more witnesses could be heard. The practical effect of this would be that, of some 140 witnesses assembled by
the Government, only the handful who had already appeared
on the witness stand would be permitted to give their testimony. If the Chief Justice were to rule in favor of the motion
of the defense it was tantamount to his taking from the jury
the privilege of deciding what testimony was relevant and ar-
rogating it to himself.

Therefore if the motion were sustained and, subsequently,
Colonel Burr acquitted, it took no exceptional prescience to
foresee that the enemies of Judge Marshall could charge that
Burr's acquittal resulted from the fact that the Chief Justice
had suppressed the Government's evidence. In refusing to com-

mit Burr for treason the Chief Justice had then declared that the Government had not produced sufficient evidence. So the Government had gone out into the highways and byways and come up with more than a hundred witnesses, which in all conscience should have been enough to convict Aaron Burr of anything. And now, if the Chief Justice granted the defense's motion, he would put himself on record as refusing to admit the testimony of the witnesses that the Government had so zealously gathered together in Richmond

No question about it—the Chief Justice found himself in a tight spot.

Chapter XV

IT IS NOT every day that a lawyer has a Vice-President of the United States as his client. And subsequent history has shown that it is exceptional indeed for a lawyer to have the privilege and honor of exercising his talents to save a Vice-President of the United States from the gallows. As John Wickham rose to defend his motion, with his shrewd sense of values, he could not have failed to be aware that this was the greatest moment in his career.

Obviously counsel for the defense were not surprised when the Chief Justice granted Mr. Wickham the right to make the motion. As learned in the law as the gentleman was known to be, he could not have made the finished argument he did without long and careful preparation.

He approached his task with an air of confidence derived from his acknowledged leadership at the Virginia bar and the many victories to his credit, a number of them over the plodding Hay. This confidence was fostered by his realization of the great difficulty of sustaining any charge of treason under the Constitution of the United States and of the weakness of the evidence in this particular case. Suave, refined, and elegant, he was the envy of his less distinguished legal brethren.

The weather had turned hot again but neither Mr. Wickham nor his colleagues were to let themselves be discouraged by so trifling a matter, or to shorten their arguments so much as a sentence in order to save themselves exertion.

In introducing his case, Mr. Wickham proceeded at once to scotch the suggestion put forward by the prosecution that the motion to disqualify witnesses had been presented because the defense wished to suppress evidence. On the contrary, said his lawyer, the prisoner was more than willing that everything should be disclosed. But, the speaker pointed out, there was a practical difficulty resulting from the great number of witnesses the Government had summoned. If, he said, all of the 140 were examined, not only weeks but months would elapse, and throughout it all his client would be under confinement just as though he had been found guilty and was serving a sentence.

Having dealt with that matter to his satisfaction Mr. Wickham next directed his attention to the most obvious weakness in the prosecution's case. That was its admission that when the alleged overt act had taken place on Blennerhassett Island Colonel Burr was many miles away.

To refresh the minds of the jury, he quoted from Article III, Section 3 of the Constitution which deals with treason against the United States and lays down that it "shall consist only in levying war against them, or in adhering to their enemies, giving them aid and comfort" and adds the safeguard that "No person shall be convicted of treason unless on the testimony of two witnesses to the same overt act, or on confession in open court."

To Mr. Wickham's way of thinking the language of the Constitution made it abundantly clear that no person in the United States could be convicted of treason in levying war who was not personally present at the commission of the act.

And what was the prosecution doing? It was resorting to artificial rules of construction so that the words of the United States Constitution would be made to take an artificial meaning based on the statute law and common law of England. Mr. Wickham denied emphatically that the statute and common law of England could properly be applied to the Constitution of the United States. Mr. Wickham would go even farther than that. He would assert that no rule which holds a person guilty of treason who is absent from the scene of the overt act had ever practically obtained even in England.

Oh yes, Mr. Wickham, master of precedent that he was, knew that there were instances in English history which might be cited by the prosecution. But he had a remedy for that. He would mention them himself before the prosecution had a chance to do so. So he frankly admitted that Lord Coke, eminent English jurist and legal authority, and other writers after him, had laid down that there are no accessories in treason either before or after the fact, but that all are principals.

However, said Mr. Wickham, in spite of the principle declared by the authorities, no actual adjudications bear them out except that in the case of Sir Nicholas Throgmorton in the reign of Bloody Mary.

Mr. Wickham was well aware that there was not a lawyer of any standing at the Virginia bar who was not conversant with the account of the Throgmorton case as presented by Judge St. George Tucker in his appendix to *4th Blackstone's Commentaries.* Throgmorton had been charged with imagining the Queen's death. At his trial the doctrine of constructive treason was insisted on by the prosecution and sanctioned by the judges. When Throgmorton requested that the law books be consulted the court told him none might be brought in, that they knew the law sufficiently without a book. And when the jury brought in a verdict of not guilty contrary to the wishes of the judges, the court committed them all to prison and fined them heavily.

But, said Mr. Wickham, the court on that occasion was so contrary, not only to the rules of law and justice, but even to those of decency, that he persuaded himself counsel on the other side would not rely on it as authority.

Mr. Wickham, intimating that he had made a diligent and exhaustive search of all the authorities, declared that he could find no case in English law where a person who was not present at the scene of the overt act had been convicted or even brought to trial, except that of Mary Speke, in the fourth year of the reign of King James II, at the time of Monmouth's Rebellion. But that, Mr. Wickham made clear, was when the spirit of persecution was high. He thought it probable that it was one of the cases decided by the execrable Judge Jefferies at the Bloody Assizes.

Mr. Wickham agreed that in England there was a treason for compassing the death of the King where the mere agreement to do the act itself constitutes the crime. He thanked God that in this country there was no subject to whom such a law applied and that the United States Constitution strictly forbade that intention alone—which was so liable to be misunderstood and misrepresented—should in any case be construed into treason.

He cited also the cases of Mrs. Elizabeth Gaunt, an Anabaptist who was burned alive, and Lady Lisle, widow of a regicide, as persons convicted as accessories merely for receiving traitors. But in both instances, he emphasized, sentence had been passed by the wicked Judge Jefferies. After Mr. Wickham had thus associated these possible precedents with such outrageous circumstances the prosecution would be daring indeed to use them.

Having warmed to his task, Mr. Wickham proceeded to give his audience an impressive demonstration of his legal erudition. He referred to Foster's *Crown Law* and from that skipped to Hume's *History of England*. He quoted passages from Tremaine's *Pleas of the Crown* and boldly plowed his way through Hale, Stanford, Brooke, and Hawkins. He alluded to the conduct of the Duke of Cumberland after the Battle of Culloden, and made mention of Flora Macdonald who had helped with the escape of the Pretender. Surely, asserted Mr. Wickham, she would have been charged with treason if the doctrine that persons absent and not in arms had prevailed in England!

From citing the authorities in English, Mr. Wickham turned to Latin declaring that *"Dixit quod in hoc quod factume est proditio, non potest esse accessarius felonice et proditire non potest esse accessarius."* Not content with Latin he lapsed into some strange tongue that must have confused Mr. Robertson, the reporter, in spite of his knowledge of five languages. But

Mr. Robertson did his best and set it down thus: "*Nota P. Hus-sey C.I. que accessory ne poet este a treason; le recetment de traitor, ne poet este tantum felony, mes est treason.*" Mr. Wickham's was a brilliant display of erudition. Perhaps the passage quoted was as familiar to his fellow lawyers as the golden bird of prey on the sign in front of the "Eagle Tavern." One wonders what the jury made of the gentleman's scholarship and in which direction they were swayed.

Again Mr. Wickham repeated the strict definition of treason as set down in the Constitution—the levying of war against the United States, the overt act and the two witnesses. Its object, he said, was clear. It was to perpetuate the liberties of the people of this country. The framers of the instrument well knew the dreadful punishments inflicted and the grievous oppressions produced by constructive treason in other countries. That is why their language was plain, simple, and perspicuous.

Mr. Wickham demanded of opposing counsel what security would be afforded by the Constitution to the best or meanest man in the country if the construction on which they insisted was correct. If it was correct then all that was wanted to fix the guilt of treason on an individual was to have an insurrection existing somewhere in the United States, no matter where.

Now, he said, suppose the Government should wish to destroy any man. They find him in Georgia, and the insurrection happens in New Hampshire. This would suffice for the purpose. But if their cause was to go on the prosecution would have to contend that even less would suffice to create treason, that even an insurrection was not necessary, but that a peaceable assemblage going down the Ohio River would be sufficient for their purpose.

Continuing to expound his hypothetical case Mr. Wickham suggested that under the prosecution's construction a man might be seized and hurried by force from New Hampshire to Georgia, or to any part of the United States which his accusers might choose as best for the purpose. Obviously he had reversed the journey of his client from Alabama to Virginia. It would be in vain for him to prove that he was not present when the offense of which he was accused was committed, that he never at any period of his life had been there, that the actors and the scene were alike unknown to him. Wretches who from interest or revenge were ready to further the views of his oppressors, would present themselves and he might be convicted of levying open war against the Government with people whom he never saw and at a place where he never was!

The hour was now growing late and Mr. Wickham had talked the better part of the day. His argument might have proved tedious to his audience composed entirely of men. Surely a little ribald humor was in order after all the heavy reasoning he had forced them to endure. So, casting aside his dignity, Mr. Wickham gave it to them.

He noted that by an act of Parliament in the reign of Henry VIII, it was made treason for any woman the king should marry, thinking her to be a true maid, or virgin, to marry him if she were not so.

Now, ventured the speaker, the paramour of such a woman (Mr. Wickham supposed her to be a maid of honor and he a lord of the bedchamber) might aid her in imposing on the king. She is tried, found guilty, and executed. How would her lover be charged? Would he be indicted by the name A. B., Gentleman, or by his title of Lord, for marrying the king, not being an unspotted virgin or, to use the language of the act, "a pure and clean maid"?

"This," concluded Mr. Wickham, "may seem to be treating the subject with more levity than I could wish to do, but the argument directly applies . . . for it is as much a physical impossibility that Colonel Burr should be at Blennerhassett's Island and in Kentucky (places several hundred miles distant) at the same time, as that an individual should be at the same time a man and a woman."

Shortly thereafter the court adjourned for the day. No doubt those who had been present retired to their taverns for a spot of brandy and laughed over Mr. Wickham's merry argument about the maid of honor and the lord of the bedchamber who was made to marry the king in the indictment. No doubt there

were some instances where the quick-witted had to repeat the
argument and help the slow-witted to see the point of the joke.

Of Richmond's public establishments for food, refreshment,
and shelter for the night none—including even The Eagle—surpassed the Swan Tavern. Standing on Broad Street that separated the Capitol Square and its public buildings from the
stylish residential quarter of Shockoe Hill, identified by a sign
bearing a white swan on a pale blue background, it was largely
favored by the judges of the Court of Appeals and legislators of
high rank. Its proprietor, Col. John Moss, was a man of great
natural dignity enhanced by starched linen. The Colonel had
the reputation for setting an excellent table over which he presided in person. His ham was always prime, his fresh meats the
best the market could afford. If any criticism was heard it was
only that Colonel Moss was "a nice calculator who aimed to
give his guests just enough but no more." But if his food was
the best he ought not to be condemned for seeing that none of
it was wasted.

Also reflecting the Swan's high standards were its wine cellar
and its bar. The former was stocked, as the popular expression
of the day defined quality, with "the best London Particular."
The bar was a favorite place of assemblage for the lawyers
after a hard day in court. It was presided over by one Lovell,
a droll fellow whose wit was as dry as his wines and spirits.

It was perhaps not entirely accidental that the house which
Colonel Burr was sharing with Luther Martin was situated close
to the Swan and its bar. There, when he was not otherwise engaged, Mr. Martin was likely to be found.

On retiring to the Martin house between sessions the Colonel
often found Theodosia and little Aaron there. Theo was exercising a careful supervision over the housekeeping and the
house was becoming a popular meeting place for Burr sympa-
thizers. Many noticed and remarked that, in spite of his years,
old Martin was beginning to exhibit a romantic attachment
for Theodosia.

To Blennerhassett, under lock and key at the penitentiary
and alone, Burr wrote apologetically: "I am surrounded by

visitors, which prevents me from adding more than the assurance of my respect and attachment."

One emissary between the two accused reported to Blennerhassett that "Burr lives in great style and sees much company within his gratings, where it is as difficult to get an audience as if he were really an emperor." Another described Burr as being "as cheerful as ever. But as a jockey might restore his fame in the course, after he had injured it on a tight rope, so perhaps the little 'Emperor' at Cole's Creek, may be forgotten in the attorney at Richmond."

Blennerhassett's use of the word "Emperor" as applied to Burr is peculiarly reminiscent of the language Peter Taylor attributed to him on their journey back to the island from Kentucky in the fall of 1806.

The heat was oppressing Blennerhassett again. "I find it very agreeable," he wrote in his diary, "to get upon a chair by which I am enabled to raise my mouth to the lower tier of openings in the gratings of the windows and breathe another air for half an hour."

When Court convened next day Mr. Wickham took up the question of what constituted an overt act of levying war, which must be proved before the guilt of treason can attach to the principal.

Here the Chief Justice interrupted to inquire if any adjudged case could be produced where the court was called upon to decide, and did decide, that the evidence submitted to the jury did or did not amount to proof of overt act. Mr. Hay broke in to say that he never knew the attempt to be made but once. That was before Judge Patterson, of the Supreme Court, and it had been unsuccessful. Mr. Wickham, notwithstanding, insisted that, "It is the right and duty of the court to instruct the jury what amounts in law to an overt act of levying war." That was an important point and more was to be heard of it. Mr. Wickham concluded his argument with a satiric peroration of which Mr. Hay was the butt: "But what did the gentleman say in defining the 'levying of war'? That there is no necessity for arms, nor for the employment of force! That there is no necessity even for potential force to effect the intended purpose by terror! That there is no necessity for the act to be public! That an overt act of treason may be committed without arms, without force, either actual or potential. If this were the law there would be no safety!"

In the time allotted to him Mr. Wickham had fairly well covered the English precedents touching on the case and exhibited other evidences of his profound legal knowledge. Had the poet Tom Moore been present he would have had even more tangible reason than enjoying the gracious hospitality of the gentleman's house for saying that Mr. Wickham could hold his own in any court.

At this point Mr. Hay surprised the Court and the defense by announcing that he had two more witnesses to the alleged overt act whom he had somehow overlooked. One was Israel Miller who had come down from Pittsburgh with Comfort Tyler's party. The other was Purley Howe, an Ohioan, who had made forty boat poles for Blennerhassett and, on the fateful evening of December 10, had come to the Ohio bank of the river to deliver them. The two witnesses added little to the testimony that already had been given. Miller made an estimate of men and arms and Howe testified to having seen two sentinels armed with rifles on the flatboat that came to the Ohio bank to pick up the boat poles.

The burden of the defense was now assumed by the ponderous Edmund Randolph. As befitted an elder statesman he announced that his duty as counsel to Mr. Burr was fortified by something more important, namely his duty as a citizen to combat and, if possible, refute the pernicious doctrine of constructive treason. He quoted Montesquieu to the effect that, "If the doctrine of treason be undeterminate in any country, however free its form of government, it is sufficient to make it degenerate into tyranny."

In his zeal to protect his fellow man the gentleman was so bold as to lecture the Chief Justice. He adverted to Judge Marshall's embarrassing statement in the case of Bollman and Swartwout that to be guilty of treason a person need not be present at the scene of the alleged overt act. Mr. Randolph said he could not bring himself to believe that the Supreme Court meant to uphold constructive treason. He contended that even if the language of Judge Marshall in his capacity as Chief Justice had been explicit and imperious, nevertheless the same Judge Marshall as the presiding officer in the subordinate court ought not to conform to it.

Realizing that this was rather a large order Mr. Randolph hastened to add, "I do not, I dare not, ask you to rebel nor prescribe what you should do. But let us pray Heaven to stay the arm of the destroying angel!"

Having thus adjured the Chief Justice, Mr. Randolph cited the opinions of the American justices—Patterson, Iredell, and Chase—claiming that they showed that an assemblage without force could not be regarded as treason. He agreed with his fellow counsel, Mr. Wickham, that such a contention was repugnant as well to the English doctrine. "Foster, Hale, Hawkins, Coke, Kelynge, Reeves and all other writers," he asserted, "you will find concur in proving that not a single indictment for treason in levying war has ever been carried into complete effect in England without actual force." Mr. Hay interrupted to explain that he had only meant to say that the provisions of the Constitution ought to be construed according to the principle of common sense.

Mr. Randolph pricked up his ears at the words "common sense." With the ferocity of a tiger attacking its helpless prey he sprang upon the poor District Attorney.

"Common sense," he sneered. "Common sense, it seems, creates an accessory and introduces him as a principal, contrary to the Constitution. Common sense does not say, like the Constitution, that treason consists in levying war, but brings in a new person to participate in the guilt and punishment of treason. This common sense extends, instead of restraining, the rigor of capital punishment. This common sense is oppression and tyranny. I pray Heaven to save us from the deductions of such common sense as this!"

Mr. Randolph next complained of the vagueness of the in-

dictment. The accused, he charged, must shape his defense to
what does not appear. The laws of this country called on him
to defend himself, but they had not apprised him against what.
He must, lamented Mr. Randolph, sit down and conjecture
what the charge was. And where, he asked, was the accused to
obtain the information? Was he to write to the President, or
to the Federal Judge, or to the public prosecutor?

In his little essay on "Common Sense" Mr. Randolph mentioned its having created an accessory and introduced him as
a principal. He now returned to that theme, contending that
before anybody else could be tried, the principal in the case
had first to be convicted. If, he argued, the previous conviction
of the principal was not necessary, then the Government could
bide its time until the death of the principal so that the accessory might thus be deprived of the main chance of disproving
his offense and thereby be unjustly oppressed. This seemingly
profound reasoning was the defense's subtle means of insinuat-
ing that if there had actually been an overt act the principal
in it was not Burr, who was many miles away, but Harman
Blennerhassett who was actually present at the scene.

The arguments of Mr. Wickham and Mr. Randolph completed for the time being the presentation of the defense's side
of the case. It now came the turn of the prosecution. But Mr.
Hay pleaded for time. He called Judge Marshall's attention to
the fact that it was then Friday and expressed the hope that
further discussion of the motion made by the defense could be
postponed until Monday. That, he said, would give the prosecution time to reflect on the matter.

Mr. Wickham, Mr. Martin and Mr. Botts at once joined
forces in protesting so long a postponement. But Mr. Hay and
Mr. Wirt held out stoutly for a delay. An argument, they said,
which had occupied two whole days in the delivery before the
Court must have required considerable labor and reflection to
arrange and digest. It was, they contended, unreasonable therefore to suppose that such an elaborate argument could be fully
comprehended and an answer prepared in a single day.

Mr. Wirt observed that five or six gentlemen of great professional experience were united in the defense. He suggested that the motion might be regarded as a mere *ruse de guerre* which they have sprung on counsel for the United States as from an ambuscade. More vital still, he reminded that if the motion were to succeed there would be an end of the case.

Judge Marshall, impressed by the arguments of counsel for the prosecution, removed any possible charge of favoritism to the defense on such an important issue by granting Mr. Hay's request. Argument was forthwith postponed until the following Monday.

Nevertheless the Court did meet briefly on Saturday. It was for the purpose of arraigning Mr. Blennerhassett, who up until now had been present at the sessions in a somewhat anomalous capacity. So he was asked to stand while the indictment for treason was read to him. Here Mr. Botts interrupted the proceedings to call attention to the fact that there was a misnomer in the indictment and he had not had a chance to consult with his associates on the subject. He asked that the arraignment therefore be postponed. The request was granted by the ever obliging Chief Justice.

The two attorneys for the defense had made it emphatic in their arguments that the fundamental issue was whether treason as strictly defined in the Constitution was to prevail, or whether the broader and vaguer principle of constructive treason was to be admitted. If the definition of treason as laid down in the Constitution were followed to the letter the chances were good that Aaron Burr would go free.

But had not the President of the United States openly declared him guilty? Did not half the people in the United States believe him so, condemning him on the sensational evidence that had been spread by the public press? Was the evidence of General Eaton and Commodore Truxtun and of the lesser witnesses to be dismissed? Mr. Hay had alluded to common sense. Mr. Randolph had sneered. But the prosecution had not yet been heard.

Chapter XVI

ON THE DAY following the postponement of his arraignment Harman Blennerhassett received an important visitor in his quarters in the penitentiary. He was William Duane, formerly a partner of Benjamin Franklin and Edward Bache in the publication of the *Aurora*. Duane was now the fiery editor of that newspaper which he had made into an organ of the Jeffersonian administration.

Duane expressed great sympathy for Blennerhassett. He told him his friends were making a scapegoat of him. Then, according to Blennerhassett, Duane tried to lure him into a confession of having written certain papers then in the hands of the prosecution. But the chief purpose of his visit was to try to persuade Blennerhassett to betray Burr.

This Blennerhassett steadfastly refused to do. And that was strange since he was himself convinced that, as Duane charged, he had been made a scapegoat. Less than a week after Duane's visit he posted in his diary: "You were right, therefore, honest Hay, on observing the other day to Woodbridge while expressing your concern for my situation 'that I must now think Burr has duped me,' but you were wrong in supposing I am indebted to you for that discovery; I am possessed of it these nine months."

Burr, who had his informants everywhere, was immediately apprised of Duane's visit and lost no time getting word to

Blennerhassett to be on his guard against spies who came to him under the mask of friendship. This precaution was unnecessary. Whatever Blennerhassett may have confided in his diary he was always completely disarmed when he came into the presence of Burr, and even when they were apart he seemed still to feel Burr's influence.

Blennerhassett's determination not to turn state's evidence against the man who had duped him after pretending to be his friend has been attributed to the mildness of his temper or lack of courage. Perhaps each was a factor. However, Blennerhassett was not a bright man. His romance with his niece is evidence of an impetuosity that led him to act without counting the cost. From the time of their first meeting Burr had courted him assiduously, protesting that his vegetating on the island was a fraud on society and holding out brilliant prospects. Blennerhassett would have been easy prey for an even less skillful flatterer. What chance did he have with a man who had duped some of the best minds in the country and once through oratory alone had provoked the Senate of the United States to adoration and tears?

When Court convened on Monday morning MacRae opened for the prosecution and proceeded to live up to his reputation for wielding a meat axe. He was not the least restrained by the consciousness that his remarks were being made in the presence of, and only a few feet away from, Aaron Burr.

The prisoner, he charged, had with unexampled dexterity contrived from the very beginning to quit his situation as the accused. Instead of Aaron Burr defending himself he was found taking the high ground of public accuser and assailing others.

Mr. MacRae charged that Wilkinson, whom he called "the savior of his country," and who had prevented the execution of this detestable plot, had incurred the hatred and resentment of the prisoner and his associates in proportion as he deserved well of his fellow citizens. Let others question General Wilkinson's integrity. Mr. MacRae would not do so, at least not in open court. In MacRae's language Wilkinson was "the patriotic and meritorious officer (like those who opposed and

overthrew Cataline, the Roman conspirator) who defeated this
daring scheme against American liberty." He would not be forgiven by the conspirators.

"If he [Burr] be innocent and pure as the child unborn,"
sneered Mr. MacRae, "if he knew nothing of the transaction,
why is it that this motion is made to exclude the evidence?"

What though the prisoner was not on Blennerhassett Island
when the overt act was committed? The speaker contended
that nevertheless he was guilty if anybody was guilty.

"Is there," he asked, "any human being who having heard the
evidence of General Eaton . . . the evidence of the Messrs.
Morgan and the evidence of the witnesses who speak of the
overt act on the island, especially Jacob Allbright and Peter
Taylor, who can doubt his guilt?"

Mr. MacRae professed he could not see why it should be
necessary for Colonel Burr to be on the island if he enlisted
the men, and sent them to the place, and acted himself in another place. Nor would he bring up the cases of Lady Lisle
and Elizabeth Gaunt who had been mentioned by Mr. Wickham. Why should he? These women were accessories after the
fact. But Mr. Burr had never been regarded as an accessory.
He was the first mover of the plot; he planned it; he matured
it; he contrived the doing of the overt acts which others did.
Burr, charged MacRae, was the alpha and omega of this treasonable scheme, the very body and soul, the very life of this
treason!

So, observed Mr. MacRae, Mr. Wickham had said the prosecution must prove that the accused was personally present. "No,
Sir," he objected, "it is necessary to prove that some act laid
has been committed. . . . If the law pronounce that he is liable
for the acts of his agents, and if the fact be that his agents by
his commands and at his request committed the act, where is
the necessity of producing proof that he was on the spot
himself?"

Counsel for defense had complained of construction. "Our
construction we think correct," said Mr. MacRae, "because it
is calculated to secure the rights of the citizen and to render

the government permanent; whereas if the construction of the gentlemen on the other side be correct, the government cannot be permanent. Let them have the power of ubiquity. The conspirators will always contrive to avail themselves of this plea that they were not present."

Mr. MacRae turned to the Old Testament to support his argument. He used the story of David and Uriah to illustrate it, confident that it was well known to all the members of the jury in an age when everybody read the Bible. David, he recalled, placed Uriah in the front of the battle in opposition to a very powerful opponent in order that he might be slain and that David might afterwards take his wife. If people were asked who killed Uriah, David or the antagonist by whose sword Uriah fell, the answer of all would be that—having placed him in the front of the battle in a place of the greatest danger, in immediate opposition to a man of great strength and power, with the intention that he should be killed—David killed him.

The speaker now applied the principle to the case before the court: "We suppose the prisoner, by himself and agents, to have been acting at or about the same time at Beaver, Kentucky, and Blennerhassett's Island. We suppose that the prisoner enlisted men before he came to Beaver and at it. We suppose that afterwards his men proceeded by his orders to Blennerhassett's Island and were there increasing their numbers by more enlistments and providing the means of transporting his troops down the river towards the scene of his expedition, while he was himself enlisting more men in Kentucky and making arrangements preparatory to his meeting and assuming the command of the whole at the mouth of the Cumberland; and that in fact, pursuant to this plan of operations, he did meet and take the command of all the conspirators at the latter place."

Were there precedents in the law to sustain this argument? Mr. MacRae cited the case mentioned in Hale's *Pleas of the Crown* of the Lord Dacre and divers others who came to steal deer in the park of one Pelham. Rayden, one of the company, killed the keeper of the park, the Lord Dacre and the rest of

the company being in other parts of the park. Yet it was held
that it was murder in them all and they died for it. And, said
Mr. MacRae, there was American authority, too. He cited
Dallas's *Reports* and the case of the United States against
Mitchell in the Whiskey Rebellion in which Judge Patterson's
charge to the jury showed that a man did not have to be present at the overt act.

Mr. MacRae then took his fling at the Chief Justice's opinion in the Bollman and Swartwout case. So the defense considered that it was not a regular, solemn opinion? That it was not
delivered on a point depending before the judges, but extrajudicial and therefore not authority? Why, declared Mr. Mac-
Rae, the language was so explicit and pointed that it could not
possibly be misunderstood!

"I consider it as completely proved by the opinion," he continued, ". . . that if an unlawful assemblage of men meet together for a treasonable purpose, it is not necessary that arms
should be in the hands of those who are concerned, in order to
make them traitors. I have imagined that their meeting together
in this manner (in military array) would be sufficient to show
that their purpose was treasonable." The speaker considered
also that the reason of East on the subject was conclusive
where, among other things, he held that "any assembly of persons met for a treasonable purpose, armed and arrayed in a
warlike manner, is *bellum levatum,* though not *percussum!*"

On that note MacRae ended his argument. *"Bellum levatum,*
though not *percussum"*—that theme with variations was to get
exhaustive treatment from the next speaker. But the court had
heard enough for one day.

When, on the morning of the 25th, the bailiff called for
order, the dashing 34-year-old William Wirt entered the lists
as champion for the prosecution. Critics of the Administration
complained bitterly of President Jefferson using the public
money to employ private counsel when there were official
prosecutors on the payroll for the purpose of performing that
particular task. But the President felt he could not leave so
great a responsibility to the plodding Hay, especially after the

defense had assembled such a dazzling array of counsel. On this hot August morning the time had come for Wirt to prove to the public that the fee he would receive from the Government was well earned.

Wirt was faced with a dilemma. At this phase of his career his chief asset was a natural flow of words that was surpassed only by that of James Wilkinson. While eloquence might be counted on to sway a jury its effect on the Chief Justice was highly problematical. Judge Marshall's style was logical and free from embellishments. He also had a keen sense of the ridiculous. Thus, as Wirt warmed to his task and instinctively soared to rhetorical heights, he found himself being rudely brought down to earth out of anxiety over what mischievous thoughts lay behind the solemn countenance of the Chief Justice.

The speaker commenced his dissertation by undertaking to clear himself of personal malice toward the accused. The humanity and justice of the nation, he observed, would revolt at the idea of a prosecution pushed on against a life which stood protected by the laws.

"I would not," he declared, "plant a thorn, to rankle for life in my heart by opening my lips in support of a prosecution which I felt and believed to be unjust."

Mr. Wirt noted that the gentlemen of the defense appeared to feel a very extraordinary and unreasonable degree of sensibility on this occasion. They seemed to forget the nature of the charge and that he and his colleagues were the prosecutors. But the lawyers of the prosecution did not stand there to pronounce a panegyric on the prisoner. They were there to urge on him the crime of treason against his country!

The lawyers of the prosecution, Mr. Wirt warned, were not going to mince matters. When they spoke of treason they must call it treason. When they spoke of a traitor they must call him a traitor. When they spoke of a plot to dismember the Union, to undermine the liberties of a great portion of the people of this country and subject them to a usurper and a despot, they were obliged to use the terms that conveyed those ideas.

Why, then, were the gentlemen of the defense so sensitive?
Why on those occasions so necessary, so unavoidable, did they
shrink back with so much agony of nerve, as if instead of being
in a hall of justice they were in a drawing room with Colonel
Burr and were barbarously violating towards him every principle of decorum and humanity?

The speaker then proceeded to deal facetiously with Wickham's erudition. The latter, he reminded, had invited them to
consider the subject abstractly. But would there not be danger
in that? While they were mooting points, pursuing ingenious
hypotheses, chasing elementary principles over the wide extended plains and Alpine heights of abstracted law, was there
not danger that they would lose sight of the great question
before the Court?

The motion before the Court, Mr. Wirt agreed, was a bold
and original stroke in the noble science of defense. It marked
the genius and hand of a master. For, said he, it gave the prisoner every possible advantage. Yet at the same time it cut off
from the prosecution all the evidence which went to connect
the prisoner with the assemblage on the island, to explain the
destination and objects of the assemblage, and to stamp beyond controversy the character of treason upon it.

If, asked Mr. Wirt, the views of the prisoner were, as they
had been so often represented by one of his counsel, highly
honorable to himself and glorious to his country, why not permit the evidence to disclose those views?

"No, Sir," he protested, "it is not squeamish modesty. It is no
fastidious delicacy that prompts these repeated efforts to keep
back the evidence. It is apprehension! It is alarm! It is fear,
or rather the certainty, that the evidence whenever it shall
come forward will fix the charge."

And now Mr. Wirt, with the instinct of a good showman,
was reminded that he was speaking to an audience of men and
must season his discourse with a little spice. "I will not," he
asserted, "follow the example which he [Mr. Wickham] has
set me on a very recent occasion. . . . I will not, like him, in

reply to an argument as naked as a sleeping Venus—but certainly not half so beautiful—complain of the painful necessity I am under, in the weakness and decrepitude of logical vigor, of lifting first this flounce and then that furbelow, before I can reach the wished for point of attack." Mr. Wirt's metaphor must at least have provoked smiles from the audience, if not downright laughter.

On the contrary, said Mr. Wirt, he would endeavor to meet the gentleman's propositions in their full force and to answer them fairly. He would not, as Mr. Wickham had done, as he was advancing toward them with his mind's eye, measure the height, breadth and power of the proposition; if he found it beyond his strength, halve it; if it still was beyond his strength, quarter it; if still necessary, subdivide it into eighths; and when, by this process, he had reduced it to the proper standard, take one of those sections and toss it with an air of elephantine strength and superiority.

Mr. Wirt would not, in commenting on the gentleman's authorities, thank the gentleman with sarcastic politeness for introducing them, declare that they conclude directly against him, read just so much of the authority as serves the purpose of that declaration, omitting that which contained the true point of the case which was made against him. Nor, if forced by a direct call to read that part also, would he content himself with running over it as rapidly and inarticulately as he could, throw down the book with a theatrical air and exclaim "Just as I said," when he knew it was just as he had not said.

Having thus performed this little exercise in satire at Mr. Wickham's expense, Mr. Wirt got down to the case in point. He noted that Mr. Wickham had read the Constitutional definition of treason and given the rule by which it was to be interpreted. After he had done that it would have been natural for him to proceed directly to apply that rule to the definition and give the result.

But no. Even while they had their eyes on the gentleman he vanished like a spirit from American ground and was seen no more until he turned up in England, "resurging by a kind of intellectual magic in the middle of the 16th century, complaining most dolefully of my Lord Coke's bowels."

"Before we follow him in this excursion," proposed the speaker, "it may be well to inquire what it was that induced him to leave the regular track of his argument. I will tell you what it was. It was, Sir, the decision of the Supreme Court in the case of Bollman and Swartwout. . . . Sir, if the gentleman had believed this decision to be favorable to him, we should have heard of it in the beginning of his argument."

And so the prosecution was back again, lunging at the chink in the defense's armor which the Chief Justice, in one rare moment of careless workmanship, had left there.

What said the Supreme Court? Mr. Wirt read the offending passage: ". . . if a body of men be assembled, for the purpose of affecting by force a treasonable purpose, all those who perform any part, however minute or *however remote from the scene of action,* and who are actually leaguered in the general conspiracy, are to be considered as traitors."

The constant reiteration of his error must have brought a blush to the tanned cheek of the Chief Justice. Or had constant repetition by now rendered him immune to embarrassment?

Counsel for the defense, said Mr. Wirt, had taken the bold and difficult ground that the passage which he had read was extrajudicial, a mere *obiter dictum.* They were, he insisted, mistaken. It was a direct adjudication of a point immediately before the Court.

The speaker referred to the fact that Judge Marshall had been asked by the defense to disregard the Bollman-Swartwout decision. But, he asked, how could an inferior court control the decision of the superior court? If the Chief Justice, sitting as a circuit court, had the right to disregard the rule decided by the Supreme Court and to adopt a different rule, then every other inferior court had a right to do the same. Then there would be as many various rules as to treason as there were courts. The result, Mr. Wirt insisted, might be—and certainly would be—that what would be treason in one circuit would not be treason in another, and a man might be hanged in Pennsylvania for an act against the United States, of which he would be perfectly innocent in Virginia.

And, continued Mr. Wirt, if treason requires the actual presence at the scene of the assemblage, how easy it would be for the principal traitor to avoid this guilt and escape punishment forever. He might go into distant states and from one state to another. He might secretly wander, like a demon of darkness, from one end of the continent to the other. He might enter into the confidence of the simple and unsuspecting. He might pour his poison into the minds of those who were before innocent. He might seduce them into love of his person, offer them advantages, pretend that his measures were honorable and beneficial, connect them in his plot and attach them to his glory.

Mr. Wirt's hypothetical case was beginning to show a striking resemblance to what Aaron Burr was charged with having done. And he was not yet through. This imaginary man might prepare the whole mechanism of the stupendous and destructive engine and put it in motion. Let the rest be done by his agents. He might then go a hundred miles from the scene of action. Let him but keep himself from the scene of the assemblage and the immediate site of battle and he would be innocent in law, while those whom he had deluded would suffer the death of traitors!

"Who," he asked, "is the most guilty of treason? The poor, weak, deluded instruments, or the artful and ambitious man who corrupted and misled them? There is no comparison between his guilt and theirs. And yet you secure impunity to him, while they are to suffer death! Is this according to the rule of reason?" Here Mr. Wirt launched forth on a lengthy dissertation on the subject of principals and accessories before and after the fact that did credit to his familiarity with legal precepts and the dicta of the authorities both in this country and in England.

And now the speaker poised himself for the supreme effort, while a hush of anticipation fell over the assemblage.

"Who is Blennerhassett?" he inquired in his melodious voice. "A native of Ireland, a man of letters, who fled from the storms of his own country to find quiet in ours. His history shows that war is not the natural element of his mind. If it had been, he never would have exchanged Ireland for America. So far is an army from furnishing the society natural and proper to Mr. Blennerhassett's character that, on his arrival in America, he retired even from the population of the Atlantic States and sought quiet and solitude in the bosom of our western forests."

Let the Chief Justice be secretly amused. Mr. Wirt was not going to deny himself the superb opportunity of holding his audience spellbound with his oratorical gifts. "But he carried with him taste and science and wealth; and lo, the desert smiled!

"Possessing himself of a beautiful island in the Ohio, he rears upon it a palace and decorates it with every romantic embellishment of fancy. A shrubbery that Shenstone might have envied, blooms around him! An extensive library spreads its treasures before him. A philosophical apparatus offers to him all the secrets and mysteries of nature. Peace, tranquillity and innocence shed their mingled delights around him.

"And to crown the enchantment of the scene, a wife, who is said to be lovely even beyond her sex and graced with every accomplishment that can render it irresistible, had blessed him with her love and made him the father of several children. The evidence would convince you that this is but a faint picture of the real life."

The speaker's countenance changed from joy to distress and his voice assumed a solemn tone. "In the midst of all this peace, this innocent simplicity and this tranquillity; this feast of the mind, this pure banquet of the heart, the destroyer comes. He comes to change this paradise into a hell. Yet the flowers do not wither at his approach. No monitory shuddering through the bosom of their unfortunate possessor warns him of the ruin that is coming upon him.

"A stranger presents himself. Introduced to their civilities by the high rank which he had lately held in this country, he soon finds his way to their hearts, by the dignity and elegance of his demeanor, the light and beauty of his conversation and the seductive and fascinating power of his address. The conquest was not difficult. Innocence is ever simple and credulous. Conscious of no design itself, it suspects none in others. It wears no guard before its breast. Every door and portal and avenue of the heart is thrown open, and all who choose it enter.

"Such was the state of Eden when the serpent entered its bowers. The prisoner, in a more engaging form, winding himself into the open and unpracticed heart of the unfortunate Blennerhassett, found but little difficulty in changing the native character of that heart and the objects of its affection. By degrees he infuses into it the poison of his own ambition. He breathes into it the fire of his own courage; a daring and desperate thirst for glory; an ardor panting for great enterprises, for all the storm and bustle and hurricane of life.

"In a short time the whole man is changed, and every object of his former delight is relinquished. No more he enjoys the tranquil scene. It has become flat and insipid to his taste. His books are abandoned. His retort and crucible are thrown aside. His shrubbery blooms and breathes its fragrance upon the air in vain; he likes it not. His ear no longer drinks in the rich melody of music; it longs for the trumpet's clangor and the cannon's roar. Even the prattle of babes, once so sweet, no longer affects him; and the angel smile of his wife which hitherto touched his bosom with ecstasy so unspeakable, is now unseen and unfelt.

"Greater objects have taken possession of his soul. His imagination has been dazzled by visions of diadems, of stars and garters and titles of nobility. He has been taught to burn with restless emulation at the names of great heroes and conquerors. His enchanted island is destined soon to relapse into a wilderness; and in a few months we find the beautiful and tender partner of his bosom, whom he lately permitted not the winds of summer 'to visit too roughly,' we find her shivering at midnight, on the winter banks of the Ohio and mingling her tears with the torrents that froze as they fell.

"Yet this unfortunate man, thus deluded from his interest and his happiness, thus seduced from the paths of innocence and peace; thus confounded in the toils that were deliberately spread for him, and overwhelmed by the mastering spirit and genius of another—this man, thus ruined and undone and made to play a subordinate part in this grand drama of guilt and treason—this man is to be called the principal offender, while he, by whom he was plunged into misery, is comparatively innocent, a mere accessory. Is this reason? Is it law? Is it humanity? Sir, neither the human heart nor the human understanding will bear a perversion so monstrous and so absurd! So shocking to the soul! So revolting to the reason!"

Thus ended Wirt's classic accusation of Burr. The time remaining to the speaker was devoted to a prosaic discussion of *bellum levatum* as distinguished from *bellum percussum*. Gentlemen on the other side, said Mr. Wirt, asked for battles, bloody battles, hard knocks, the noise of cannon. But there was none. There did not have to be. The Constitution said "levying war," not "making war." He had recourse to his dictionary to show that the word "levy" means "to raise." So there needed to be no force. The word force was used figuratively merely to signify the assembled body and not any deed of violence.

Nevertheless, if the defense insisted upon force, did not the assemblage on Blennerhassett Island exert a species of potential force on the surrounding country? Did not Comfort Tyler and his party put that country into a state of consternation? What urged the state government of Ohio to send a body of men to take that party and seize its boats? What induced the State Legislature to deliberate with closed doors? What caused the militia of Wood County, Virginia, to be put in motion and marched to the island? The speaker traced the wave of alarm as it moved from the island southward all the way to New Orleans.

The day was almost spent when, with a sigh of weariness, Mr. Wirt announced that he had finished what he had to say. He begged pardon for consuming the time of the Court so long. He thanked it for its patience and polite attention. He pleaded that he was much too exhausted to recapitulate his argument. But to such a Court as that of the Chief Justice's he was sure that was unnecessary.

After his masterly effort Mr. Wirt would not have been human had he not felt a glow of satisfaction over his performance. Even those on the other side must have conceded that he had more than earned his fee. All that came after the portrayal of the relationship between Blennerhassett and Burr was anticlimax. That passage, duly recorded by Mr. Robertson, found its way into books of elocution and became one of the most popular pieces of literature to memorize and declaim. The Chief Justice was kind enough to remark that he had been greatly impressed by the speaker's eloquence. What effect it had on the members of the jury for whose consumption it was chiefly intended only they could say, and they left behind them no record of their reactions.

There was also the effect on the prisoner whose misdeeds had been so vividly described. The Colonel sat through it all calmly, but with his alert mind he took in every word of it. It is said that in later years he entertained himself and his friends by reciting the more florid passages and that his performance seldom failed to be rewarded with peals of derisive laughter.

Chapter XVII

WIRT'S ARGUMENT had consumed the better part of the day, but there still was a little time left before the regular hour for adjournment. Two of the lawyers for the prosecution having held the floor in succession it was again the turn of the defense.

Of Colonel Burr's lawyers none was better equipped by temperament to counterbalance William Wirt than was Benjamin Botts. He, too, could boast the vigor and abandon of youth. In fact he was the youngest of all the array of legal talent which had been attracted to the case. He was distinguished for his wit and he was a master of ridicule, for which Mr. Wirt's florid oratory made an excellent target. As Wirt had set out after Wickham in his opening remarks, so young Botts turned his guns on Wirt.

"I cannot promise you, Sir, a speech manufactured out of tropes and figures," he began with mock apology. Then, alluding to Wirt's reference to "an argument as naked as a sleeping Venus," he continued: "Instead of the introduction of a sleeping Venus, with all the luxury of voluptuous and wanton nakedness to charm the reason through the refined medium of sensuality, and to convince us that the law of treason is with the Prosecution by leading our imaginations to the fascinating richness and symmetry of a heaving bosom and luscious waist, I am compelled to plod heavily and meekly on through the dull doctrines of Hale and Foster." Mr. Botts, too, was not without skill in playing up to the gross humor of an all-male audience.

"So far though from reproving the gentleman's excitement of the boiling blood of such of us as are in the heyday of youth, without the previous caution of clearing the hall of those whose once panting desires have been chilled by age, and upon whom the forced ecstasy sat unnaturally and uneasy, I only lament my utter incapacity to elicit topics of legal science by an imitation of so novel and tempting an example. Nothing but the impossibility of success would prevent me also from grasping at the fame and glory on this grave occasion, and at this time of pleasure, of enriching the leering lasciviousness of a like bewildering thought to transport anew the old and the young."

In such manner Mr. Botts soon put the assemblage in good humor. Even the Chief Justice, who enjoyed a joke as much as the next man, must have joined in the fun. Having thus ingratiated himself with his audience by this gay introduction he proceeded to present his serious argument. His first proposition he told them would be to endeavor to establish the fact in support of the motion that the acts proved to have taken place on Blennerhassett Island were not in themselves acts of war and that no intention could make them acts of war.

What had actually happened? According to Mr. Botts about thirty men had landed on the island and remained there for two or three days. It is true, they had some arms and ammunition. They guarded their property at the boats. They prepared provisions to take with them down the river. At a place contiguous to the island it was admitted they had killed some squirrels. As notable a circumstance as any in this overt act was that they had had what one of the witnesses called "a watchword." All but Blennerhassett and Tyler were confessedly ignorant of the plan. They got alarmed on hearing the report of a mob and fled secretly in the night after Comfort Tyler had declared his purpose not to resist constituted authorities.

Now, said Mr. Botts, the proposition of the opposing side was that these were acts of war, that they were intended first against the people of Wood County, Virginia, in which the island was situated, and then against New Orleans.

He would suppose first that the acts were against Wood County. Very well, then, the boats, the oars, the provisions for a long journey, the after-descent of the river were overt acts of levying war against Wood County.

"But, Sir, the party was armed!" he exclaimed, imitating the manner of the prosecution. Why? Mr. Botts contended that it showed they were expecting the people of Wood County would attack them. In other words Mr. Botts apprehended that the people of Wood County meditated war on the people of the island, not that the islanders meditated war against the people of Wood County.

Then, continued Mr. Botts, it was found that the people of the island had fled silently in the night from those of Wood County. And because they fled, it seems they were guilty of acts of war!

On the other hand, said Mr. Botts, pursuing his argument, "if the war was not against Wood County it was against New Orleans. And New Orleans was 2200 miles away!"

In the same playful mood, Mr. Botts suggested that the defendant might claim that these persons had no arms, or if they had guns that they were not long enough to shoot all the way from the island to New Orleans. He presumed that the reply the prosecution would make to that was that no arms were necessary, that they might make war with their fingers. Or the defendant might urge that persons in this country have a right to carry arms, that it is also conformable to usage for people going down the river to kill ducks and other such game.

"The prosecutor," Mr. Botts presumed, "would answer that arms are not necessary; that they had three or four guns, a little powder and shot even to kill fowls and ten or twelve boats; that it was a most bloody war indeed; that without arms it would be war, but with these arms it was a most dangerous war against the United States!"

If this was making war against the United States, declared Mr. Botts, then "If I run away and hide to avoid a beating, I am guilty and may be convicted of assault and battery!" Here Mr. Botts suggested the propriety of adjourning.

When Court met next morning and Mr. Botts resumed his argument he was in the same facetious mood. Once more he went back to the charge of levying war and recalled the failure of the grand juries in Mississippi and Kentucky to indict.

"The Mississippi Territory and Kentucky, as we are informed, were the seat of war," he observed. "But the simpletons of that State and Territory hunted but could not find the war. They were so stupid as not to perceive in a collection of men without arms, without any possible means of annoyance, without any hostile disposition and without the possibility of getting away their women and families, anything criminal, much less any aptitude to overturn two mighty empires.

"It remained for us, the proud members of the Virginia bar, to come out and astonish the world with the profundity of our learning in matters of war. They have ascertained that there was a terrible war. I ask you what manner of war was it? We have had a much more serious war here than on the island. We have had here a carnage of breaths, sour looks and hard words and the roaring of vocal cannon. We have had a battle with the laws and the Constitution fought courageously and furiously by our enemy.

"Is it not a mockery to speak of the war on Blennerhassett's Island? Shall we not be the sport of Europe and the world by such a discussion?"

In spite of the nation's independence, which it now had enjoyed for a matter of more than thirty years, the Virginia bar still did obeisance to that of England. Though Burke had died in 1797 and Charles James Fox and the younger Pitt had gone to join their fathers within the year, counsel in the Burr case transferred their veneration to their successors in Westminster. They seemed to have imagined fatuously that this spirit of camaraderie was reciprocated and that the great men of England had temporarily put aside the affairs of empire to follow every move being made by opposing counsel in the hall of the Virginia House of Delegates in Richmond.

Now, continued Mr. Botts, Mr. Hay had said that constructive treason in this country would not be dangerous. Mr. Botts would suppose an imaginary case. He would suppose there had been well-grounded apprehension of an approaching war with a neighboring and powerful nation. He would suppose that the United States had a feeble army in the neighborhood of the boundary line between the two countries, and that the American general had orders to fall back. Mr. Botts, be it noted, was as good at making hypothetical cases for the defense as was Mr. Wirt for the prosecution.

He would suppose that the populous rich city of New Orleans was in danger of invasion. He would suppose that a hero distinguished for military science and valor and as patriotic as he was ambitious of honorable fame—but whose good name was blighted and blasted by the malice of his countrymen—should have seen the dangers hanging over his country: New Orleans threatened with invasion and conquest by a Spanish force, the citizens there in danger of murder and captivity, their wives and daughters ready to be a prey to Spanish lust, and all else in that favored country exposed to desolation.

He would suppose that the hero knew that a band of faithful patriots could be collected immediately around his standard. He would suppose that with this band of patriots the hero should at this fortunate and critical moment have rescued the country, the army, the people, by a reasonable relief to the decrepit and half baffled forces of the United States. He would suppose that in the same magnanimous spirit the hero should after this have gone on his enterprise to establish the independence of the Mexicans and give liberty to millions now groaning under bondage.

Suppose he had done all this: he would have acquired immortal glory and be renowned in future ages as the deliverer of his country, worshiped as its idol and called its savior as Washington was.

Thus Mr. Botts artfully contrived to present the character of Aaron Burr as his defenders chose to imagine it. The defense scored the prosecution for trying to introduce constructive treason into the United States. It did not object to introducing constructive heroism, provided the hero was Colonel Burr. The

Colonel laughed at William Wirt's extravagant language. Is it not possible that he stifled a cynical smile as he heard himself thus being glorified by young Botts?

Mr. Botts's supposing ended, he next described in heart-rending language the manner in which the well-meaning and patriotic Colonel had been basely betrayed and thwarted. In what some might have considered not too good taste he recalled that Christ himself had been abused, mocked, and spit upon. Why then should not a mere mortal man be in like manner abused?

The young champion next raised his lance against the President of the United States. He charged that Mr. Jefferson's interference with the prosecution of the case was improper, illegal, and unconstitutional. He had no doubt, he said, that the President had acted from good intentions, without sufficiently reflecting on the subject, and that he was inadvertently following one of the very worst English examples in the most arbitrary reigns. He wished Mr. Jefferson could be at his side now to hear what could be said on the subject. Young Mr. Botts was sufficiently sure of his powers of persuasion to believe that under those circumstances Mr. Jefferson would be convinced that he had done wrong.

Then Mr. Botts came to his concluding peroration. "We are told," he said, "that the virtue of the people will do everything; that the voice of the people must be heard and must decide where they are sovereign; that the voice of the people is the voice of God; and that a majority of the people must always do right. . . .

"I hope the gentlemen . . . will not refer the fate of individuals accused to the sudden and violent impulse of their feelings and passions. . . . There are cases where individuals have been sacrificed by the voice of the people. Socrates was made to drink the hemlock, and Aristides was banished by the people. . . . Admiral Byng was made to die for the same cause. Jefferson was run down in the year 1780 by the voice of the people." Mr. Botts's reference here was to the unpopularity of Mr. Jefferson during the Revolution when he was Governor of Virginia and the state was invaded by the British and complaints of

Mr. Jefferson's ineffectiveness in meeting the crisis raised murmurs for his impeachment.

After that Mr. Botts was back again appealing to Holy Writ
to drive home his point: "Reformation and Christianity itself
prove the general errors subject to pervade the people. Jesus
Christ himself was crucified by the people."

On this sacred note Mr. Botts closed his discourse. He had
proved himself to be as entertaining as any of his elder brethren
of the bar.

The industrious Mr. Robertson rendered yeoman service in
recording the lengthy and often tedious proceedings. Even he
was beginning to tire. He concluded it was not necessary to
set down all that was said. Instead he contented himself with
making the entry, "here some facetious and pleasant remarks
passed between Mr. Botts and Mr. MacRae; which afforded
amusement for the moment, but are omitted as irrelevant to
the report." Irrelevant? Who knows but that if Mr. Robertson
had recorded the facetious and pleasant remarks that Mr. Mac-
Rae made in his exchange with Mr. Botts, Mr. MacRae might
have been spared the ignominy of going down to posterity as
a sour Scotsman.

Soon after there appeared the entry: "Here a desultory conversation ensued between Mr. Botts and Mr. Wirt in which
some warm and animated observations were made respecting
the evidence, and Mr. Wirt's comments thereon." Had Mr.
Botts's ridicule got under Mr. Wirt's skin? At this point the
Chief Justice poured oil on the troubled waters by remarking
that the evidence was such that different gentlemen might draw
different inferences from it.

After Botts came the District Attorney's turn again. "I
cannot," he confessed with his customary modesty, "instruct
you by my learning, amuse you by my wit, make you laugh by
my drollery nor delight you with my eloquence. All I can do
is to express to you in plain language the convictions perhaps
of a mistaken judgment." Here was no mock humility, but
the sincere outpouring of a spirit oppressed by the knowledge
that among his colleagues of the Richmond bar he was labeled

as a mediocrity. Hay would have been even duller of wit than public opinion made him out to be if he had not noted the special consideration assigned to such of his contemporaries as Wickham, Botts, and Wirt. He could have consoled himself with the reflection that in such an assemblage humility was a rare and welcome virtue.

Mr. Hay had no sooner fairly begun on his discourse than he made an allusion to Justice Samuel Chase and his conduct in the Fries case in which he had strained the law to convict for the Government. The censure the judge brought on himself, observed Mr. Hay, was not on account of his opinions but for his arbitrary and irregular conduct at the trial. Chase, he reminded, attempted to wrest the decision from the jury and prejudge the case before hearing all the evidence in it. It was, said Mr. Hay, the identical thing this Court was being called on to do by the gentlemen of the defense. At this the gentlemen of the defense pricked up their ears. Mr. Hay was to hear from them later.

The remark about Justice Chase was preliminary to a dissertation on the institution of trial by jury. "If," Hay averred, "it ever shall be determined by this Court that it has it in its power to take the decision of facts from the jury, the trial by jury, one of the greatest bulwarks of civil liberty, may be struck down and destroyed."

The great question at issue in this case, he said, was compounded of law and of fact, of which latter the jury were the judges. Therefore every allegation which related to the indictment, all the evidence relating to and bearing on the issue, ought to be brought forward and heard by the jury. The prosecution held that Colonel Burr was guilty of levying war against the United States. Colonel Burr said he was not. The evidence the defense sought to exclude bore directly on the point at issue. Mr. Hay expressed himself as positive the framers of the Constitution never intended to take the decision of the general issue in a criminal case away from the consideration of the jury and give it to the judge.

The speaker paused for an impressive moment and then, selecting his words with care, addressed the bench: "I consider this principle of the trial by jury, preserved in its uttermost purity and independence, as connected with the best principles of the human heart. It ought to be viewed and approached with the utmost reverence and caution; and when a judge is called to do what may lead him to encroach on this principle, he will advance with the utmost circumspection and awe. I will take the liberty to say that it will be far more safe and correct to remain a thousand miles on this side of the line which separates the rights of the Jury from those of the Court, than to go a hair's breadth beyond it; and if he should encroach he ought for no human consideration to touch it. If ever he do, he undermines civil liberty." That short dissertation on trial by jury must have made some of those present wonder if they had misjudged when they wrote George Hay off as a mediocrity.

The District Attorney returned to the old question of whether actual presence of the accused at the scene of the overt act was necessary to sustain a charge of treason. Suppose, he said, Colonel Burr had never been on the spot where the overt act was committed. Suppose he knew his men were there and about to be attacked. Suppose he sent more men there to help them, along with arms, ammunition, and provisions and all other things necessary for their defense. Suppose an attack was made and repelled and thousands fell in the battle. Would it be contended by the gentlemen of the defense that Aaron Burr, not having been personally present when this overt act of his procurement was committed, was not a principal but an accessory? That his soldiers were principals in treason, but he was not? To prove the fallacy Mr. Hay proposed that they look at the result. He is innocent and safe. They are guilty and punished.

"Is it possible," he asked, "that the human mind can be so perplexed by learning and so misled by ingenuity, so totally bereaved of all its powers, as to adopt a conclusion like this?"

Mr. Hay closed his argument by reverting to Mr. Wickham's expressed fear that the doctrine the prosecution asked the Court to sanction would be fatal to the liberty and happiness of the people of the United States. He pictured Mr. Wickham trembling for his country, himself, and his posterity lest the prosecution succeed.

"I too am a citizen of this country," he declared, "and the father of children for whose happiness and welfare I feel a solicitude as lively and affectionate as any parent can feel. To the true happiness of my country I hope I know that I am sincerely and ardently attached. But I see no danger. I apprehend none for myself or my posterity. I am perfectly willing to risk my own life, liberty and happiness, and those of my posterity on the propriety of the principles which we recommend. Let them avoid traitorous conspiracies and designs fatal to the liberty and happiness of their fellow citizens; let them avoid traitorous assemblies, overt acts of war, and they will be safe."

Thus concluded Mr. Hay. Next on the list of pleaders was Luther Martin, but he sent word to the Court that he was not ready. So Mr. Charles Lee, of the defense, arose to fill the breech. It was one of the rare occasions when he was recorded as having spoken.

Counsel for the defense had been waiting impatiently for a chance to pounce on the District Attorney from the moment he brought up Justice Chase and the Fries case. Now Mr. Lee had that agreeable opportunity.

"The gentleman said in substance there was no difference between the opinion which we desire you to give and that for which Judge Chase was impeached," charged Mr. Lee, addressing the Chief Justice. "It was very kind of the gentleman to remind the Court of the danger of a decision of the motion in favor of the prisoner, a decision like that which has already produced the impeachment of another judge."

Mr. Lee knew full well he was touching a tender spot. By thus accusing the District Attorney he was acting on the popular belief among Judge Marshall's friends that the Chief Justice was himself as much on trial as was the prisoner at the bar. Mr. Hay was prompt to do what he could to counteract that impression.

"The cases are different," he replied. "What I said was only said to put Mr. Botts right in his misrepresentation. It was innocently said and compatible with the highest respect for the Court, not with the design which the gentleman (I will not say candidly) insinuates."

Here the Chief Justice intervened. "I did not consider you as making any personal allusion, but as merely referring to the law," he assured Mr. Hay. Thus, with an exhibition of his customary common sense, Judge Marshall graciously accepted Mr. Hay's explanation, whatever his innermost thoughts might have been.

Mr. Lee, however, persisted. "The gentleman plainly insinuated the possibility of danger to the Court from a favorable opinion to the prisoner," he protested, "because he said that the opinion which we claimed for him was the same in substance as had occasioned the impeachment of one judge already. It certainly would not be unfair to infer that it was intended to show that the same cause might again produce the same effect."

Colonel Burr's urgent request that the trial be expedited seemed doomed to failure. Mr. Lee, having been less long-winded than his colleagues, completed his argument some time before the hour of adjournment. The proposal was made to send a messenger to summon Mr. Martin whose appearance was next on the agenda. But the lawyers of the defense who were present declined to do so, stating again that Mr. Martin was not yet ready. The Court therefore adjourned for the day.

It was not until Friday morning, August 28, that Mr. Martin at last made his entry and rose to address the Court. In speech and appearance he was coarse and crude. Toward his enemies he could be vindictive, as he already had shown in the previous proceedings of the trial. His emotions were as violently stirred in behalf of those he called his friends. On the other hand no one surpassed him in his knowledge of the law and in the application of that knowledge to whatever case he might be pleading.

At the moment Colonel Burr enjoyed his complete loyalty.

And since his introduction to her a few weeks before he had developed a consuming admiration for Theodosia Alston. Now came the supreme opportunity to serve them both.

Mr. Martin opened his address with an expression of regret that the artifices and persecutions of his enemies had placed Colonel Burr in his present predicament. But, he continued: "I shall ever feel the sincerest gratitude to Heaven, that my life has been preserved to this time, and that I am enabled to appear before this Court in his defense.

"And if the efforts of these highly respectable and eminent gentlemen with whom I have the honor to be associated, united with my feeble aid, be successful in rescuing a gentleman for whom I with pleasure avow my friendship and esteem, from the fangs of his persecutors—if our joint efforts shall be successful in wiping away the tears of filial piety, in healing the deep wounds inflicted on the breast of the child, by the envenomed shafts of hatred and malice hurled at the heart of the father—if our efforts shall succeed in preserving youth, innocence, elegance and merit from despair, from distraction—it will be to me the greatest pleasure. What dear delight will my heart enjoy. How ineffable, how supreme will be my blessings."

The solicitude of the elderly gentleman for the prisoner's daughter was not lost on his audience. The old and kindly disposed no doubt heard them and were touched. The young and cynical were amused that the old man's infatuation for the beautiful young matron was capable of producing such eloquence. It was one of the current jokes of the town.

However, pursued the speaker, private friendship for the accused and his connections was not his only inducement. He was as well thankful to Heaven that when a question as to the right construction of the principles of treason was to be decided—on which the happiness or misery of the present and future ages depended—he was to have an opportunity to exert to the utmost his feeble talents in opposing principles which he considered so destructive as those advanced on the present occasion. If he and his colleagues, said Mr. Martin, were able

to satisfy the Court that the principles the reverse of those contended for on the part of the prosecution ought to be established, he would think he had not lived in vain.

Mr. Martin took pains to make it clear that neither Colonel
Burr nor his counsel had ever admitted or suggested that Harman Blennerhassett was guilty of treason. What then was the
propriety of Mr. Wirt saying that they were willing to sacrifice him, and that he might be hanged without pity or remorse
on their part?

Mr. Martin then brought to bear all the wisdom acquired
during his thirty-six years at the bar. He referred to Hale and
Hawkins. He recalled the Statute of 39 Elizabeth Cap. 15,
wherein A and B both consented to enter a house to rob and
only A entered and B stood by, wherefore A was "ousted of
his clergy" while B still had it. He cited the case of Pudsey
in 1 Hale 534 to show how it came within the general principles of the cases of constructive presence as stated in Foster 349.

He, too, mentioned the case of My Lord Dacre who came
with a band of men to steal deer in the park of one Pelham.
And he noted that Hawkins, in his second volume, Chapter 9,
section viii, page 442, also explained very clearly the principle
of constructive presence. He admitted that in Great Britain
there was a species of treason which consisted in the intention
without any act consummating the guilt of treason. He meant,
of course, compassing the death of the king when the crime
was only imagined. But in America, since there was no king,
there were only two species of treason, which were levying
war against the United States or adhering to their enemies,
giving them aid and comfort.

"Sir," he exclaimed, "I execrate a contrary doctrine as highly
tyrannical and oppressive. And here I beg leave to enter my
censure against the decisions of the court in Pennsylvania on
this subject in the cases of what are called the Whiskey and
the Hot Water Insurrections."

Having thus abruptly paid his compliments to the American
judges with whose decisions he differed he went back across
the sea to England and John Wedderbourn's case and Deacon's

case and that of the king versus Captain Vaughan, who went aboard a vessel called the *Loyal Clencartie* in the service of the French king to cruise against the subjects of the English king. As he expounded the law in this masterly fashion how could he have failed to bring a blush to the cheek of Mr. Ritchie of the *Enquirer* who had used his columns to belittle Luther Martin and scoff at the absurdity of importing a Maryland lawyer to try a case in a Virginia court.

It was gossiped that during the preparation for his appearance Mr. Martin had drunk even more freely than was his usual custom. If so the indulgence had done nothing to befuddle his brain or dim his memory of precedents. Next he turned to the incident of Lord Balmerino entering the gates of Carlisle and holding the city for the Pretender. He cited other allegedly treasonable acts having to do with the efforts of the Stuarts to regain their throne. This was a fruitful field for English precedents for acts of treason. But, he contended, those who had levied war in Perth were charged with levying it in Perth. So, too, were those who levied war in Aberdeen charged with levying it in Aberdeen. He could find no case in which a person was charged with levying war in a place where he was not present.

"But," he observed, "if the counsel for the Crown in Great Britain had found out this new doctrine discovered by the ingenuity of the counsel for this prosecution, prosecutions would have been easily conducted and much trouble saved. If this new doctrine be as the gentlemen effect to believe, unanswerably correct, then it shows incontrovertibly great ignorance on the part of the lawyers who prosecuted in Great Britain in encountering so much unnecessary trouble and adopting a mode of prosecution so difficult as they did, and the superior ingenuity of the gentlemen in discovering this very easy and plain mode."

Then Mr. Martin was off after Nicholas Throgmorton, following his case with allusions to the cases of Alice Lisle and Mary Speke, who were so despitefully treated by Judge Jefferies of the Bloody Assizes. He delved into the eighteenth year

of the reign of King Edward I to bring forth the case of
Bago de Clare to whose house one John Wallis, a clerk, brought
a letter of citation from the Archbishop of Canterbury, and
some of de Clare's family forced Wallis to eat the process and
wax seal affixed thereto. And de Clare pleaded that he was not
required to answer the suit brought against him until the principal actors had been convicted. So he was released on bail to
answer after the principals had been convicted. From which
incident, which had happened more than five centuries before,
Mr. Martin sought to prove that in the State of Virginia in the
year of Our Lord 1807, Colonel Burr could not legally be
brought to trial until Harman Blennerhassett had been tried and
convicted. If Mr. Botts's allusion to the Crucifixion and Mr.
MacRae's use of Uriah's death through the connivance of David
are excepted, Mr. Martin deserved the prize for going farthest
back into history for a precedent.

The speaker had occupied the time of the Court for the
entire day and the hour was growing late. When asked if he
could finish his argument that evening he replied that he could
not. So the Court was adjourned until the usual hour on the
morrow and judge, jury, learned counsel, prisoner, witnesses,
and spectators drew a sigh of relief and went off to refresh
themselves and enjoy as much of a night's rest as the hot, hu-
mid atmosphere permitted.

When Court reconvened on Saturday morning, August 29,
Mr. Martin resumed his argument. Here he gave his attention
to the opinion in the case of Bollman and Swartwout. He
brought out that when the opinion was given only four of the
seven judges of the Supreme Court were sitting. Would four
judges in an extrajudicial manner have undertaken to settle
the construction of the law so infinitely important to the
United States? Would they have decided so important a question in a collateral, irregular manner on a point not immediately
before them? And that also without the aid of the other three
judges?

Even if they had done so, contended Mr. Martin, their decision "certainly deserves no credit as binding on this Court.

As a binding judicial opinion it ought to have no more weight than the ballad or song of Chevy Chase."

Mr. Martin alluded to Mr. Hay's statement "with great zeal and pathos, that he pledged his own and the life of his children and posterity, on the propriety of the doctrine which he has advocated: that, if they avoid conspiracies, that if they be innocent, they will be safe."

"A most delusive doctrine," he exclaimed. And he warned Mr. Hay: "If he be now in the full tide of successful experiment, in the enjoyment of the approbation of his country and his government, so was, not long ago, the gentleman whom I advocate. He was as highly distinguished by the kind favor of the people as he could be by their suffrages.

"It was then incredible that their favor should so soon be changed to calumny and rancor of party into the most malignant hatred. The gentleman may now think himself perfectly safe, by the prevalence of his party and his principles; but the day very possibly may come when he may find himself as obnoxious as the gentleman whom I defend.

"He may possibly by the same means, the malice, the injustice and violence of party spirit, like my client, not only find himself reviled and calumniated, but his dearest friends abused and persecuted. I should be sorry that such a prediction should be realized with respect to any gentleman; but, such are the natural consequences of his own pernicious doctrine, and those we oppose."

And now the speaker arrived at the end of his argument. Those of the assemblage whose minds may have wandered now and then in the course of Mr. Martin's exposition of the technicalities of the law were brought to attention by the solemnity of his countenance and the careful weighing of his words:

"When the sun mildly shines upon us, when the gentle zephyrs play around us, we can easily proceed forward in the straight path of our duty. But when the bleak clouds enshroud the sky with darkness, when the tempest rages, the winds howl and the waves break over us—when the thunders awfully roar over our heads and the lightnings of heaven blaze around us

—it is then that all the energies of the human soul are called into action.

"It is then that the truly brave man stands firm at his post. It is then that by an unshaken performance of duty man approaches the nearest possible to the Divinity. Nor is there any object in the creation on which the Supreme Being can look down with more delight and approbation than on a human being in such a situation and thus acting."

The speaker turned to look straight into the eyes of the Chief Justice as he continued: "May that God who now looks down upon us, who has in his infinite wisdom called you into existence and placed you in that seat to dispose justice to your fellow citizens, to preserve and protect innocence against persecution—may that God so illuminate your understanding that you may know what is right; and may he nerve your soul with firmness and fortitude to act according to that knowledge."

So saying, Mr. Martin shuffled over to his seat. It is a safe assumption that the Chief Justice was not a little moved.

There were souvenir hunters even in those early days. In the *Gazette and General Advertiser*, organ of Richmond's Federalists, on the morning of August 31 appeared this advertisement:

> The Gentleman—who while I was on Sat. last addressing the court, TOOK MY CANE from the seat behind me and carried it away—is respectfully requested to send it when he has done with it, to the Bar of the Swan Tavern. Luther Martin.

It hardly required a public notice to let people know where Mr. Martin in his moments of relaxation was most likely to be found.

Chapter XVIII

ONE OF THE principals who failed to hear Luther Martin's masterly argument was Harman Blennerhassett. He felt unwell on Thursday; on Friday he awoke with a continuation of his indisposition attended by a fever which made him so miserable he returned to bed without waiting for breakfast. In keeping with the prevailing custom he dosed himself with three or four grains of calomel.

Blennerhassett was a hypochondriac but on this occasion his ailment was not imaginary. He was a victim of influenza which suddenly struck Richmond in epidemic form. Next day the news reached him in the penitentiary that half the families in the town were afflicted. The disease hit the staff of the *Enquirer* so hard that it was with the greatest difficulty that popular organ of public opinion continued publication.

Kind Mrs. Gamble heard of Blennerhassett's illness and did what she could to contribute to his comfort. On Sunday she sent him fruit and fresh butter and fine calf's foot jelly nicely chilled in ice. The same day he was honored by a call from Mr. Martin and was by that time sufficiently recovered to receive the visitor. Mr. Martin appeared none the worse for wear as a result of his very strenuous labor in court. Blennerhassett recommended his brandy as being considered superior and put a pint tumbler before the Marylander.

No ceremonies retarded the libation. Blennerhassett's ab-

sence from the court during the time Mr. Martin held the floor
was not to deprive him of the privilege of getting a generous
sample of the gentleman's eloquence and wisdom. The visit
did not exceed thirty-five minutes. Yet so fluent was the
speaker that he delivered an account of an entire week's proceedings in the trial. He not only quoted verbatim long extracts from his own speech but also extracts from the speeches
of other lawyers on both sides of the case.

Mr. Martin also regaled his host with whole columns, from
a series of papers, which he had written under the pen name
of Investigator. He also caricatured Jefferson and gave a history of his acquaintance with Burr, expatiating on the latter's
virtues and suffering. These last were not received enthusiastically by Mr. Blennerhassett. At the moment he happened to
be feeling particularly aggrieved over the manner in which he
had been duped by the adventurer. In fact, the laudatory comments on Burr made by Martin raised the suspicion that he
had been deliberately sent by Burr to restore Blennerhassett's
good humor as a precaution against the ever-present danger
of his turning state's evidence.

Among other things Martin expressed the opinion that because Burr had alleged he expected a war between Spain and
the United States his expedition was lawful. But, countered
Blennerhassett, "may not a jury think Burr did *not* expect war
and find their verdict then on the confession?"

If Burr supposed that Blennerhassett would be favorably
impressed by Martin he was greatly mistaken. The latter had
hardly left his presence before Blennerhassett sat down and
went to work drawing one of those pen portraits which were
so much the vogue at the time among those who laid any claim
to literary talent.

"His manner," wrote Blennerhassett, "is rude, and his language ungrammatical, which is cruelly aggravated upon his
hearers by the verbosity and repetitions of his style. . . .
Fancy has been as much denied to his mind as grace to his
person or habits. These are gross, and incapable of restraint,
even on the most solemn public occasions."

The influenza skipped the Chief Justice. Perhaps it considered it futile to attempt an assault on his hardy constitution. It was just as well for, over the weekend, he had strenuous work to do. Court had adjourned late Saturday afternoon. It was scheduled to reconvene early Monday morning. In the approximately thirty-six hours between adjournment and reconvening, it was Judge Marshall's task to review the arguments presented, weigh them against each other, and arrive at a conclusion to be contained in a written opinion. The Judge was taking no chances. He knew that whatever opinion he might render would be immediately scanned in Washington and perhaps misconstrued, that any slip he might make would be used against him.

Sunday was an important day in Richmond when almost everybody went to church. The Roman Catholics were ministered to by the Abbé du Bois, a refugee from the French Revolution, who said mass in the courtroom of the Capitol. Methodists and Baptists were numerous and had their own churches.

The House of Delegates was the scene of an unusual example of denominational co-operation between the Episcopalians and the Presbyterians. The two sects were led respectively by Parson John Buchanan and Parson John Blair, devoted friends who, in their lighter moments, discussed philosophy and punned in Latin. Buchanan was a bachelor and well heeled. Blair had numerous progeny and was hard pressed to make ends meet. So Parson Buchanan applied his logic to the practical end of convincing Parson Blair that all of Parson Buchanan's fees for marriages, funerals, and the like should by right go to Parson Blair.

The Presbyterians did not yet have a church and the only Episcopal church was St. John's, on a high hill to the east and hard to reach. The upshot of it was that Episcopalians and Presbyterians worshipped together in the House of Delegates, with Parson Buchanan and Parson Blair occupying the pulpit on alternate Sundays.

Whether Sunday, August 30, 1807, was Parson Buchanan's

turn in the pulpit or Parson Blair's history does not record.
Judge Marshall was an intimate of both parsons and a devout
churchman as well. But it is unlikely that, with the exacting
business in hand, he found time to attend church that day.

Even with that allowance there was not much time for reflection. A plausible explanation is that while the lawyers were
debating the Chief Justice was formulating his opinion. This
one was to be the longest in the whole trial and the one containing the most references to the authorities. It may well be
that he made notes of these authorities cited by the speakers
as the argument proceeded.

Did he work by candlelight long into the night? Did he
wake up with the birds and labor during the cool hours of the
early morning? Or did he sit under the trees in his spacious
yard during the day, braving the critical looks of his neighbors as they returned from church? Whatever the Chief Justice's method, when court met on Monday morning, August
31, he was ready to deliver his opinion. Counsel, jury, and
public in attendance knew that the crisis in the trial had been
reached.

The ever-courteous Marshall made use of his introduction
to compliment counsel on both sides. The motion, he said, had
been argued in a manner worthy of its importance and with
an earnestness evincing the strong conviction felt by opposing
counsel that the law was with them.

"A degree of eloquence," he declared, "seldom displayed on
any occasion has embellished a solidity of argument and a
depth of research by which the court has been greatly aided
in forming the opinion it is about to deliver."

The Chief Justice restated the issue which was that, the testimony having shown that the prisoner was not present when the
overt act mentioned in the indictment took place, objection
had been raised that testimony offered to connect him with
those who committed the overt act was totally irrelevant and
therefore must be rejected.

His first task was to clarify the confusion arising out of the
opinion in the Bollman and Swartwout case, which already

had been brought up by counsel on both sides. It was said that it was on the basis of that opinion that the Grand Jury had seen fit to bring in the indictments for treason. The offending phrase was the one which said: "If a body of men be actually assembled for the purpose of effecting by force a treasonable object, all those who perform any part, however minute, or however remote from the scene of action, and who are actually leaguered in the general conspiracy, are to be considered as traitors."

If the phrase meant what it seemed to mean then, surely, the absence of Colonel Burr from Blennerhassett Island at the time of the alleged overt act in no way relieved him of his guilt. Was the phrase a mere *obiter dictum* or chance remark as the defense maintained, or was it a formal declaration of the court changing the previous conception of treason as laid down in the Constitution as the prosecution assumed it to be? The time had come for the Chief Justice to make known which interpretation was correct.

He had heard, said Judge Marshall, that his opinion had been construed to mean that any assemblage whatever for a treasonable purpose, whether in force or not in force, whether in condition to use violence or not in that condition, was levying war. It had not been expressly advanced by the bar, but he understood it had been adopted elsewhere. (Anyone who was at all conversant with the existing political situation knew that the interpretation referred to was that of President Jefferson. It had been adopted by his partisans, and it was because it had gained such a firm hold that the incidents of Blennerhassett Island, mild as they were, were assumed by the prosecution to fulfill the Chief Justice's definition of an overt act of levying war.)

Judge Marshall pointed out that the court which gave the opinion was composed of four judges. Of these he said one was sick. He seemed uncertain as to this judge's opinion. Three judges were absent. Therefore, said the Chief Justice, if the three judges who were absent concurred with the sick judge who was present "and perhaps dissents," a majority of the judges might overrule the decision. A critical observer might have charged that the Chief Justice was falling back upon a good many suppositions.

What, he asked, was levying war? He had, he said, looked at all the English authorities and, so far as he could see, levying war meant just that. The words had received no technical meaning different from their natural meaning. The assemblage must be a warlike assemblage, carrying the appearance of force, and in a situation to practice hostility. The Chief Justice added for good measure that the American judges, so far as their opinions had been quoted, seemed to go even farther than the English authorities and require the actual exercise of force.

But, he reminded, it had been said that all these authorities had been overruled by the decision of the Supreme Court in the case of the United States versus Bollman and Swartwout. Now it would be expected that an opinion which was to overrule all former precedents and to establish a principle never before recognized would be expressed in plain and explicit terms. Had the intention been to make so material a change, then the Court ought to have expressly declared that any assemblage of men whatever who had formed a treasonable design constituted the fact of levying war. Yet no such declaration was made.

What was more, said the Chief Justice, in the case of Bollman and Swartwout there was no evidence that even these two men had met for the purpose of executing a plan. In their case the issue of an assemblage did not appear. In short, the Chief Justice asserted that general expressions ought not to be considered as overruling settled principles without a direct declaration to that effect.

Thus at last the ghost of the opinion in the case of Bollman and Swartwout was laid by the same hand that had raised him. At least the Chief Justice must have hoped so. It was not often that his rare gift of logical reasoning was put to so severe a test. By this time counsel for the prosecution must have seen

how the wind was blowing, if they had ever harbored any
doubts about it.

The Chief Justice now got to the nub of his opinion. It was
essential, he said, that an indictment be explicit as to the nature
of the crime and the place where it was committed. Otherwise
the accused would not know how to defend himself. The
whole treason laid in the indictment was the levying of war
on Blennerhassett Island and the whole question was whether
the prisoner was legally present. It was as if no other overt
act ever had existed. Therefore, said Judge Marshall, the only
point the Court was examining was the constructive presence
of the prisoner at the fact charged.

Now, said he, had Burr arrived on the island he would have
been present in fact. Or, had he taken a position near enough
to co-operate with those on the island, the question of whether
he was constructively present would be a compound of law
and fact which the jury would decide with the assistance of
the Court as respected the law.

On the other hand, if the prisoner was not with the party
at the time, did not intend to join it, and if his co-operation
was at a great distance, in fact in a different state, then he was
not constructively present. Therefore the Judge confessed that
he was strongly of the opinion that proof of the actual or legal
presence of the prisoner on the island by the evidence of two
witnesses could not be made.

But, continued the Judge, the prosecution might contend
that the indictment did not charge the prisoner with actually
being present at the assemblage on the island, but that though
he was not at it he caused it. If the law was as the prosecution
maintained then the procurement of the assemblage took the
place of presence at the assemblage. In that case, he insisted,
under the Constitution procurement of an assemblage should
be testified to by two witnesses just like presence at an overt act.

Judge Marshall pointed out that, because the advising of
treason or the procuring of treason was a secret matter of the
mind rather than an actual deed, it might be objected that it

would be hard to prove. But, he retorted, the mere difficulty of proving a fact surely did not justify a conviction without proof.

Was the testimony the Government proposed to offer to prove the overt act laid in the indictment? No, it was evidence of subsequent transactions at a different place and in a different state. Such testimony, he declared, was not relevant. It could be produced only as corroborative or confirmatory testimony, if it could be produced at all.

The Chief Justice had now dealt with the decision in the Bollman and Swartwout case and made it clear that it had not been intended to serve as a new rule of law introducing constructive treason into the United States. He had followed that up by showing that neither Colonel Burr's actual presence nor legal presence on the island at the time of the overt act had been proved. This done he was coming to the end of his opinion. The words he was about to speak had evidently been carefully chosen. He must have been aware of the solemnity of the moment even though he may not have foreseen that he was speaking for posterity as he began:

"Much has been said in the course of the argument on points on which the Court feels no inclination to comment particularly; but which may, perhaps not improperly, receive some notice.

"That this Court dares not usurp power is most true.

"That this Court dares not shrink from its duty is not less true.

"No man is desirous of becoming the peculiar subject of calumny. No man, might he let the cup pass from him without self reproach, would drain it to the bottom.

"But he has no choice in the case, if there be no alternative presented to him but a dereliction of duty or the opprobrium of those who are denominated the world, he merits contempt as well as the indignation of his country, who can hesitate which to embrace."

There spoke the soldier of the American Revolution. Not all the power that could be exerted by the presidential office, not all the threats of public violence nor the prospect of public scorn could frighten John Marshall from doing his duty as he saw it. If Aaron Burr was to be found guilty of treason it would be only after he had been granted all the protection that was due him under the Constitution and the laws of the land.

If that be an undue encroachment of the Judiciary on the powers of the Executive and the Legislature, let Mr. Jefferson make the most of it!

"The result of the whole," concluded Judge Marshall, returning to his customary calm, judicial language, "is a conviction as complete as the mind of the Court is capable of receiving on a complex subject, that the motion must prevail."

He observed that the jury had heard the opinion of the Court on the law of the case. They would now apply that law to the fact and would find a verdict of guilty or not guilty as their conscience might dictate.

Although the great probability of an opinion ruling out the rest of the evidence must have been foreseen by the prosecution, Mr. Hay was momentarily confused as to how next to proceed. So, as soon as the Chief Justice had concluded his remarks to the jury, the District Attorney requested that the Court grant him time to consider it. Judge Marshall readily agreed and an adjournment was taken until the morrow.

Whatever courses the counsel for the prosecution may have discussed among themselves during the evening they came upon no plan to counter the opinion of the Chief Justice. So, when the Court met next day, Mr. Hay announced that he had nothing to offer the jury either of evidence or argument and must, therefore, leave the case to it.

At the order of the Chief Justice the jury then retired. The assemblage was not kept long in suspense. Soon the jury was on its way back to the courtroom led by its foreman, Colonel Carrington. Asked by Judge Marshall if a verdict had been reached, the Colonel arose and replied: "We of the jury say that Aaron Burr is not proved to be guilty under this indictment by any evidence submitted to us. We therefore find him not guilty."

Not guilty "by any evidence submitted to us." Did the jury
then mean to imply that had some of the evidence not been
withheld under the motion made by the defense and sustained by the Chief Justice, it would have found Aaron Burr
guilty? Would that not be the impression made on the public?
If such an impression were made on the public could the verdict
then be regarded as an exoneration?

Colonel Burr did not think so. He was on his feet at once
protesting and he was supported in his protest by other counsel
for the defense. The Colonel called the verdict unusual, informal and irregular. He demanded that the objectionable
qualification be stricken out.

Luther Martin called it a tempest in a teapot. Colonel Carrington interposed to say that if the objections to the offending passage were continued the jury would strike it out. He
was immediately contradicted by his fellow juryman Richard
E. Parker, an ardent Jeffersonian, who shouted that it had
been inserted deliberately and that it would stay there.

Judge Marshall listened patiently throughout the controversy and compromised the issue by stating that, in the opinion
of the Court, the verdict was in effect the same as a verdict
for acquittal. He would therefore let it stand in the bill as
the jury had pronounced it. The entry made on the record
would be simply, "Not Guilty."

With his customary courtesy the Chief Justice thanked the
jury for its patient attention during the whole course of the
long and tedious trial and dismissed it. Attorney Hay, recognizing the hopelessness of getting a verdict of treason on the
basis of the assemblage on Blennerhassett Island therefore entered a *nolle prosequi* to the indictments of Blennerhassett and
the other alleged conspirators. That is to say, having failed to
convict Burr, the Government would drop the charges against
his subordinates. However, Hay asked that they and Burr as
well be still held on charges of treason on the possibility of
some other overt act elsewhere being charged against them.
This move was made by Mr. Hay at the instigation of President Jefferson. Again the Chief Justice listened patiently

through another long argument over the legal point involved. When it was over he ruled against the request, pointing out that all of them still had to be tried before the present Court on a charge of misdemeanor.

Yet another protracted argument arose over the proper bail for Aaron Burr. His counsel contended that he should give none at all. Now that the Colonel's neck was safe it was no longer necessary for the Chief Justice to make every concession the defense requested. He insisted upon bail and ordered it set at $5,000. In spite of the defense's contention that no one dared perform this favor for Colonel Burr because of public opinion two sureties at once presented themselves and, on September 8, Aaron Burr found himself a free man. For nine weeks he had been under confinement.

This being the sickly season in Washington the President had retired to Monticello. Postmaster Gideon Grainger had installed a special courier service between Washington, Richmond, and Monticello and Secretary of State Madison's summer home, Montpelier. It was to Monticello that Hay reported to the President on the Government's defeat which he attributed to the unfriendly attitude of Judge Marshall. To show that this was not his opinion alone he stated that "Wirt, who has hitherto advocated the integrity of the Chief Justice, now abandons him. This last opinion has opened his eyes, and he speaks in the strongest terms of reprobation."

Jefferson was willing enough to adopt this excuse for the failure of the prosecution. He replied at once, "Yours of the 1st came to hand yesterday. The event has been what was evidently intended from the beginning of the trial; that is to say, not only to clear Burr, but to prevent the evidence from ever going before the world.

"But this latter must not take place. It is now, therefore, more than ever indispensable that not a single witness be paid or permitted to depart until his testimony has been committed to writing. . . .

"These whole proceedings will be laid before Congress, that they may decide whether the defect has been in the evidence of guilt, or in the law, or in the application of the law, and that they may provide the proper remedy for the past and the future."

There was no doubt as to where the President believed the defect to lie. Burr had escaped conviction of treason. But in his trial on the charge of a misdemeanor there was a prospect that the witnesses, who had been refused opportunity to testify by the Chief Justice, would be heard.

"Not proved to be guilty by any evidence submitted to us." The President in his letter made it clear that Mr. Hay was to be responsible for seeing that the evidence which had been withheld reached the eyes and ears of Congress. Then Congress would know where the defect lay and provide the proper remedy.

The President had abandoned the hunt for Aaron Burr. He was now hot on the trail of the Chief Justice.

Chapter XIX

An Act of Congress of 1794 provided that if any person should, within the jurisdiction of the United States, begin or set on foot a military expedition against the territory of any foreign power with whom the United States was at peace, he would be guilty of a high misdemeanor. It was under this statute that Burr, Blennerhassett, and their fellow conspirators now were to be tried. The specific charge against them was that they had begun or set on foot an expedition against Mexico, then a possession of Spain with whom the United States was at peace.

It was the opinion of some people that, in their effort to have Burr exonerated of the charge of treason, his counsel had virtually admitted the misdemeanor. Blennerhassett, it will be recalled, criticized one of Luther Martin's arguments for just that reason.

In the few days that intervened between the two trials Colonel Burr was making the most of his new freedom. With the beautiful Theodosia on his arm he strolled through the town in order to give the Richmond populace full opportunity to see and admire her. The most serious crisis in her father's affairs having passed, she was on the point of returning to South Carolina with her husband and son.

Blennerhassett too had now been relieved of the ignominy of confinement behind bars. Released from the penitentiary

he went to board in town while Colonel Burr moved from
Luther Martin's house to the one that had previously been occupied by the Alstons. It was not long before Blennerhassett
received a visit from the Colonel. According to his own account he represented distinctly and with firmness that he expected to be repaid for all the financial losses he had suffered
either through endorsing Burr's papers or buying supplies for
him. And, since he was no doubt quite aware that such payment was beyond the Colonel's powers, he let him know that
he intended to hold Alston answerable for any losses he might
have sustained over and above the amount of Alston's guaran-
tee by letter.

Both men were the objects of courtesies at the hands of the
fashionable element who composed the Federalist society in
Richmond. Blennerhassett's interest in music was immediately
rewarded by invitations to meetings of the Harmonic Society.
Though at the outset he could not assist in the program because he had no spectacles, he was granted an honorary membership for the length of his stay in town. He found the flutes
good, four violins moderately good, and three excellent singers
who performed some charming trios by Dr. Calcott, inspired
by extracts from Ossian. These were new to Blennerhassett's
ears and, on the whole, he enjoyed himself so much that he
stayed listening to the music until midnight.

The visitor was more fortunate at a meeting of the society
a few nights later. Somebody lent him a pair of spectacles, thus
enabling him to read notes and take part in a symphony and
also in a quartet by Pleyel; but, he lamented, "with less effect
than if I had been provided with my own."

In fact now that Blennerhassett was free, on Sundays when
the Court was not sitting and in the evenings, he found many
opportunities to enjoy the best Richmond society. He made a
special visit to Mrs. Gamble, no doubt to thank her in person
for the calf's foot jelly and butter she had sent him while he
was in prison. He found her to be "a most amiable old lady,
so fraught with the generous humanity characteristic of her
sex, as to suffer not the connections of her daughters . . . to

prevent her expressing not merely a concern for the general hardships we have suffered, but even to censure the last two days' proceedings in court." The "connections" of her daughters were of course Agnes's husband, Governor Cabell, and Elizabeth's husband William Wirt who, had it not been for Hay's *nolle prosequi*, would at that very moment have been using his eloquence to get Blennerhassett hanged.

Mrs. William Brockenbrough, too, was among the ladies expressing solicitude for the poor persecuted prisoners. The former mistress of Tuckahoe and present wife of the rising young banker was, observed Blennerhassett, the nearest approximation in Richmond to a *savant bel esprit*. Her reputation for intelligence was, perhaps, somewhat enhanced in Blennerhassett's estimation by her insistence that she must get a copy of "The Querist" to read. The proud author of that series of articles just then was under the impression that David Robertson, who had done such a fine job of taking notes on the trial in shorthand, was going to give them a longer life by including them in the book he proposed to compile on the trial. In this expectation he proved to be mistaken. "The Querist" articles were not made a part of Robertson's two classic volumes.

After his long years on his island with no settlement closer than Marietta, Blennerhassett evidently relished the cultivated society that the capital of the Commonwealth of Virginia provided. He experienced great delight in the piano performance of a talented young Frenchman. It lasted two hours and introduced Blennerhassett to the most recent compositions of Haydn who, at the age of 75 years, was still producing his melodious music. At another meeting of the Harmonic Society he enjoyed the company of Mrs. Wickham and of Mrs. Chevallié. It did not quite compensate for the separation from his wife, but the Blennerhassetts were not entirely out of touch. "I had this morning," he exulted, "a long double letter from my adored wife. Its red seal was as welcome to my eyes as the evening star to the mariner."

However, these delightful diversions could not entirely erase the fact that the Messrs. Burr and Blennerhassett were in

Richmond for other than social affairs. On September 9 the petty jury to hear the case of misdemeanor against the Colonel was sworn in and the trial of witnesses commenced. The trial was less than a week old when the same obstacle presented itself that had halted proceedings in the treason trial. Defense counsel again objected to what they regarded as quantities of irrelevant matter in the testimony.

After the issue had been debated at length the Chief Justice again issued one of his long and learned opinions sustaining the defense's objection. The testimony, he ruled, must include only that which showed the expedition to have been military in nature and designed against the dominions of Spain. He ruled further that the testimony must deal only with the acts charged in the indictment and which were alleged to have occurred within the jurisdiction of the Court.

Again the District Attorney confessed he had presented all the testimony answering the description of that which the Chief Justice had ruled to be admissible. So, like the treason trial, that on the misdemeanor charge came to an abrupt conclusion. It took the jury not more than half an hour to find Aaron Burr not guilty of a high misdemeanor. Again, as in the treason trial, on hearing the verdict Mr. Hay entered a *nolle prosequi* in the cases of Blennerhassett and the other accused men.

The defeat of the Government was now well nigh complete. The gallant Wilkinson, observing the proceedings in Richmond, wrote a letter of condolence to his chief.

"The disgraceful and dishonorable scenes which have been passing in review here are drawing to a close," he lamented. "Burr has just been acquitted on the trial for misdemeanor and now a motion will be made for his transmittal to Kentucky, which will go off the same way. The chief [Marshall] has stepped in too deep to retreat, and indeed, his enterprise and hardihood almost justify the suspicion that he has been a party to the conspiracy." Wilkinson spoke of reforming the Federal courts and getting rid of a "corrupt judge."

Mr. Jefferson, in a letter to a friend took his cue from the

General, remarking: "The scenes which have been acting at Richmond are sufficient to fill us with alarm. We supposed we possessed fixed laws to guard us equally against treason and oppression; but it now appears we have no law but the will of the judge."

Once more it looked as though many of the Government's witnesses, who had been gathered together with such great pains and who had been waiting all these weeks to testify, would go home without being heard. But Mr. Hay had one more trump card to play. He moved that the alleged conspirators be committed both on charges of treason and misdemeanor which might have taken place in Ohio and Mississippi. Through this motion the Chief Justice found himself transformed into an examining magistrate. As such he regarded it as essential that all the evidence be heard. So at last, in spite of the protests of defense counsel, the Court was thrown open to any and all witnesses the Government chose to present.

For the most part they were youths and humble folk who had joined the expedition or had had dealings with the party on Blennerhassett Island.

Edmund P. Dane—the Blennerhassetts had come to his house at Belpré to buy cider. They had invited him to go on the expedition, assuring him it was not hostile to the Government and aimed only at settling the Washita lands.

Israel Miller—he was with the expedition when Burr met it at the mouth of the Cumberland. He mentioned a few weapons.

"Do they kill ducks and turkeys with bullets?" inquired Mr. MacRae, who was familiar only with hunting on the eastern coast.

"If the gentleman had ever been in Kentucky," remarked Burr dryly, "he would have known that it was considered inglorious there to kill a squirrel, or even ducks, with anything but bullets."

James McDowell—he went with the expedition as far as Chickasaw Bluffs, the present site of Memphis. He saw a few guns with bayonets, but no boxes of arms. It appeared to him that Burr was in command. Recalled to the stand, he admitted that after leaving the mouth of the Cumberland he saw six or seven boxes that were so heavy he could not lift them.

Stephen S. Welch—he joined the party at the mouth of the Cumberland. He said the proposition put up to him was settlement of the Washita lands. Samuel Moxley and Chandler Lindsay, John Mulholland and Hugh Allen told much the same story.

"Had you any reason to suspect that any of the party meditated hostility against the United States?" inquired Burr of Allen. "Never," Allen replied.

A prize witness for the prosecution was Sergeant Jacob Dunbaugh, a member of Captain Bissell's command at Fort Massac when the Burr expedition passed there. Dunbaugh testified that Burr invited him to join the expedition and go down the river, for which purpose Captain Bissell gave him a furlough of twenty days. After the expedition had left Bayou Pierre he said he saw Colonel Burr and another man go to the bow of the boat and set to work with an ax, augur, and saw, chopping and sawing. According to Dunbaugh two bundles of arms tied up with cords were sunk. On being questioned he estimated the arms at from forty to forty-three stands. He said he also saw pistols, swords, blunderbusses, fusees, and tomahawks.

Dunbaugh testified further that, after Captain Bissell had given him leave to go with the expedition, Colonel Burr had called him into his cabin and asked him if he could persuade ten or twelve of the best men in the garrison to go along. He protested that he had repelled any such suggestion. On further questioning it was brought out that what the Sergeant meant to convey was that Colonel Burr wanted the men to desert.

The reason for the alleged sinking of the arms was in order to hide them from the Mississippi authorities when they made a search of the boats. Dunbaugh said one man had been delegated to take out a hogshead of potatoes with which to fill an arms box to make it look like a box of potatoes. The arms, he declared, suspended by cords, were down so deep that the boat could not get to within fifty yards of the shore.

Dunbaugh's evidence was the strongest that yet had been given to show the military aspects of the expedition. But it lost much of its force when, under cross examination, the Sergeant confessed that he had overstayed his twenty-day furlough, had been arrested and found guilty of desertion and imprisoned, and that he had written to General Wilkinson promising him that if he were released he would be in New Orleans in three days, presumably to do the General's bidding in the trial.

More impressive because of its source was the evidence of Alexander Henderson, a respected citizen of Wood County. Mr. Henderson described a visit from Mr. and Mrs. Blennerhassett who mentioned to him the advantages to be gained by the West in separating from the Union. The Blennerhassetts had remained for dinner and after the meal was over Harman enlarged on the same theme in the presence of Alexander and his brother John. He told them, said Alexander, that New Orleans was to be seized, and that artillery to the number of fifty pieces belonging to the French was to be commandeered.

"Did you understand whether he said anything for Mr. Jefferson?" asked Mr. Wirt, evidently with an end to refreshing the witness's memory. Alexander replied that "Mr. Blennerhassett said that if Mr. Jefferson was any way impertinent that Colonel Burr would tie him neck and heels and throw him into the Potomac."

"What did he say of his means of opposition to the Government?"

"He mentioned," said Henderson, "that with three pieces of artillery and 300 sharpshooters he could defend any pass in the Allegheny Mountains against any force the Government could send."

The witness testified further that Blennerhassett had shown them two numbers of "The Querist" and told them he had written them.

"It is remarkable," observed Mr. Wirt, addressing the Court, "that Colonel Burr was at the island on the 1st of September and the first number of 'The Querist' is dated the 4th."

John Graham, Secretary of the Mississippi Territory, who

had been directed by the Government in Washington to investigate Burr's activities in the West, was next called to the stand.
He told of his meeting with Blennerhassett who, with his customary gift for blundering, at first mistook him for a friend of
Colonel Burr and one who was sympathetic with the expedition. Yet he admitted that Blennerhassett had mentioned the
settlement of the Washita lands as being the object. Furthermore, according to Graham, when he tried to discourage him
from taking part, Blennerhassett replied that the expedition was
legal, that he and Burr were familiar with the law and knew
what they were doing. As for the separation of the western
country from the Union, he and Burr held that it would be
beneficial for the people of the West but realized that they
were not yet ready for it.

Saturday, September 26, was a red letter day in the trial since
it brought two colorful figures to the witness stand in the persons of General Eaton and General Wilkinson. Eaton now was
permitted to include in his testimony that part of his affidavit
which Judge Marshall had forbidden in the treason trial on the
ground that it was irrelevant to the doings on Blennerhassett
Island. The evidence was sensational enough but, having been
published in the newspapers throughout the country months
before, it was an old story that had lost most of its original force.

According to Eaton, in the course of their conversations in
Washington during the winter of 1806, Burr told him that if he
could win over the Marine Corps and secure the interest of
Truxtun, Preble, and Decatur, he would turn Congress out
neck and heels, assassinate the President (or what amounted to
that), and declare himself the protector of an energetic government. Eaton insisted that Burr had used such expressions as
"hang him," "throw him into the Potomac," and "send him to
Carter's Mountain." Carter's Mountain was that eminence overlooking the town of Charlottesville, Virginia, on whose edge
lay Monticello.

In response to these boasts Eaton claimed he had observed to
Burr that one solitary word would destroy him. When Burr
inquired what the word was Eaton replied, "Usurper." Burr,

continued Eaton, smiled at the General's want of confidence, quoted examples of dictators from ancient history and, if Eaton's memory served, mentioned Caesar, Cromwell, and Bonaparte.

Yet who could believe Eaton, a mere adventurer who had not yet had time to spend the $10,000 indemnity presented to him by the Government so shockingly close to his appearance as its witness? Eaton's blustering and braggadocio while he was hanging around during the summer waiting his summons to testify also had created an unfavorable impression in the town. The story was spread that one disgusted Richmonder had threatened to kick the Hero of Derne out of a saloon. Nevertheless Eaton's account of Burr's lurid boasts bore an astonishing resemblance to those the Morgans had claimed Burr had made to them, and those that Alexander Henderson had charged that Blennerhassett had made to him.

Now at last, when the proceedings were almost through, General Wilkinson was allowed to give his version of the conspiracy in open court. It was the story of Samuel Swartwout's arrival at Wilkinson's headquarters at Natchitoches with the cipher letter from Burr, and of Eric Bollman's arrival at New Orleans with the duplicate. It provided a fresh opportunity for the General to present himself to that large and attentive audience in the role of the savior of his country. But the cross questioning to which he was subjected by the defense made him squirm, while the explanations he gave in reply were a major test of his ingenuity.

Had he made an erasure in the letter? Yes, he had erased the sentence "yours, postmarked 13th of May, is received." The sentence was a clear giveaway that he had been in previous communication with Burr.

"Have you ever sworn that this was a true translation?" asked Mr. Botts.

"No, only substantially so," was Wilkinson's reply.

When the questioning drove him into a corner he excused his conduct on the ground that at the time he had many military duties to perform in defense of his country and was in a hurry.

Besides, he had been upset by the death of his wife. No doubt there was truth in that for his devotion to her was universally acknowledged.

Why, Mr. Wickham asked him, had he waited from October 10th, when Swartwout handed him the cipher letter, until October 21 to notify the Government? Mr. Wickham's implication was that he had needed the time to make up his mind. But the General had a different and plausible explanation. He said he took that time in order to get out of Swartwout all the information he could about the conspiracy. Why had he asserted in his first letter to the President that he did not know the leader? Wilkinson pleaded that he was not at that time sure since he could not fully trust what Swartwout told him.

September gave way to October and Wilkinson was still on the stand being badgered by the defense. Counsel for Colonel Burr were desirous of linking the General's high-handed conduct in New Orleans with orders issued by the Government. This line of questioning brought a protest from Hay.

"It has been the constant effort of the counsel on the other side to identify General Wilkinson with the Government," he charged. "We have heard of the plundering of post offices, violating of oaths and prostrating of private rights. Now it is asked if the Government approved of these acts. Is it proper, is it decorous to pursue this course?"

"Do you recollect expressing to any person that he would confer the highest obligation on the Government by seizing Colonel Burr?" Wilkinson was asked by the defense. The General admitted that he might have said that since those were his sentiments. His great object, he declared, was to apprehend Burr and deliver him to the civil power for trial. The city of Washington was the place he wished to have him sent. But personal injury to the Colonel had not entered his head. He recollected a German had come to him and proffered his services to take the Colonel "dead or alive."

"I was shocked at the very idea," declared Wilkinson, "and declined employing him."

When Mr. Wickham demanded a letter purported to have

been written by President Jefferson to Wilkinson approving the measures the General had taken, he set off another argument almost as acrimonious as that which had attended Burr's request for the *subpoena duces tecum.*

"These gentlemen, it seems, are carrying on an impeachment against the President of the United States," asserted Mr. Wirt, not unmindful of the political effect of the charge. "What is their object in demanding this letter? It is no more than vainly to attempt to inculpate the President and to gratify their spleen and their resentment against him. Is that their object? Is Aaron Burr more or less guilty because he [the President] has approved or disapproved the measures of General Wilkinson?"

"They want to ask you," continued Wirt, pursuing the same line of criticism, "which is the most guilty, Thomas Jefferson or Aaron Burr? Are you, then, trying the President? And even if you were, would you not have him here and give him an opportunity of answering his accusers?"

"It has already been decided in this Court," retorted Martin, "that the President has no more rights than the man who walks the street in rags. 'What!' says the gentleman. 'Will you then violate the sanctity of private correspondence?' Sir, when the gentleman made this declaration, I looked at his face to see whether it did not blush with shame, and even burst with blood, at expressing such a sentiment."

"I hope, Sir," observed Wirt, "the redness of a man's face is no evidence of a man's guilt." This indirect allusion to Martin's own physiognomy, red presumably as a result of his addiction to the bottle, was surely not lost on the audience.

The Chief Justice expressed regret that the question of producing the letter had arisen. It was irksome to him, he declared, and it was with considerable reluctance that he must insist on its being produced. He did only what his duty prescribed. However, Judge Marshall concluded, though he did not know what the letter contained he saw no need for it to be read aloud.

Now the tables were turned by the prosecution. They had contended all along that there was nothing in the letter which reflected against the President. So MacRae stated that the prosecution preferred to read the letter to the Court as being "the only way to avert the misrepresentations of its contents."

No sooner had the argument over this one letter been settled than Wickham was up again demanding that the whole of another letter from the President to Wilkinson be produced. The Chief Justice reminded him that the President had certified his reasons for communicating only certain parts of the letter. He believed that the withheld parts had no application to the present prosecution.

Mr. Martin was on his feet again protesting. He hoped the Court had not definitely decided the point. Once more he displayed his personal animosity toward Mr. Jefferson. "Has not the Court already declared that the President has no more power here than any other man? If this be law, for which gentlemen now contend, God forbid that I should remain a citizen of the United States.

"And is Mr. Jefferson to be the judge of the relevancy of evidence, in a prosecution in which he has taken so active a part against the accused? Mr. Jefferson, Sir, is a man of no legal knowledge. He was of no celebrity as a lawyer before the Revolution, and he has since been so much engaged in political pursuits that he has had time enough to unlearn the little law he ever knew."

Hay rose to the defense of the President against Martin's vituperation. "The only end of this conversation is abuse of Mr. Jefferson," he declared.

"Sir," retorted Martin, "we shall use Mr. Jefferson so as not to abuse him. Remember that the life and liberty of Colonel Burr are shown to be no longer dependent on Virginians, and therefore I am free from any restraint in declaring what I think." In this scornful thrust at Virginians might be discerned a reply to Editor Ritchie's belittlement of the capacity of a certain Maryland lawyer.

It now came General Wilkinson's turn to take the offensive in explaining his actions in New Orleans by presenting the warning letter dispatched by Andrew Jackson to Governor Claiborne. He also offered a deposition stating that Burr's stepson, Judge Prevost of New Orleans, had saluted a public officer there and congratulated him on the arrival of General John Adair, of Kentucky, as second in command to Burr. The Chief Justice ruled that it would not be correct to permit the deposition to be read. The episode nevertheless set the stage for another of Wilkinson's patriotic outbursts. Striking an attitude, he declared: "I was prompted by that pure patriotism which has always influenced my conduct and my character which I trust will never be tarnished. I shall continue to defy the utmost art, fraud, deception and villainy that my enemies can practice toward me." Never was the General more eloquent than when he was proclaiming his virtue.

The proceedings now and then were enlivened by verbal exchanges between Martin and Wirt. General Wilkinson offered a letter that Mr. Martin had requested the day before. Mr. Martin looked at it and remarked that it was "only an extract." The General replied that he had no other.

"We take no extracts," retorted Mr. Martin, returning the paper to Wilkinson.

"Unless it be of molasses," commented Wirt, sotto voce. At this stage of the trial Blennerhassett noted that Martin was "more in his cups than usual."

The defense counted heavily on the evidence of a Major James Bruff to discredit Wilkinson. Bruff testified that the General had held out inducements to him to join an expedition against the Spaniards. He stated that on a visit to Washington he had called on both the Secretary of War and the Attorney General and warned them that Wilkinson was acquainted with Burr's plans and involved in them. According to his story, Secretary of War Dearborn replied that it would be impossible at this point for the Government to discredit Wilkinson.

The Government, however, had foreseen Bruff's testimony and prepared itself to meet his charges. It had on hand as witnesses Lt. Edmund Pendleton Gaines—the same Gaines who had accepted Burr's arrest—and a Commodore Shaw. These military gentlemen had traveled to Richmond in the same stagecoach with Bruff and testified that Bruff had announced in their presence that he was going to get even with General Wilkinson. Bruff had recently been sentenced by a court martial. The testimony of Gaines and Shaw supported that of Wilkinson who asserted that Bruff had long borne toward him an implacable hatred.

In replying to Bruff's testimony Wilkinson artfully contrived to work into his evidence damaging details of Burr's behavior at their meeting at St. Louis in the autumn of 1805, which hitherto he had been given no opportunity to present. He attributed to Burr a reference to the imbecility of the Government, the prophecy that it would moulder to pieces, and his observation that the people of the western country were ready for revolt.

"To this I recollect replying," said the General unctuously, "that if he had not profited more by his journey in other respects, he had better have remained at Washington or Philadelphia; for surely, said I, my friend, no person was ever more mistaken. The western people disaffected to the Government! They are bigoted to Jefferson and Democracy." The General no doubt was not unmindful of how that would sound when the President got around to reading the testimony.

Wilkinson concluded with a parting shot at Major Bruff: "But I can state before you, Sir [addressing the Chief Justice], and before God [turning his eyes up to Heaven and placing his hands over his heart] that this whole narrative is either a vile fabrication or a distortion of fact." After a whole week of cross-questioning the General's spirit was unquenched and his flair for histrionics as keen as ever.

During all these tedious proceedings the "culprit" Burr, too, contrived to enjoy himself. Even though he had confessed that he had been duped, Blennerhassett still could not resist the Colonel's magic charm. The two were constantly in each other's company. Blennerhassett found Burr as gay as ever and busy speculating on the reorganization of his projects just as though they had never suffered the least interruption. He observed to the Irishman that within six months all their schemes would be

remounted. What was more, said the Colonel, they could re-
model them in a better mould than formerly since they now
had a clearer view of the ground and a more perfect knowledge
of men.

Blennerhassett listened in silence while he thought to himself
". . . time will prove him as incapable in all his future efforts
as he has been in the past."

The day after the jury had declared Burr "not guilty" of a
misdemeanor the Colonel celebrated at a dinner party which
included Martin, Blennerhassett, and a cousin of Judge Prevost.
The dinner itself featured all the delicacies Richmond's lavish
Main Street market afforded and it included also three or four
wines.

"Splendid poverty!" Blennerhassett exclaimed.

During the chit-chat after the cloth had been removed a note
was handed the Colonel. Blennerhassett, who sat next to him,
detected the odor of musk and mentioned it. This was the cue
for his host to enliven the company with the story of a flirta-
tion. Blennerhassett gave space to it in his diary "only to convey
an idea of the temperament and address which enabled this
character on certain occasions, like the snake, to cast his slough,
and through age and debauchery, seem to uphold his ascend-
ancy over the sex."

Yet, in spite of this caustic criticism, Blennerhassett did not
cease to marvel at Burr's ingenuity. He discovered in the Colonel's possession a complete file of all the depositions made before the Grand Jury. "It must be confessed," he remarked,
"that few other men in his circumstances, could have procured
these documents out of the custody of offices filled by his inveterate enemies. I have long been at a loss to imagine the means
he used, of which I am not yet fully informed."

Burr, too, succumbed to the malady which had laid low so
many people in Richmond. On one of his visits Blennerhassett
found him in bed. He suggested that a doctor be called, to
which Burr replied that he had no confidence in the local physi-
cians. Blennerhassett expressed himself as being of the same

opinion, unless he excepted Dr. McClurg. This was an unwarranted reflection against some of Richmond's outstanding members of the medical profession.

Blennerhassett thoughtfully went to a druggist and returned with medicine carefully prepared which he left with the Colonel. When he returned in the evening to see how his patient was faring, Burr confessed that, instead of taking Blennerhassett's medicine, he had given himself a dose of laudanum. He defended his action on the ground that he felt weak and in need of an opiate.

At one of their meetings Burr confided to Blennerhassett that as soon as the trial was over he proposed to set off immediately for England, there to collect money for his projects.

"In London, no doubt," commented Blennerhassett bitterly, "he will pledge himself to appropriate every guinea they will advance him to the promotion of such operations on the continent as will best serve the interests of Britain; and if he had not already exposed his duplicity and incapacity in his favorite area of intrigue to Yrujo, he would again as readily promise to advance, with Spanish dollars and Spanish arms, the fortunes of the Spanish minister and his master."

Toward the close of the trial Blennerhassett had the pleasure of drinking tea and spending the evening at the Chevalliés'. There he met Mrs. David Randolph, formerly the mistress of Moldavia, and the sister of a son-in-law of Jefferson. Moldavia, derived from the names of Molly and David Randolph, was Richmond's fashionable boarding house. Mrs. Randolph was famous as a provider and the author of a cook book. She, it will be recalled, was credited also with having designed a tin-lined ice chamber for storing perishable foods that was used as model for the first American refrigerator. Blennerhassett found her accomplished, charming in manner, and possessing a masculine mind. He recorded that, in spite of her relationship to the President, "I heard more pungent strictures upon Jefferson's head and heart . . . and she certainly uttered more treason than my wife ever dreamed of, for she ridiculed the experiment of a republic in this country." No wonder since the President had deprived her husband, a Federalist, of the lucrative post of U.S. Marshal of Virginia.

The last days of the trial were enlivened also by a personal encounter between General Wilkinson and young Sam Swartwout. They ran into each other on a narrow sidewalk and the injured young man shouldered the portly major general off into the street, uniform and all. He followed this insult with a challenge to a duel to which Wilkinson did not reply. He would have no correspondence with traitors, and conspirators, he declared. Swartwout therefore was reduced to publishing in the *Virginia Gazette* an open letter to the General which read:

"Sir—I could not have supposed that you would have completed the catalogue of your crime by adding to the guilt of treachery, forgery and perjury, the accomplishment of cowardice. . . .

"Having failed in two different attempts to procure an interview with you, such as no gentleman of honor could refuse, I have only to pronounce and publish you to the world as a coward and poltroon."

Burr's gaiety, which Blennerhassett noted, was not at all times apparent in the courtroom. As the Chief Justice began to show greater leniency toward accepting the prosecution's testimony the Colonel became progressively more bitter. He made little effort to conceal his irritation at what he conceived to be weakness and vacillation on the part of Judge Marshall.

At last the prosecution came to the end of its list of witnesses and left to the Court a decision on Hay's motion that the conspirators be held on charges of treason and misdemeanor outside the jurisdiction of the Virginia circuit. On October 20 the Chief Justice delivered his final opinion. Weighing the whole of the testimony, he said, it appeared to him to predominate in favor of the belief that the enterprise was really designed against Mexico. If there had been any plan for dismembering the Union it was known only to Burr and Blennerhassett. Even the witnesses offered by the prosecution had asserted that they had heard nothing and suspected nothing hostile to the United States. How then could the assemblage of men be said to have levied war against the United States? He therefore concluded that, in his judgment, it would be improper to commit the accused on the charge of treason.

As to the charge of misdemeanor, it appeared to the Chief Justice that Burr's purposes were to settle the Washita lands and to invade Mexico if opportunity offered, perhaps only in the event of war with Spain. But this was a matter which should be left to the decision of the jury, and he would make no comment on it one way or the other to influence their judgment. He therefore would commit Burr and Blennerhassett for preparing and providing the means for a military expedition against Spain. In this instance the misdemeanor was alleged to have occurred in Ohio. Therefore Burr and Blennerhassett were released on bail for the action of the Circuit Court in that state at its next meeting on January 4, 1808.

Hay interpreted the decision as a defeat for the Government forces. He immediately said that he would advise the Government to desist from further prosecution. No man on either side had labored more indefatigably than he. But his patience was now at an end. And so in the last days of the trial he threw aside all restraint and confided in Jefferson his true sentiments with respect to Wilkinson. To the President he wrote: "The declaration which I made in court in his favor some time ago was precipitate; and though I have not retracted it, everybody sees that I have not attempted the task, which I in fact promised to perform. My confidence in him is shaken, if not destroyed. I am sorry for it, on his account, on the public account, and because you have expressed opinions in his favor; but you did not know then what you will soon know, and what I did not learn until after—long after—my declaration above mentioned."

Whatever Mr. Jefferson's innermost feelings may have been on receipt of this letter from the District Attorney surely he was then in no position to confess any misgivings about the man whom he had taken as his chief ally in the proceedings in Richmond.

Burr was no better pleased with the Chief Justice's decision on the Hay motion than was its author. In his disappointment at not being granted complete exoneration he ignored the courageous behavior of Judge Marshall in his behalf at the critical moment when the mob was hot on Burr's heels.

Three days after the rendering of the final decision he wrote in disgust to Theodosia: "After all, this is a sort of drawn battle. The Chief Justice gave his opinion on Tuesday. After declaring that there were no grounds of suspicion as to treason, he declared that Burr and Blennerhassett should give bail in $3,000 for further trial in Ohio.

"This opinion was a matter of regret and surprise to the friends of the Chief Justice, and of ridicule to his enemies—all believing that it was a sacrifice of principle to conciliate Jack Cade."

Gratitude was not one of Colonel Burr's most conspicuous attributes.

Chapter XX

I<small>T WILL BE</small> recalled that when Aaron Burr was under suspicion in the Fall of 1806 he made haste to assure his friends in no uncertain language that there was no truth in the rumors.

Senator John Smith of Ohio, who had received the Colonel cordially on his visit to Cincinnati, was among the first to grow alarmed and to make direct inquiry. Burr replied that he was "surprised and hurt" at the unusual tenor of Smith's letter. He then went on to say: "If there exists any design to separate the Western from the Eastern States, I am totally ignorant of it. I never harbored or expressed any such intention to anyone, nor did any person ever intimate such design to me."

A month later, in November, Burr addressed a letter to Governor William Henry Harrison, of the Northwest Territory. "Considering the various and extravagant reports which circulate concerning me," he said, "it may not be unsatisfactory to you to be informed (and to you there can be no better source of information than myself) that I have no wish nor design to attempt a separation of the Union, that I have no connection with any foreign power or government, that I never meditated the introduction of any foreign power or influence into the United States, or any part of its territories, but on the contrary should repel with indignation any proposition or measure having that tendency; in fine, that I have no project or views hostile to the interest, or tranquillity, or union of the United States, or prejudicial to its government; and I pledge to you my honor for the truth of this declaration."

Within the space of a few days he was assuring Henry Clay that: "I have no design, nor have I taken any measure, to promote a dissolution of the Union or a separation of any one or more States from the residue. . . . I do not own a musket nor a bayonet, nor any single article of military stores, nor does any person for me by my authority or with my knowledge."

On top of all that General Andrew Jackson was himself authority for the statement that, in reply to his inquiries, Burr had given "the most sacred pledges that he had not, nor never had, any views inimical or hostile to the United States, and whenever he was charged with the intention of separating the Union the idea of insanity must be ascribed to him."

Here then from the lips of the accused himself were the most categorical denials of the serious charges that had been brought against him. To the truth of his assertions he pledged his honor as a gentleman. It was a pledge supported by many generations of Burrs and Edwardses representing the purest blood of Puritan New England. Only by hair-splitting with the deliberate intention of misleading could his declarations be otherwise construed.

Since then Burr's innocence of the crimes of treason and high misdemeanor, so far as his actions within the territory of Virginia were concerned, had been attested by two juries of his peers in a tribunal presided over by the Chief Justice of the United States. The only mark against him that remained unresolved was his commitment by Judge Marshall for possible misdemeanor in the State of Ohio.

In the light of this exoneration the Federalists might well claim that their charge had been sustained: to wit, that Burr was an unoffending man who had been subjected to merciless political persecution at the hands of Thomas Jefferson and his followers. On the basis of the decisions rendered in Richmond future generations might perpetuate that belief.

Some eighty years were to pass before fresh evidence was disclosed touching on the activities of Aaron Burr at the turn of

the century. It was on or around the year 1890 that Henry
Adams, the historian, gained access to the British and Spanish
archives which contained the written reports of their representatives in this country during the administration of Thomas Jefferson. The ministers of these two countries were respectively
Anthony Merry and the Marquis de Casa Yrujo.

Anthony Merry came to the United States highly recommended by our Minister to the Court of St. James's, Rufus
King. Merry sought the office and, according to all accounts,
was eager to do a good job. Unfortunately for that ambition
he arrived at a time when Jefferson's ingrained antipathy toward England was at its peak. It also was at a time when the
President was showing his greatest persistency in applying his
theories of equality to the official society of the capital. The
unhappy Merry proved to be an ideal subject on which Mr.
Jefferson could practice his theories.

The first opportunity came when Mr. Merry went with
Secretary of State Madison to present his credentials at the
White House. The traditional story is that the President received the emissary from his Majesty King George III in his
bedroom slippers. Of course there was no rule against such
informality. Mr. Jefferson's indifference to dress was notorious.
No slight may have been intended. Yet the British Minister,
wearing the full regalia of his office, was made to look somewhat foolish. He not unnaturally assumed that the author of
the Declaration of Independence was being deliberately rude.

That impression gained support soon thereafter when, at his
official dinners, the President abolished the rules of precedence
and substituted that of "pêle mêle," under which the company
marched from the drawing room to the dining room in whatever order they found themselves. The system deprived the
British Minister of the place to which he felt entitled.

It so happened that Mrs. Merry was a lady of fiery temper
who rejoiced in the clash of battle. She was more eager than
her husband to pick up the gantlet Mr. Jefferson had thrown
down. The result of all this was a tempest in official circles in

Washington which the critics and enemies of the President rejoiced in and did nothing to allay.

Such was the unfriendly relationship between the President and the Merrys when, in July of 1804, following his duel with Hamilton, Colonel Burr appeared as a refugee in Philadelphia. The Merrys were spending the summer there. It was not long before the Colonel, with his unerring eye for singling out malcontents in the prospect of working them into his plans, made a contact with Merry. In a letter to Lord Harrowby, then the British Foreign Secretary, dated August 4, Merry informed his superior of the details of a visit he had just received from Colonel Williamson, an emissary of Burr, whom he described as the "actual Vice-President of the United States (which situation he is about to resign)." On that point Merry was definitely misinformed.

Burr, said Merry, had made an offer through Colonel Williamson to lend his assistance to his Majesty's Government in any manner in which they might think fit to employ him, "particularly in endeavoring to effect a separation of the western part of the United States from that which lies between the Atlantic and the mountains." Burr's proposition, said Merry, would be fully detailed to Lord Harrowby by Williamson who was to embark for England within a few days.

Merry alluded to Burr's profligacy of character. He then sketched his existing situation, describing how he was now cast off by both the Democratic and Federalist parties but still preserved connections with some people of influence. He called attention to Burr's great personal ambition and the spirit of revenge he harbored against the Jefferson administration. These circumstances Merry thought might possibly induce him to exert his talents and activity with fidelity to his employers. That, in substance, was Merry's first communication with his superiors on the subject of Burr.

In the succeeding months Burr made his trip to the South, then returned to Washington and presided at the trial of Justice Chase before retiring from the Vice-Presidency. Meanwhile his friend Colonel Williamson had journeyed to England where he held conferences with the British ministers trying to get the co-operation of their government in Burr's plans. Burr's next contact with Merry was shortly before he set out on his first trip to the West.

About this time there arrived in Washington a delegation from Louisiana to lay their grievances before the Government. Under the treaty by which the territory had been ceded to the United States its people were promised all the rights and privileges of United States citizens. But the United States Government was slow in carrying out its commitments. Here was another discontented group.

To Lord Harrowby on March 29, 1805, Merry directed another letter which he marked "Most secret." Merry mentioned that Burr had been very intimate with the Louisiana deputies during their visit to Washington. From Burr he learned that the people of that territory seemed determined to make themselves independent of the United States and that the execution of their design was delayed only by the difficulty of obtaining previously an assurance of protection and assistance from some foreign power.

Burr, according to Merry, then alluded to the possibility of the inhabitants of the western parts of the United States joining in this independence movement since Louisiana must always have command over them because of their rivers joining with the Mississippi. Burr as usual threw out hints without definitely committing himself. "It is clear," commented Merry, "that Mr. Burr (although he has not as yet confided to me the exact nature and extent of his plan) means to endeavor to be the instrument of effecting such a connection."

Merry went on to quote Burr as saying that for obvious reasons the people of Louisiana would prefer having the protection and assistance of Great Britain to that of France; but that if His Majesty's Government should not think proper to listen to his overture, application would be made to the Government of France. Burr claimed that the French Government was eager to embrace such an opportunity and that, even while at war with

England, it could find means for sending to America the small force that would be needed for the purpose.

As to the military aid from the British that would be required for the enterprise Burr, according to Merry, thought that two or three frigates and the same number of smaller vessels, stationed at the mouth of the Mississippi to prevent its being blockaded by any such force as the United States could send, and to keep open the communications with the sea, was all that would be required.

Then Burr came to the vital matter of cost. Merry said Burr conceived that a "loan" of about £100,000 would be sufficient for the immediate purposes of the enterprise. Burr went even further to suggest a way to prevent any suspicion of His Majesty's Government being involved in the transaction until the independence of Louisiana had been declared. Such suspicion would be raised if remittances were made from England to the United States or if bills were drawn in this country. Burr knew that a payment of £200,000 was due from the United States to England in the coming July. He proposed that the British Government appropriate part of this sum to his plan. If they would do that, Burr told Merry, he could devise the means to get the money into his possession without its destination being either known or suspected.

Merry gave no intimation of being surprised at this proposal. If the British Government had been as naïve as its minister in Washington, imagine the change in Burr's declining fortune on finding himself possessed of the equivalent of approximately $500,000 out of the British Treasury and under conditions that would prevent the British Government from confessing its source or protesting any purpose to which Burr might put it.

Shortly after this interview Burr set out for the West. It will be recalled that some careless talk, which gave rise to rumors, alarmed Daniel Clark in New Orleans and caused him to sound a warning to Burr through General Wilkinson. Merry, who by this time imagined that he was a party to the intrigue, also heard the rumors and expressed his anxiety in a letter to Lord Mulgrave who had succeeded Harrowby in the ministry of

William Pitt. He wrote: ". . . I learn that that gentleman [Burr] has commenced his plans in the Western country, and apparently with much success, although it would seem that he or some of his agents have either been indiscreet in their communication, or have been betrayed by some person in whom they considered that they had reason to confide, for the object of his journey has now begun to be noted in the public prints, where it is said that a convention is to be called immediately from the States bordering on the Ohio and the Mississippi for the purpose of forming a separate government."

There was a more favorable interpretation of the leak which Merry thought worth mentioning. "It is, however, possible," he said, "that the business may be so advanced as, from the nature of it, to render any further secrecy impossible." Merry concluded by noting that Burr had been received everywhere with the most marked attention.

When Burr returned from his western trip in November he lost no time in calling on the British Minister. Merry faithfully reported their conversation to Lord Mulgrave in a letter dated November 25. Burr, according to Merry, opened the conversation by stating that he had supposed the British Government disposed to give him assistance. However, continued Burr, the information he had received on this head was not sufficiently explicit to warrant his sending a confidential person to London to make the necessary communication as he had promised to do. He had therefore to content himself by speaking through Merry.

His disappointment at the hesitation of the British Government, Burr told Merry, had given him the deepest concern because his journey through the western country and Louisiana as far as New Orleans, not to speak of a visit to a part of West Florida, had been attended with so much more success than he had even looked for. Everything, he said, was completely prepared in every quarter for the execution of his plan. Therefore he had been induced to enter into an agreement with his associates and friends to return to them in March to commence operations.

Again Burr refrained from entering into details with Merry. He thought enough had been said to start the project and that the rest of the arrangements could be made through authorized persons he recommended to accompany the British ships. These would cruise off the mouth of the Mississippi, commencing April 10 at the latest and continuing there until the commanding officer should receive information from him or from Daniel Clark that Louisiana had declared itself independent.

Burr, according to Merry, suggested that his former estimate of naval strength needed to be increased by a number of smaller vessels since he had learned on good authority that East and West Florida and other parts of the Spanish dominions on the North American continent were impatient for independence. Therefore the increased British force and whatever he himself could provide would be required for this additional task.

Burr mentioned no names in his conversation with Merry, contenting himself with presenting his plans in broad outline. "Throughout the Western country," Merry quoted him as reporting, "persons of the greatest property and influence had engaged themselves to contribute very largely towards the expense of the enterprise; at New Orleans he represented the inhabitants to be so firmly resolved upon separating themselves from their union with the United States, and every way to be so completely prepared, that he was sure the revolution there would be accomplished without a drop of blood being shed . . ."

Merry concluded with Burr's reference to Wilkinson's army: ". . . the American force in that country (should it not, as he had good reason to believe, enlist with him) not being sufficiently strong to make any opposition." It was accordingly settled that the revolution would begin at the end of the coming March or the beginning of April, provided always that the British Government should "consent to lend their assistance toward it, and the answer, together with the pecuniary aid which would be wanted, arrived in time to enable him to set out the beginning of March."

To spur the British Government to action Burr once more threatened them with the prospect of the people of Louisiana turning to France. Then he presented another impelling argument for British help in the enterprise though at the expense of his own loyalty to his native land.

"He observed," reported Merry, "what I readily conceived may happen, that when once Louisiana and the Western country become independent, the Eastern States will separate themselves immediately from the Southern; and that thus the power which is now risen up with so much rapidity in the western hemisphere will, by such a division, be rendered at once informidable. . . ."

Despite Burr's pleading and Merry's indorsement, the British Government remained apathetic. The last hope of assistance from that quarter vanished when in January, 1806, William Pitt died and was succeeded as Prime Minister by Charles James Fox, an avowed friend of the United States.

Burr, however, had more than one string to his bow. If he could not wring money from the British he might still try his luck with the Spaniards. The most convenient victim was Yrujo, the Spanish Minister. Yrujo had married a daughter of Thomas McKean, signer of the Declaration of Independence and at the moment Governor of Pennsylvania. He was well informed as to what was going on in the United States. As early as the summer of 1805, when Burr was in the West and the rumors were beginning to fly, he reported to Cevallos, Spanish Minister of State: "The supposed expedition against Mexico is ridiculous and chimerical in the present state of things; but I am not unaware that Burr, in order to get moneys from the English Minister or from England, has made to him some proposition, in which he is to play the leading role."

Having thus early divined Burr's purpose of extracting money from the British he should not have been surprised when, six months later, he found himself the object of financial solicitation. Burr did not personally approach Yrujo. He sent as his emissary his old friend Jonathan Dayton, the ex-Senator from New Jersey. The visit took place in Philadelphia where Dayton was already present and to which Burr repaired after his last apparently futile appeal to Merry.

Dayton, according to Yrujo's report to Cevallos, explained that the reason of his visit was that he had information, known only to three persons in the country, which he thought would be worth thirty or forty thousand dollars to the Spanish Government. When Yrujo encouraged him to proceed Dayton disclosed the story of Burr's secret conferences with Merry. It included the plan for taking the Floridas and for effecting the separation and independence of the western states. The Floridas, said Dayton, were to be associated with the new federated state, and for her share in bringing it about England was to receive a preference in matters of commerce and navigation. The plan, he continued, had obtained the approval of the British Minister who had recommended it to his Government. Dayton added that on his trip to the West Burr had found the people of that section not only disposed toward independence but also anxious to make an expedition against the kingdom of Mexico. The proposal, said Dayton, had been well received by the British Cabinet.

In his previous letter to Cevallos, Yrujo had spoken of Burr's proposed expedition into Mexico as chimerical. Surely nothing was more chimerical than his present plan to help pay for it by frightening the Spaniards into giving him money for warning him of what was going to happen to them. General Jackson and other prominent westerners who were enthusiastic over such an expedition and had hailed Burr as the leader no doubt would have been astonished had they known that he was thus divulging his plans to the Spaniards in the hope of getting money from them.

But in this instance Yrujo was not so easily fooled. He did not believe that the British Government had fallen for the plan as Dayton asserted. Yrujo reasoned that, had they done so, Burr and Dayton would not now be coming to him. He was quite aware that Dayton, while pretending to betray the plot, had actually been sent by Burr.

Yrujo did not commit himself. He dismissed the ex-Senator courteously, promising to talk to him again. Burr and Dayton appear to have realized that they had overplayed their hand. A few days later Dayton paid a return visit. This time he confessed that Burr's plan had not been received with enthusiasm by the British ministry.

Dayton now unfolded another. It was that a certain number of men were to be introduced into the city of Washington, in disguise and well armed. At a signal from Burr they were to seize the President, Vice-President, and the President of the Senate, thus securing the heads of government. Next they were to take the public money which was on deposit in the banks in Washington and Georgetown and possess themselves of the arsenal on the eastern branch of the Potomac and also the Navy Yard. The vessels would be burned except two or three which were ready for service. Burr, according to Dayton, hoped to paralyze the opposition and make favorable agreements with the individual states. But, failing this, he would board the vessels in the Navy Yard with his followers and sail for New Orleans and there proclaim the emancipation of Louisiana and the western states.

In reporting the interview to his Government, Yrujo observed that for one who did not know the country it would appear almost insane, ". . . but I confess, for my part, that in view of all the circumstances it seems to me easy to execute, although it will irritate the Atlantic States. . . . It is beyond question that there exists in this country an infinite number of adventurers, without property, full of ambition, and ready to unite at once under the standard of a revolution which promises to better their lot. Equally certain it is that Burr and his friends, without discovering their true object, have succeeded in getting the good-will of these men, and inspiring the greatest confidence among them in favor of Burr."

After what Merry imagined to be valiant service for his own country in abetting the dissolution of the Union, the end of his mission to the United States was distressing. His correspondence, intended for Pitt's ministers, was read by Fox who wrote to Merry accepting his resignation. It did no good for Merry to protest that he had not offered his resignation. But even while he waited for his successor to arrive he sent off one final dispatch warning that if Britain refused to support Burr's enterprise recourse would be had to France, and that even without the help of any foreign power Burr proposed to go ahead.

From the foregoing evidence various conclusions may be drawn. Apologists for Burr might question the accuracy of the reports sent to their governments by Merry and Yrujo. It is hard to believe they would have made them up.

Or, Burr's proposals may be accepted, as Merry at least accepted them, at their face value. If so, and had he gone on with his plans, a substantial charge of treason could be laid against Burr.

Still another conclusion would be to accept Burr's own protest of innocence and to assume that the propositions he made to the British and Spanish governments were dishonest and insincere, merely designed to wring money from them for services which he never intended to perform.

Whichever conclusion is accepted, had the reports of Merry and Yrujo been made public at the time of the trials, one wonders whether in October, 1807, Aaron Burr would have walked out of the Circuit Court for the Fifth District of Virginia a free man.

Chapter XXI

THE TRIAL ENDED, those of the principals whose homes were in Richmond returned to their normal pursuits in the city, while those from a distance departed to pick up the threads of their various careers elsewhere. What became of them in later years and what changes were wrought in the scene of their activities during the long hot summer of 1807 are the proper subject for a closing chapter.

Richmond itself continued to grow and prosper. Its important status as capital of the State of Virginia, the seat of the administrative branch of state government, of the legislature and the judiciary, and its favorable location as a center of commerce contributed toward a continued activity of which the Burr trial was merely one outstanding episode.

Prosperity had its reflections in the physical appearance of the city. As Lawyer Wickham's practice became more lucrative, and as his increasing progeny began to tax his domestic establishment, he bethought himself of building a new house. For this project he engaged the services of the distinguished young architect Robert Mills. The result of their combined efforts was the handsome house, with its graceful spiral stairway, which survives to this day as the home of the Valentine Museum.

Another actor in the drama, who played a modest role as a member of the Grand Jury, also took advantage of increasing good fortune to employ Mr. Mills to build a mansion commensurate with it. Dr. John Brockenbrough, advanced from cashier to president of the Bank of Virginia, chose a site on Shockoe Hill on an eminence with a sweeping view to the east. The new abode was a fitting setting for his wife Gabriella's salons. It has been destined to go down in history as the White House of the Confederacy.

They were but two of many other ambitious houses that altered the modest, homely face of Shockoe Hill. Even as they were rising, however, fashion was shifting westward. Within a few decades it was to sound the death knell of the Hill as a desirable residential quarter.

The only dwelling of distinction which stood there at the time of the Burr trial and which stands today is the house of Chief Justice Marshall. Restored and reverently cared for, it enables visitors to visualize what life on the Hill was like when, under its roof or in the shade of the trees on the lawn, the master penned his famous opinions.

The master himself and his beloved Molly have moved a few blocks away. They and their family and friends occupy more restricted quarters in Shockoe Cemetery. In death as in life fashion predominates. As in life fashion moved from the Hill to the West End, so in death fashion has shifted to Hollywood Cemetery. Hollywood, with its presidents and post-bellum aristocracy, has become a showplace. Only the rare visitor finds his way through a poor and forgotten quarter to Shockoe.

After his long and arduous experience presiding over the trial the Chief Justice was in need of a rest and he hurried off to the Blue Ridge Mountains. In a letter to his friend Judge Peter thanking him for the gift of a book he revealed his sense of relief: "I received it while fatigued and occupied with the most unpleasant case which has ever been brought before a Judge in this or perhaps any other country, which affected to be governed by laws."

In those days much of the work of the Supreme Court was conducted on circuit. So the Chief Justice was able to spend a great deal of his time on official business in the congenial atmos-

phere of Richmond. There, after the indignation of his political
opponents over his conduct of the trial had somewhat died
down, he once more enjoyed the affection and respect of his
neighbors.

Even after Mr. Jefferson came to the end of his term of
office and retired to Monticello the feud between the Chief
Justice and himself went on. In the summer of 1821 a series of
articles by Judge Spencer Roane, of the Virginia Court of
Appeals, attacking the Chief Justice and presenting the states'
rights argument against the extension of Federal power, appeared in *The Enquirer*. In a letter to his colleague Justice
Story, Judge Marshall attributed the vulgarity of their tone to
Roane, but imagined the "acerbity of language increased by his
communications with the Great Lama of the mountains." And
even when Jefferson died the Chief Justice, kindly though he
was in most human relationships, could not bring himself to the
point of expressing distress or offering a word of praise.

Edmund Randolph, the elder statesman, did not long survive
the trial. That, in fact, was his last memorable appearance. He
died in 1813 at the age of 60 years. By an irony of fate the
youngest of the counsel in the trial was the first to go. The
prospects of a brilliant career were cruelly blasted when Benjamin Botts and his young wife met death in the burning of the
Richmond Theater on December 26, 1811. So, save for his part
in the defense of Aaron Burr, he is best known in local history
as the father of John Minor Botts, a Virginia statesman.

William Wirt's participation was a prelude to greater achievement. His distinction as a lawyer increased with the years and
he eventually became Attorney General of the United States
in three administrations. Wirt combined with the law the avoca-
tion of a man of letters. He wrote a life of Patrick Henry and
a series of essays under the title of *Letters of a British Spy* in
which he portrayed some of his contemporaries. These publica-
tions gave him momentary fame. He was alert to seize any inspiration for a literary composition whether it was the death of
an acquaintance or an early morning stroll.

Of the two warriors who figured in the trial the futures were in striking contrast. Winfield Scott appeared there only as a youthful spectator. He won his spurs in the War of 1812 where he proved beyond a doubt that his natural calling was that of a soldier. Between military assignments he occasionally returned to Richmond to pursue his courtship of the lovely and talented Maria Mayo. It was said that he wooed her as lieutenant, captain, major, and colonel, and finally as general won her hand. He eventually rose to be Commander-in-Chief of the United States Army. But when, in that position, he was delegated the task of invading and conquering his native state, Virginia erased his name from the list of her distinguished sons and has never restored it.

The other warrior was Major General James Wilkinson. Battered and bruised from his experience at the hands of the Grand Jury and counsel for the defense he returned to the Southwest to resume his command. When, in the War of 1812, General Dearborn demonstrated beyond any doubt that he was unequal to the task of commanding the United States Army of the North, the nation once more in her dire need called on the leader who, according to his own account, had saved her from the threats of Aaron Burr.

Wilkinson, with the same lethargy of movement that had characterized his entry on the scene at the Burr trial, eventually reached the northern theater in the middle of the summer of 1813. His ensuing campaign was as disastrous to American arms as that of his predecessor had been. After a succession of failures he gladly welcomed relief from command though he had still to face a court-martial. This exonerated him from blame, which no doubt under the circumstances was a just decision. The nation at last seemed to have arrived at the conclusion that it could be saved without intercession of the General. He was not called on again. The remaining twelve years of life that fate generously granted him were spent in retirement in Mexico. His position there, though comfortable enough, was something less than it would have been had he appeared there as the commander of the conquering army of Emperor Aaron I.

George Hay who had battled so bravely, if unsuccessfully,

for the Government eventually won his reward as a Republican stalwart. He was elevated to the bench as Judge of the Federal District of Virginia. Further to seal his connection with the "Virginia Dynasty," he took as his second wife Eliza, daughter of James Monroe.

Hay's colleague MacRae, following his appearance as counsel for the prosecution, passed through various vicissitudes of fortune. Soon after the trial he was appointed American consul in Paris. He remained in Europe a few years before returning to Richmond. What then happened to him is obscure. One account has it that he met with financial reverses. However that may be he disappeared from Richmond, leaving his wife behind, and never returned. He is reported to have died in England.

Of Andrew Jackson and Washington Irving nothing needs to be said. Their later careers are too well known to require a recapitulation here.

Following his release on bail to await the action of the Ohio Grand Jury Colonel Burr set out for the North. He was accompanied by the ever faithful young Samuel Swartwout, Luther Martin, and Harman Blennerhassett. Blennerhassett's excuse was that he was sticking with the Colonel in the hope of recovering more of his money. Whatever the reason he seemed always ready to answer the Colonel's beck and call and to enjoy his company, however much he might abuse him behind his back.

As they proceeded on their journey the report of the outcome of the trials in Richmond went ahead of them. It was a report of the miscarriage of justice painted in the lurid colors of the most extreme animosity of political partisanship.

The crisis came with the arrival of the party in Baltimore on November 3. That city was a hotbed of Republicanism and its frequent emotional outbursts already were conditioning it for the popular name of "Mobtown." Handbills had been printed and distributed announcing the hour for the hanging in effigy of the Chief Justice, Burr, Blennerhassett, and Martin.

On learning of the proposed demonstration Burr, accompanied by Swartwout, discreetly embarked in a stagecoach for

Philadelphia. Martin retired to his house where he enjoyed the protection of some of his law students and other friends who armed themselves and prepared to resist if the house were attacked.

Blennerhassett repaired to an inn where he was supposed to be guarded by the police—a doubtful security in the event of a public demonstration. At the frantic urging of the landlord he sought the greater safety of the attic and from a window looked down at the disorderly procession as it passed by the inn.

In the lead was a fife and drum corps playing "The Rogues' March." Behind it came a cart in which were the effigies of the aforesaid gentlemen on their way to be strung up on Gallow's Hill. It was a motley array which the living models for the effigies did well to escape. Fortunately the demonstration ended without violence or bloodshed.

Burr was still under indictment in New Jersey and New York despite the fact that the death of Hamilton had occurred three years before. He did not therefore dare to show his face in public, but lived in New York City as a fugitive, cared for by devoted friends, until six months later he took passage for Europe under an assumed name.

He arrived in London in the middle of July and, because of his former distinction as well as his personal attractions, he was welcomed by such accomplished persons as Charles Lamb, William Godwin, and Jeremy Bentham. Burr was still obsessed with the idea of playing a vital part in the achievement of independence by the Spanish colonies in America. He gained an interview with the British statesmen Castlereagh and Canning and revealed a plan of action, but without obtaining either their interest or support. On the contrary, for whatever reason, the official attitude stiffened. His apartment was searched and his property seized. The property was returned but with it came an order to leave England. Some people saw in this the avenging hand of Jefferson.

Once more an exile, Burr wandered through Sweden, Denmark, and Germany, always out of funds, depending on the charity of friends, but still with enough of the old unconquerable spirit to set down in his diary a lively record of his various amours.

The Colonel at last reached Paris where he sought an interview with Napoleon in the hope once more of pushing his plans for exploiting the Spanish colonies. But the Emperor was too busy with his immediate problems in Europe to give ear to those of Burr. The latter's situation was more desperate than ever. The only recourse left to the outcast was to return home. The American representatives in Paris, on orders from Washington, refused him a passport. By one of those odd coincidences so often encountered in life, one of the American representatives was Alexander MacRae who so short a time before had sought his conviction in Richmond.

In these trying days the Colonel, if he ever needed consolation, could still count on Theodosia. In fact the harder he was treated by the world the greater was her adulation. It reached its climax in a letter which she addressed to him in Europe:

"I witness your extraordinary fortitude with new wonder at every new misfortune. Often, after reflecting on this subject, you appear to me so superior, so elevated above all other men, I contemplate you with such a strange mixture of humility, admiration, reverence, love and pride, that very little superstition would be necessary to make me worship you as a superior being, such enthusiasm does your character excite in me.

"When I afterwards revert to myself, how insignificant do my best qualities appear. My vanity would be greater if I had not been placed so near you; and yet my pride is our relationship. I had rather not live than not be the daughter of such a man."

At last in 1812 the Colonel was permitted to return home. By this time public opinion even in New York had relented. The war with England and other more immediate matters served to erase from the public conscience the Hamilton episode. Burr could resume his practice and his native brilliance soon restored to him his earlier reputation as a leader at the bar.

But more tragedy was in store. This time it took the form of domestic sorrow, as though fate were trying to see what else it could do to break his indomitable spirit. From Charleston came the distressing news of the death of Aaron Burr Alston, to whom the grandfather was so devoted and on whom he had counted to carry on the family tradition.

There was still more to come. Theodosia, stricken with grief and herself fatally ill, sought solace in the company of her father in New York. At noon on December 30, 1812, accompanied by her maid, she set sail from Charleston aboard a vessel named *The Patriot*. Not long after, a terrific storm blew up on the Atlantic. *The Patriot* was never heard of again. The vessel's fate has continued to be a mystery.

The North Carolina coast in the neighborhood of Cape Hatteras was notorious in those days for "wreckers," men who, by the ingenious shifting of lights on shore, lured ships on the shoals and, when the ships had broken up, preyed on the wrecks. There were as well rumors of the operations of pirates. In later years legends sprang up of deathbed confessions in which Theodosia Burr Alston figured as a victim of one of these bands of marauders. But convincing proof is lacking.

Whatever his innermost thoughts, Burr accepted this last and bitterest loss with the stoicism he had shown on earlier occasions. His pride demanded that he do no less.

Meanwhile retribution had caught up with another figure in the trial. Luther Martin's constitution broke down under his persistent and unrestricted drinking. His law practice fell away. Burr learned of his condition and repaid him for past favors by giving him asylum in his home in New York.

Eventually Martin returned to Baltimore, his once brilliant mind shattered by the steady inroads of senility. He often wandered through the court rooms which had been the scene of so many of his triumphs, a drooling derelict, for whose support, in recognition of his great past achievements, each member of the bar accepted a small annual assessment.

Shortly after the episode in Baltimore Blennerhassett parted company with Burr and went to join his beloved Margaret in Natchez. He was now approaching the end of his resources, burdened with an accumulation of debts, and badgered by insolent and exacting creditors. His library, research apparatus and the furniture in the mansion on the island had to be sold. The mansion itself was allowed to go to ruin. It was taken over along with the rest of the island by a tenant who used them for the culture of hemp and the manufacture of cordage. It was not long, however, before the mansion was mercifully rescued from its humiliation by a fire which leveled it to the ground.

Despairing of ever getting any money out of Burr, Blennerhassett concentrated on his son-in-law Alston, demanding $35,000 on pain of publishing a pamphlet disclosing the Governor's connection with the conspiracy. Alston, now Governor of South Carolina, is reported to have given him $10,000. Blennerhassett's next venture was the purchase of a cotton plantation in Mississippi. In spite of Margaret's loyal support this too was a failure.

At this point the acting Governor of Canada, an old and intimate friend, managed to find a seat for Blennerhassett on one of the provincial courts of the Dominion. So in 1819, disposing of what interest remained to him in the island and the plantation, he moved with his wife and sons to Canada and took up his residence in Montreal. But this solution of his problem proved temporary—he was turned out of office by what he described as the "capriciousness of the British ministry."

All that was left to him now were claims to property still existing in Ireland. So in 1822 the Blennerhassetts set sail from Canada for home. Nothing came of the claims and, after living for a time with a maiden sister of Harman's in England, the Blennerhassetts sought refuge on the island of Guernsey. That was Blennerhassett's last move. There he died in 1831, leaving Margaret with little or no money and two dependent sons.

In 1842 Mrs. Blennerhassett decided to return to the United States and petitioned Congress for payment for the boats and stores seized at Marietta, Ohio, in the winter of 1806–07. On her arrival in New York with one of her sons, Henry Clay, who was then in the Senate, interested himself in her case. He described her as living in absolute want, presented her petition, and advocated its justice. But the petitioner died before the Senate had time to act.

Thus ended the tragic story of the Blennerhassetts, though they themselves may not have considered it so. For the love that had been the cause of their adventures in the new world sustained them to the last. Yet their later years were a far cry from the romantic dreams in which Blennerhassett stood at the right hand of the Emperor Aaron I while Margaret presided as first lady in waiting to the Princess Theodosia. Such was the heavy penalty the Blennerhassetts had to pay for Harman, as his partner Woodbridge put it, having "all kinds of sense except common sense."

For some fifteen years Aaron Burr continued to practice law in New York City successfully. At the age of 77 years he had one last romantic passage which culminated in his marriage to the widow Jumel, for which nothing good could be said on either side. The episode soon ended in divorce. Time for the Colonel was now fast running out. Yet how many of his enemies had he already survived! Death came to him at last in September, 1836, at the age of 80 years.

The body of Aaron Burr was laid to rest in a grave beside those of his father and his grandfather in the cemetery at Princeton.

One evening at twilight many, many years later, two visitors stood at the foot of the grave. Instinctively both of them had removed their hats as they approached the spot. They were Burr's biographer Walter Flavius McCaleb and Woodrow Wilson, then President of Princeton University. They remained for a moment in silence. It was broken by Wilson's voice, pitched very low: "How misunderstood—how maligned—"

This from a historian who must have been acquainted with all the facts. Even in death, and in spite of the passage of time, Aaron Burr still exercised his fascination.

Bibliography

Abernethy, Thomas Perkins. *The Burr Conspiracy.* New York, 1954.
——. "Aaron Burr at Blennerhassett Island and in Ohio." *Bulletin,* Historical and Philosophical Society of Ohio, January, 1954.
Adams, Henry. *History of the United States During the Administration of Thomas Jefferson.* New York, 1930 ed.
Ambler, Charles Henry. *Thomas Ritchie.* Richmond, 1913.
Annals of the Congress of the United States. Tenth Congress, first session, 1807–08, Vol. 17.
Armstrong, Margaret. *Five Generations: Life and Letters of an American Family* (The Mayos). New York, 1930.
Bailey, Thomas A. *The American Pageant.* Boston, 1956.
Beveridge, Albert J. *The Life of John Marshall.* New York, 1929.
Bradford, Gamaliel. *Damaged Souls.* John Randolph of Roanoke. New York, 1922.
——. *Wives.* Theodosia Burr Alston. New York, 1925.
Brown, Alexander. *The Cabells and Their Kin.* New York, N.D.
Bruce, William Cabell. *John Randolph of Roanoke.* New York, 1922.
Bowers, Claude. *Jefferson in Power.* Boston, 1936.
Boushall, Frances. "Celebrated Taverns and Hotels Have Served Richmond." *Richmond Times-Dispatch,* July 18, 1945.
Christian, W. Asbury D.D. *Richmond, Her Past and Present.* Richmond, 1912.
Clark, Daniel. *Proofs of the Corruption of General James Wilkinson and of His Connection with Aaron Burr.* Philadelphia, 1809.
Coombs, J. J. *The Trial of Aaron Burr.* Washington, 1864.
Cox, Isaac Joslin. "General Wilkinson and His Later Intrigues with the Spaniards." *American Historical Review,* July, 1914.
Davis, John. *Travels of Four Years and a Half in the United States of America.* London, 1803.
Davis, Matthew L. *Memoirs of Aaron Burr.* New York, 1836–37.
Dictionary of American Biography.
Eckenrode, H. J. *The Randolphs.* New York, 1946.

Ford, Paul Leicester. *The Writings of Thomas Jefferson*. New York, 1898.

Garland, Hugh. *The Life of John Randolph of Roanoke*. Philadelphia, 1851.

Gordon, Douglas H. "John Marshall, the Fourth Chief Justice." *American Bar Association Journal*, August, 1955.

Hay, Thomas Robson, and Werner, M. P. *The Admirable Trumpeter: A Biography of General James Wilkinson*. New York, 1938.

Hecht, Arthur. "The Burr Conspiracy and the Postoffice Department." *Missouri Historical Society Magazine*, January, 1936.

Hockett, Homer C. *Political and Social History of the United States*. New York, 1925.

Hornblower, Arthur. *A History of the Theater in America*. Philadelphia, 1919.

Howden-Smith, Arthur D. *Old Fuss and Feathers: The Life and Exploits of Lt.-Gen. Winfield Scott*. New York, 1937.

Irving, Pierre M. *The Life and Letters of Washington Irving*. New York, 1865.

Jacobs, James Ripley. *Tarnished Warrior: Maj.-Gen. James Wilkinson*. New York, 1938.

James, Marquis. *Andrew Jackson, The Border Captain*. Indianapolis, 1933.

Kennedy, John P. *Memoirs of the Life of William Wirt*. Philadelphia, 1849.

Little, John P. *History of Richmond*. Richmond, 1933.

Lowther, Minnie Kendall. *Blennerhassett Island in Romance and Tragedy*. Rutland, Vt., N.D.

Macaulay, Lord. "The Trial of Warren Hastings." *Critical and Historical Essays*. London, 1909 ed.

Martin, Luther. "Letter on Logan to Mr. James Fennel, reprinted from the *Philadelphia Gazette* of March 29, 1797." *The Olden Time*, Vol. II, Pittsburgh, 1814.

Mayo, Bernard. *Jefferson Himself*. Boston, 1942.

McCaleb, Walter F. *The Aaron Burr Conspiracy*. New York, 1903.

Meade, Bishop William. *Old Churches and Families of Virginia*. Philadelphia, 1857.

Mordecai, Samuel. *Richmond in By-Gone Days*. Richmond, N.D.

Mumford, George Wythe. *The Two Parsons*. Richmond, 1884.

National Cyclopedia of American Biography.

National Intelligencer and Washington Advertiser, January, 1807.

"Old Swan Tavern." Anon. *Virginia Historical Register and Literary Advertizer*, July, 1849.

Parton, James. *The Life and Times of Aaron Burr*. New York, 1857.

——. *Andrew Jackson*. New York, 1859.

Randall, Henry S. *The Life of Thomas Jefferson*. New York, 1858.

Randolph of Roanoke, John. Correspondence with Joseph H. Nicholson, Nicholson Mss. Library of Congress.

Randolph, Mrs. Mary. *The Virginia Housewife or Methodical Cook*. Philadelphia, 1858 ed.

Richmond Bicentennial Commission History. Richmond, 1938.

Richmond Inquirer, March-August, 1807.

Richmond Portraits. Valentine Museum. Richmond, 1949.

"Richmond, Va., Fifty Years Ago." Anon. *The Land We Love Magazine*, Charlotte, N.C., May-October, 1867.

Robertson, David. *The Report of the Trials of Col. Aaron Burr*. Philadelphia, 1808.

Safford, William H. *The Blennerhassett Papers and a Memoir of Blennerhassett*. New York, 1864.

St-Mémin, Exhibition of the Work of. Valentine Museum. Richmond, 1941.

Schacher, Nathan. *Alexander Hamilton*. New York, 1946.

Scott, Lieut.-Gen. Winfield. *Memoirs*. New York, 1864.

Scott, Mary Winfield. *Houses of Old Richmond*. Richmond, 1941.

"Some Richmond Portraits." Anon. *Harpers Magazine*, April, 1885

Stanard, Mary Newton. *John Marshall and His Home*. Richmond, 1913.

———. *Richmond, Its People and Its Story*. Philadelphia, 1923.

Stanley, John S. "Luther Martin." An Address Delivered before the 57th Annual Meeting of the Maryland State Bar Association, June 20, 1952. Printed in the *Daily Record, Baltimore*, June 21, 1952.

Tucker, George. *The Life of Thomas Jefferson*. Philadelphia, 1837.

Tyler, Lyon G. *Encyclopedia of Virginia Biography*. New York, 1915.

———. An Address Given by President John Tyler at Richmond, Va., 1858. Reprinted in *Letters and Times of the Tylers*, Vol. I, 1884.

Van Doren, Mark. *Correspondence of Aaron Burr and His Daughter Theodosia*.

Virginia Gazette, 1807.

Weddell, Alexander Wilbourne. *Richmond, Virginia, in Old Prints, 1737–1887*. Richmond, 1932.

Williams, E. Randolph. Letter to Justice Harold H. Burton, October 4, 1951. Virginia Historical Society.

Williams, Stanley T. *The Life of Washington Irving*. New York, 1935.

Index

first appearance in court, 168
funds of, attachment served on, 173–174
and Graham, 160
at Harmonic Society, 246, 247
indicted by Grand Jury, 127
indiscreet talk by, 159, 160
island purchased by, 155
law studied by, 154
and Love's testimony, 185
mansion built by, 155–156
at Marietta, 155
money received from Alston, 284
in New York, arrival in, 155
niece married by, 154–155
nolle prosequi entered to indictment of, 242, 248
in penitentiary, 166, 171–172, 196, 202
  illness of, 233
  Martin's visit to, 233–234
postponement of arraignment of, 201, 202
as "Querist," 158, 159, 160, 247, 251
scholarly talents of, 156
secession discussed by, 158–159
sister of, 154
sons of, 156
and Taylor's testimony, 180–182
Theodosia admired by, 150
at thirty-one, 154
wife's portrayal of Burr's relationship to, 211–214
and Woodbridge's testimony, 186–187
Woodbridge's view of, 154, 285
Blennerhassett, Margaret, 20, 150, 154, 155, 162, 283, 284
appearance of, 156
Burr received at Blennerhassett Island, 157
education of, 156, 157, 159
in Natchez, 164, 185, 283
servants' testimony denounced by, 185
sons of, 157
Theodosia admired by, 159

as widow, 284–285
Blennerhassett Island, 128, 150, 157–160 *passim*, 187, 188, 191, 205, 237, 239, 242, 249
Bollman, Justus Eric, 38, 71, 101, 102, 111, 116, 117, 253
Bollman-Swartwout case, 71, 175, 198, 206, 210, 230, 236, 238, 240
Bott, Miles, 173
Botts, Benjamin, 66, 89, 91, 169, 200, 201, 253
argument at Burr trial, 216–222
death of, 278
Botts, John Minor, 278
Brockenbrough, John, 73, 125, 277
Brockenbrough, Mrs. William, 247
Brown, Joseph, 109
Bruff, James, 118, 257, 258
Bruin, Judge, 163
Buchanan, John, 135, 235
Buckey, 169
Buell, Maj. Gen., 161
Burling, Walter, 115, 116
Burr, Aaron, in Albany, 9, 10
appearance of, 8, 69–70
arrest of, 28
as Attorney General of New York State, 11
bail set for, 35, 44, 91
in Battle of Long Island, 9, 10
at Bayou Pierre, 163
birth of, 8
and Blennerhassett, 157, 158, 162, 165, 168, 196–197, 202, 203, 246, 251, 252, 258, 259, 260, 280
brother-in-law of, 8, 9, 145
Bruin visited by, 163
in Charleston, S. C., 16
childhood of, 8
in Cincinnati, 20, 159
and Clay, Henry, 83, 265
at Cole's Creek, Miss., 28
at Cumberland Island, 163
and daughter. *See* Burr, Theodosia.
Daveiss' accusation of, 23

290

and Theodosia (daughter). *See* Burr, Theodosia.
at thirteen, 8
treason trial of, Botts' speech at, 216–222
  Hay's opening remarks at, 175–176
  Hay's turn after Botts, 222–225
  jurymen picked for, 168–170, 172–173
  Lee's speech at, 225–226
  MacRae's opening statement for prosecution, 203–206
  Marshall's opinion on issues of, 236–241
  Martin's speech at, 226–232
  "not guilty" verdict at, 241–242
  Randolph's attack on doctrine of constructive treason, 198–200
  testimony of witnesses at, 176–177, 179–188, 198
  Wickham's motion proffered at, 188, 190–195, 197–198
  Wirt's accusation at, 206–215
Truxton's friendship for, 179
Truxton's testimony against, 178–180
uncle of, 8
in United States Senate, 11
as Vice-President of U.S., 11, 13, 17, 109, 148
and Washington, George, 9, 10
wife of, 10, 145
and Wilkinson. *See* Wilkinson, James, and Burr.
and Williamson, 267
women's education advocated by, 146
and Yrujo, 272, 273, 274, 275
Burr, Esther Edwards, 8
Burr, John, 8
Burr, Sally, 8
Burr, Theodosia (later Mrs. Joseph Alston), 10, 16, 129, 196, 282
  birth of, 145

and Blennerhassetts, 150, 159
education of, 146–147, 148
faith in father, 149
gifts to imprisoned Blennerhassett, 171
girlhood of, 145–146
as hostess at ten, 147
and husband, affection for, 149, 150
letters from father, 54, 70, 77, 128, 136–137, 144, 152, 263
lost on ship *Patriot*, 283
marriage of, 148
Martin's admiration for, 227
in Richmond, 153
at seventeen, 148, 150
son of, 149, 150
suitors of, 148
Byrd, William, 31

Cabell, Joseph Carrington, 64, 73
Cabell, William H., 67, 130, 133, 135, 247
Cade, Jack, 263
Calvo, de, Casa, 108
Campbell, George W., 77, 78, 84
Canning, 281
Carr, Dabney, 134
Carrington, Edward, 170, 173, 241, 242
Carrington, Eliza, 172
Carter, Mary Walker, 64
Castlereagh, 281
Cevallos, 273
Charleston, S. C., Burr in, 16
Chase, Samuel, 17, 35, 42, 51, 65, 69, 92, 223, 225, 267
Chesapeake-Leopard incident, 131, 133, 134, 135
Chevallié, Mrs. Jean Auguste Marie, 173, 247
Claiborne, William C. C., 21, 82, 84, 107, 114, 116, 117, 256
Clare, de, Bago, 230
Clark, Daniel, 110, 111, 269
Clay, Henry, 83, 164, 265, 284
Clinton, DeWitt, 13, 17
Clinton family, 12, 13
Coffee, John, 80, 82, 83, 159, 162